Praise for *The Inequality of Wealth*

'Very few in frontline politics have worked as long as Liam Byrne on the theory and practice of tackling inequality. This new book is essential reading for anyone who cares about tackling one of the great political and moral challenges of our time.'
Ed Balls, former Government Minister and Shadow Chancellor

'The UK is an "inheritocracy" – a country where the richest, wealth-wise, have widened the gap with the rest, amplifying social inequalities. Liam Byrne's book is ... compelling in its proposals for turning this tide, elevating opportunities and living standards for many millions of people. I hope it is not just read widely but acted on immediately.'
Andy Haldane, former Chief Economist at the Bank of England

'Liam Byrne understands the devastating costs of wealth inequality; here is a politician with a true sense of purpose. This is a must-read for those who want to shape a better society.'
Kate Pickett and Richard Wilkinson, authors of The Spirit Level

'Combining powerful social observation with a distillation of the best of today's thinking, *The Inequality of Wealth* is at once readable and passionate.'
Will Hutton, author of The State We're In

'A thought-provoking read about one of the most difficult yet most important political issues of our time.'
Lord Gus O'Donnell, former Cabinet Secretary

'Liam Byrne's new book will help the British left to understand how freedom and equality should be reconciled.'
Philip Collins, columnist for the New Statesman

THE INEQUALITY OF WEALTH

WHY IT MATTERS AND HOW TO FIX IT

LIAM BYRNE

An Apollo Book

First published in the UK in 2024 by Head of Zeus Ltd,
part of Bloomsbury Publishing Plc

9 7 5 3 1 2 4 6 8

A catalogue record for this book is available from the British Library.

ISBN (HB): 9781804543382
ISBN (E): 9781804543368

Typeset by Divaddict Publishing Solutions Ltd

Printed and bound in Great Britain by
CPI Group (UK) Ltd, Croydon CR0 4YY

Head of Zeus Ltd
First Floor East
5–8 Hardwick Street
London EC1R 4RG

WWW.HEADOFZEUS.COM

To the people of Hodge Hill,
who taught me everything

Contents

Introduction:

The Notes I Wish I'd Left

'The well-being of the Nation as a whole is synonymous
with the well-being of each and every one of its citizens.'
Franklin D. Roosevelt, speech at Soldiers' Field,
Chicago (28 October 1944)

A heavy snow lay thick on the American capital, and a heavy
cold laid up the American President. Just home from a draining
summit in Tehran, he now had a date to keep with the American
people. But his doctors were alarmed. He was forbidden to take
the short ride to Congress to deliver his tenth State of the Union
address. And so, at 8.45pm on 11 January 1944, the 62 year-
old, sun-tanned, sunny-natured and self-confident Franklin
Delano Roosevelt rolled into the White House Diplomatic
Reception Room to deliver for the first and only time the annual
State of the Union as a 'fireside chat'. And he didn't pull his
punches.

The tide of war was turning. There was a sense that the end
might be in sight. Bob Hope, the most famous comedian in
America, was smiling from the cover of *Life* magazine. So now
was the time, insisted Roosevelt, 'to begin to lay the plans... for
the winning of a lasting peace and... an American standard of
living higher than ever before known'.[1] But this lofty goal, the
president declared, would prove impossible to achieve if 'some
fraction of our people... is ill-fed, ill-clothed, ill-housed, and

insecure'. So what was now required was nothing short of a second Bill of Rights to enshrine the 'one supreme objective for the future' captured 'in one word: security'. The United States might have grown 'under the protection of certain inalienable political rights', Roosevelt explained, but '[w]e have come to a clear realization of the fact that true individual freedom cannot exist without economic security and independence'. So what was now required was an 'Economic Bill of Rights', to deliver 'economic security, social security, moral security'. It was an extraordinary performance.

Roosevelt's 'fireside chat' was the zenith of decades-worth of thinking, campaigning and – often experimentally – governing. It was a testament to his simple belief that 'we must lay hold of the fact that economic laws are not made by nature. They are made by human beings'.[2] Within fifteen months of his address to the nation, Roosevelt was dead. But his dream of freedom, guaranteed by security for all and power to each, is due a second birth. It is the unfinished business of the progressive revolution.

We like to think that we live in a free country. But some are more free than others. There are many reasons why this is so; but the most important is the *inequality of wealth*. Not so long ago, Roosevelt's successor, Barack Obama, called inequality the 'defining challenge of our time'.[3] He was right. Inequality – the market that creates it, and the politics that permit it – slows our commerce, threatens our climate, incites conflict, excites corruption, and has created, in the UK, not a sceptred isle of proud dignity but the indignity of a realm where the luckiest live like princes and the poorest live on charity.

The last twenty years have been golden years for a fortunate few. But they have been hard years for millions who are now prisoners of anxiety, fear and want, haunted by the spectre of risk, and threatened by the tyranny of poverty. This world we have built for ourselves, if left to itself, will get worse, not better, in the years to come. That imperils not only the future wealth of our *economy* but the future health of our *democracy*.

Since Obama's speech, we have been endowed with entire libraries of books dissecting the 'New Inequality'.[4] But for more than a decade, we have failed to describe solutions that voters will not merely 'like' on social media but vote for at the ballot box. Which is why I have written this book to set out a plausible path to progress.

My story begins at the White House. Or rather, next door, where the real work gets done. The Eisenhower Executive Office Building, christened 'the ugliest building in America' by Mark Twain, looks like it was lifted from the Champs-Elysées. Today, its Second Empire grandeur is home to the president's staff, and it was here, one blue and white October morning, that I sat down with a small jet-lagged team from Her Majesty's Treasury to meet the brains behind Joe Biden.

It was 2009, the year after the Great Financial Crash. The banks had been saved. The economy was healing. But the political shockwaves, like a tsunami of popular anger, had only just begun. That morning, Jared Bernstein, the vice-president's chief economist (and at the time of writing, chair of President Biden's Council of Economic Advisers), told us why. For all the so-called triumph of the West and the imperishable glory of Cold War victory, Jared explained, most American workers had not had a pay rise *in years*, in sharp contrast to the burgeoning wealth of a lucky few. While some read recent history as an affirming 'end of history', for most it felt like the end of progress.[5] I remember the feeling in my stomach as I wondered: was the same curse afflicting Britain?

I got back to the Treasury that week to talk it over with Alistair Darling, the chancellor of the exchequer. Those were difficult days in the Treasury, where I was chief secretary. I was in the middle of negotiating the biggest round of government spending cuts in decades, in order to halve our deficit in just four years without triggering another recession. It is no secret that, at the time, Prime Minister Gordon Brown and his chancellor were not getting on. Too often, I was the bridge between the two. Some mornings, I would get a call from the PM asking me to say one thing on the radio; and twenty minutes later, the chancellor would ring to insist I said the opposite. Now, I was suggesting to Alistair Darling that we might have a bigger problem, and that we needed to create something like Biden's 'Middle Class Taskforce', given the job of transforming the living standards of working families.

We agreed to set up a small team, which, I remember, decided to christen itself the 'taskforce on the future of the English working class'.[6] Assembling the picture for the first time, like a giant jigsaw puzzle of Britain, was a nightmare. But sure enough, within weeks we had discovered what came to be known as the 'squeezed middle' – the poorest third of workers, whose plight was nowhere near as grim as in the United States, but who, it was clear, were falling behind. The fruits of Britain's growth were no longer fairly shared. I took the lessons to the Cabinet a few months later with a plea that we at least talk about the problem, to show that we 'got it'. But by then, it was all too late. On Thursday, 6 May 2010, we were defeated at the polls.

Ever since those fateful meetings in Washington, I have been obsessed with the question of how we fix our country to fairly share the national harvest. I've written books on the history of our economy, to show how markets have both good entrepreneurs and bad, and how new economies like China have changed the rules of the game. I've studied how we have created a global marketplace of more than 7 billion people, only to watch new tech monopolies mushroom in America, the land of the free, while new trading autocracies multiply in the lands of the unfree, like China. I've worked across the political divide in Britain, and around the world, to try and find an overlapping consensus for ideas that might help us rebuild a more united kingdom and defend our politics from the economic crime and corruption that now infect, like a pestilence, the corridors of power. It was the US senator, Mark Hanna, who once said: 'There are two things that are important in politics. The first is money, and I can't remember what the second one is.' More often now, I feel the same about British politics.

I am by nature, an optimist. We now live not merely in an era of change, but in a change of era. The prizes of economic growth in the years ahead will be enormous.[7] But if we are to fairly share the future, we need not a revolution, but a reformation and a renaissance of a very old ideal: not simply a wealthy democracy but a democracy of wealth. You might call it a wealth-owning democracy.

For two thousand years, philosophers have celebrated the importance of property to democracy and a good life, clear-eyed about Grimmelshausen's wisdom that 'gold lendeth a man strength'.[8] From Plato to Aristotle and beyond – to Aquinas, Hegel, Hobbes, Locke, Hume, Kant, Marx and Mill – there has long been a recognition that inequality of wealth underpins all other inequalities.[9] So much political theory counsels that every citizen has a right to a fair share of the fruits of growth.

No-one has ever really proposed that assets should be somehow divided into mathematically equal shares. But from the days of Plato, there has been a persistent idea that healthy politics require a fair spread of the ownership of wealth, because, as the American jurist Louis D. Brandeis once put it, 'we can have democracy… or we can have great wealth concentrated in the hands of the few, but we can't have both'. Aristotle argued that private ownership promoted virtues like prudence and responsibility.[10] At the dawn of the Enlightenment, Jean-Jacques Rousseau declared that no citizen should 'be so rich that he can buy another, and none so poor that he is compelled to sell himself'.[11] Adam Smith believed that the 'wealth of nations' required wealth for the nation's people; he, in turn, shaped the thinking of Thomas Paine, who was a major influence on the early American republic. Both Thomas Paine and Thomas

Jefferson put the idea of assets centre-stage in the tradition of civic republican thought.[12]

On the Right in Britain, the idea of a property-owning democracy became mainstream, thanks to the work of the Scottish Conservative & Unionist MP Noel Skelton, who argued in the 1920s that 'since today practically all citizens have political rights, all should possess something of their own'.[13] It was a line of argument that profoundly influenced prime ministers like Anthony Eden, Harold Macmillan, Winston Churchill and Margaret Thatcher.

On the Left, the same idea was championed by Labour's great revisionist thinkers such as Hugh Gaitskell, Tony Crossland and Douglas Jay, in a debate transformed by the Nobel Prize-winner, Sir James Meade, who knew that an 'unequal distribution of property means an unequal distribution of power and status'.[14] Meade, in turn, convinced the great liberal philosopher John Rawls that a property-owning democracy was the best guarantor of justice, because it prevented 'a small part of society from controlling the economy and, indirectly, political life as well'.[15]

Down the ages, and from around the world, there is endless evidence that inequality in general, and wealth inequality in particular, creates the divisions that make for unhappy societies – and that is dangerous. On the walls of Renaissance council chambers throughout Europe could be found the advice of the Roman historian Sallust, that 'small states grow with concord; discord causes great ones to dissolve'. Truly great nations find ways to reconcile this conflict of factions.[16] And that is much easier in a country where *everyone* can build wealth. Democracies should be nations of freedom, happiness and justice. But as Roosevelt understood, our freedoms require security and power. And security and power require wealth. Not just for some, but for all.

★

Optimists do not need to be utopians. I was a utopian when I was younger, but now I am a politician, and the hard knocks of losing elections jolt the stars from starry eyes. I know that there are limits to the sort of changes that are possible, and I have learned that the best way to be radical is to sound reassuring, a quality that the phrase 'wealth-building' commands.[17] I might wish that this book were akin to a political trophy cabinet, but it is not. It is more a *Bildungsroman*, comprising the lessons I have learned the hard way since Maundy Thursday in 2010.

The office of the chief secretary to the Treasury looks out onto St James's Park. With a comforting precision, once a week, the Mounted Band of the Household Cavalry, impeccable in their black and silver uniforms, march under the window with full military fanfare and faded memories of greatness. From my desk, I had one of the best views of St James's pelicans, fountains and lawns, which stretch up towards Buckingham Palace. I love the park. It is where I proposed to my wife. Now, on that cool and bright April day in 2010, I looked out on the beautiful pink cherry blossom in full bloom. But it was time to go. The election was upon us. I sat down to finish a few thank-you letters to some of the brilliant civil servants I had worked with on two budgets, and then I thought I would write one more note, to my successor.

There is an old tradition of hand-over notes in the Treasury. It is a bit of gallows humour, which dates back to 1929, when Winston Churchill bounded down the Treasury steps to greet his successor, Philip Snowden, with the news that there was 'nothing in the till'. Thirty-five years later, Reginald Maudling, the departing Conservative chancellor, wrote to James Callaghan: 'Good luck, old cock... Sorry to leave it in such a mess.' I thought I would pen something in the same tradition, and just as brief: 'Dear Chief Secretary,' I wrote, 'I'm afraid to tell you there is no money.'

Politics is a rough trade. For fifteen years, that wretched leaving note has been wielded and waved by prime ministers like a rallying flag for *laissez-faire* economics, ignoring the advice of even that free-market apostle Friedrich Hayek, who warned in *The Road to Serfdom* that it was 'the wooden insistence' on *laissez faire* that had 'done so much harm to the liberal cause'. Today, a philosophy of *laissez faire*, disguised with flags not of patriotism but tribalism, is leading us not to serfdom, but to dystopia.

So, these are the notes I wish I had left. In Part I of the book, I explain what has happened to the inequality of wealth and the peril that lies ahead if we don't change the way wealth is (or is not) shared. Part II unpacks how it is we have reached this sorry state, before, in Part III, I show the way I think we should fix things. Together, these notes show how a different kind of future is possible.

That future might not be a land of milk and honey, but it *could* be a place where we all live longer, wealthier and happier lives. If we are to avoid war or revolution, we will need a reformation. That will require us to summon the moral imagination to refresh fraternity and build the coherent amity required to modernize both the state and the market for new times – and take us off the road to dystopia.

PART I

1

The Absurdity of Affluence

The lives and loves of the super-rich

The rich have lovely things. Stroll around the magical Rolls Royce factory, nestled deep in the Sussex Downs, and you can see some of them being made. Designed by the architect Sir Nicholas Grimshaw, Rolls Royce HQ is more like a clinic than a factory. Arranged around a cool slate-grey courtyard, with trees cut into neat box shapes, the immaculate five-storey buildings are home to a quiet production line from which glide engineering masterpieces that cost up to a million pounds.

Just fifteen cars are made here every day. Every one is customized to any whim and fantasy you can think of. Need the roof's interior to look like the night sky on the day you proposed to your partner? No problem. Or would you prefer thousands of peacock feathers woven into an intricate tapestry? Just say the word. Crests, logos or coats of arms designed into the upholstery are not untypical. If you would like your Phantom the same shade of green as an Amazonian tree frog, well that is perfectly do-able. Or what about a colour scheme to go with your private jets? It might take a couple of years to match the aircraft paint, but do not let that stop you. If you lack a jet, you might like instead a paint with a clear coat of crystal flakes: it lights up as the sun comes out. Inside, you can rest your own hide on the hide of cows that come from the world's highest altitudes, just to make sure they are not pock-marked by ugly mosquito bites. And as you set off on your drive you'll enjoy a ride that glides like a magic carpet, if you can imagine such a thing.

Rolls Royce sells to what you might call 'ultra luxury clients'. 'They want something very special that nobody else has,' explained one of the directors to me when I stopped by for a visit. 'They want something that matches their interests and their tastes and their desires. To a level that's completely unique to them and reflects their personalities.'

The luckiest of these owners will park their limousines outside their mansions, like the grand houses on Britain's most expensive road, Phillimore Gardens, just off London's Kensington High Street. Giant eighteenth-century townhouses line the road. Bentleys and Ferraris line the kerbs. Uniformed staff fuss around the courtyards with blowers to clear stray leaves. The gardens back onto Holland Park. When I took a stroll to have a look, one house was even offering private swimming lessons – in its basement. The average price of a home here? Twenty-four million pounds. You could buy an entire street in my constituency of Hodge Hill for that.

To move between your mansions, you may of course need a jet. Now, we do not make private jets in the UK, but we do service them, and when I asked to visit the Gulfstream hangars in Farnborough, Hampshire, the company was initially enthusiastic. Until the 'manager, public and media relations' found out, whereupon I got a terse email explaining I could not visit after all 'given the need to focus on customer support and other business priorities for the foreseeable future'.

Never mind. There's always the open water, and in the UK we do make super-yachts. And where better to choose your cruiser than the Monaco Yacht Show? Tucked into a narrow strip of the French Riviera, where the pearl-white and fern-green Alpes-Maritimes descend to the Mediterranean, the little Principality of Monaco is a theatre of luxury, in which the annual Yacht Show is its greatest production.

In the soft warmth of the September air beneath a beautiful azure sky, an alternative reality unfolds every year where everything is inexplicably expensive. It is busy but not bustling, the air is full of English, and everyone seems to be doing something, though not anything very pressing, and with the confidence that it is not that important if the things that everyone was *supposed* to be doing do not actually get done. Which is how the Monegasques like to carry themselves. Everyone is wearing Italian blazers, expensive shoes, sunglasses and enormously pricey watches. The valets park the nicest cars on the vast bone-white courtyard before the elegant marbled symmetry of the Beaux-Arts Monte Carlo casino, which looks down onto the Port Hercule.

In that first Yacht Show after Covid-19, the sunny quayside was lined with elegant peaked white tents, the principality's red, white and blue flags flew stiff in the sea-breeze, and the bay was the colour of lapis lazuli. From restaurant terraces, you could admire the sleek and dashing lines of the new 115-metre-long super-yacht *AHPO*, inspired by the LaFerrari super-car, and designed, according to its manufacturer Lürssen, 'to enable a healthy and family-focused life' while travelling 'to her destinations in utmost comfort'.[1] Alongside her, at anchor, was the 90-metre *Phoenix II*, with its New York Art Deco interiors, and the 89-metre *Here Comes the Sun*, with its on-board beach club and spa, a self-playing grand piano and a sun deck big enough to land its own helicopter. Some of the yachts in Monaco were large enough have yachts within yachts. And together, the 118 super-yachts at that year's show were worth a cool £3.1 billion. But even that is nothing compared to, say, Roman Abramovich's 162-metre *Eclipse*, a single craft costing £1.2 billion and boasting a missile-detection system and bullet-proof windows.

Apparently, no-one actually buys a yacht in Monaco. But according to Stephen Hill, the commercial director of Pendennis, Britain's most successful super-yacht builder, it is a rather nice place to nurture relationships before, perhaps, an invitation to a shipyard – like the giant Pendennis 'yard' at the mouth of Cornwall's Carrick Roads. Here, framed against the sheer 150-foot black cliff face at the edge of the Falmouth estuary, are gigantic dry docks, with sheds half the size of a football stadium. And inside, propped up on shipping containers, are huge water craft.

British yards are not as big as those in Italy, Holland or France, and to build the world's biggest yachts – a sort of Abramovich-scale affair – you would have to go to Germany, which has a naval shipyard that has turned its hand to commercial work. But what was, ten years ago, a big project for Pendennis is now small beer, for at 46 metres long, some of these vessels are still nearly half the length of a football pitch.

It was lunchtime when I arrived, so the halls were strangely quiet. The concrete floors were wet from the morning's rainstorms, and I could smell the sea as Stephen showed me around the business of selling, building and refurbishing a super-yacht. One hall houses the largest sailing catamaran in the world; it started life as a new-build project in the United States. Another hall is filled by a giant tug now converted to a pleasure-craft. Some super-craft are sheathed inside vast plastic tents to create a temperature- and air-controlled environment for repainting and respraying them. Hundreds of people might work on any one job, which could take up to eighteen months, and once the teams finish work, the front doors of the halls are opened, the dry dock flooded and the craft sails out into the harbour.

'Our model,' explained Stephen, 'is like a service industry really. We bring the people together and the skill set together to be able to take your boat and do what you want to do with it... it's not us saying, "What you want is one of these."' And no

Pendennis customer turns up with a blank sheet of paper. The act of super-yacht buying is all about having something unique and different. As Stephen put it, 'It's a bit like, "I could have a Rolls Royce but I don't want a Rolls Royce. I actually want my own car that is somewhere between a Rolls Royce, a Bentley, and a Ferrari and I'm going to pay people to build me my own car."'

Like a Rolls Royce, these enormous machines are incredible bits of engineering. All told, as much as a million man-hours of work goes into building or refurbishing one. Their state-of-the-art radar systems are so advanced, Stephen told me, that 'if you took a Royal Navy captain off one of our warships and put him on a super-yacht bridge they would probably cry with jealousy'. There is a huge amount of work simply refurbishing these things every five years to keep them ship-shape and secure a clean bill of health from the insurers. That alone might set you back £6–8 million in maintenance, on a craft that cost you £30–40 million to buy.

Can I confess that I left the Pendennis yard awestruck? Maybe it was because, when I was a boy, a super-yacht was beyond my wildest imagination. In fact, I could not imagine anything more magnificent than a Rolls Royce. But of course, these days, if you have really made it, you do not want a yacht or a Roller. You want a rocket.

At 9.12 a.m. Eastern Daily Time, on Tuesday, 20 July 2021, Amazon-founder Jeff Bezos blasted off with three fellow passengers into the azure American sky to become the first man to pay his way into outer space. Over eleven glorious minutes, his oddly phallic-looking 18-metre-high spaceship crossed the Kármán Line, which notionally divides our atmosphere from space, ascending 66.5 miles above the earth before falling back, with a sonic boom, to a dusty landing in the West Texas scrublands. 'Best day ever!' he declared. 'My expectations were high and they were dramatically exceeded.' Dressed in a blue jumpsuit and a cowboy hat, he then proceeded to lay credit where credit was due: 'I... want to thank every Amazon employee and every Amazon customer. Cause you guys paid for all this.'[2]

But that summer, Mr Bezos was not alone. Ten days before his space adventure, the 70-year-old British billionaire Richard Branson flew a 90-minute trip on his SpaceShipTwo to just below the Kármán Line. 'Welcome to the dawn of a new space age,' declared Sir Richard upon arriving home. 'To all you kids down there, I was once a child with a dream. Looking up to the stars. Now, I'm an adult in a spaceship with lots of other wonderful adults looking down to our beautiful, beautiful earth.' Lucky him. And to welcome him home, who showed up in Sir Richard's kitchen at 3 a.m? None other than Elon Musk, whose SpaceX firm launched four civilians into earth's orbit two months later for a three-day jaunt. The era of the new super-rich space barons had dawned.

The trophies of the super-rich – the exquisite toys, the gilded and gated palaces, the tiny rockets, the small jets, the giant yachts – are now the stuff of modern myth and legend. Is it not the tragedy of our age that the human genius of so many is poured into pleasing the super-human lusts of so few? It is the absurdity of affluence. But there is not just one man flying rockets. There are three. The year 2021 saw record sales of super-yachts, a total of 887 – more than *double* the number sold in 2019. In London that year, more luxury properties were sold than anywhere else in the world.[3] An 'extremely rare' North London nine-bedroom home, complete with a triple-height underground swimming pool, recently went up for sale for £110 million.[4] There are now fifteen streets in the British capital where the *average* house price is more than £15 million.[5] In 2022, sales of luxury Rolls Royce cars hit an all-time high: 6,021 vehicles, making it the best year for sales in the company's 119-year history.[6] In the same year, auction sales at

Sotheby's, Christie's and Phillips topped £11 billion, up 12 per cent on the previous year.[7] And in 2023, at the time of writing, sales of private jets were forecast to reach their *highest* ever level, the global fleet having more than doubled in the last two decades.[8] Make no mistake, the super-rich have never had it so good – and the gigantic ego-industry that serves them, pushing the frontiers of art and engineering, has ballooned alongside an extraordinary billionaire boom.

In 2019, before the Covid-19 pandemic, which cost the world an incredible £15 trillion of lost output, the world's richest 52 million people – now better known as the top 1 per cent – owned almost half of global wealth. That was £140 trillion. And then the pandemic struck. Yet, despite the worst health disaster of modern times, the super-rich actually got richer.[9] According to the *Financial Times*, in the first year of the crisis, the 'total wealth of billionaires worldwide rose by $5 trillion... the most dramatic surge ever registered on the annual billionaire list.'[10]

A casual read of the *Forbes* billionaire list helps us understand the scale of the transformation under way.[11] Over the twelve years between 2010 and 2022, the number on the Forbes billionaires list more than doubled, from 1,001 to 2,640 globally. The rise in their combined wealth was even more spectacular: it more than tripled from £2.9 trillion (in 2010) to almost £10 trillion in 2022, transforming economies – and politics – around the world.

In the United States, Bernie Sanders, the senior senator from Vermont, is probably the American politician with the most to say about his nation's super-rich. We recently found ourselves together at a British-American Parliamentary Group conference. White-haired and intense, Bernie has an electric smile that comes alive whenever someone asks for a selfie – which is all the time. I put it to him that the conspicuous consumption of the American super-rich was surely now more extreme than in the days of the Great Gatsby. 'Absolutely,' said Bernie:

... it is probably worse than it was in what we call the Gilded Age. You have people who are competing with each other as those yachts are getting bigger. You're seeing all of these people on their own jets. They live in mansions all over the world. Some of them own their own islands. I mean, the absurdity of this affluence is so great that you're seeing people like Bezos or Musk literally going off into outer space on their little spaceships.

'So yes,' he concluded, 'you are seeing an extraordinary level of greed, of opulence, of contempt for ordinary people.'

The Americas now possess more billionaire wealth than anywhere else on earth. But Asia isn't far behind, and the best student of their rise is an old friend, James Crabtree, whose best-selling book tells the inside story of India's *Billionaire Raj.*[12] Back in the 1990s, there were just two Indians on the *Forbes* billionaire list, worth around £2.4 billion between them. Nowadays, India's most exclusive club has ballooned to over one hundred members, which is more than in any other country bar the United States, China and Russia. So how, I asked James, do Indian billionaires enjoy their wealth?

'I think the Indian super-rich have the same habits as the global super-rich,' he told me, 'but the very wealthy in India, like the Gulf, now almost abandon the entire country during the intolerable heat of the summer months.' 'I put it this way,' he joked, 'instead of retreating to the hill stations of Simla, as the English did in the days of the Raj, they retreat to the hill stations of Kensington and Chelsea.'

But if you want to stay at home, you might need the biggest home possible. For James, nothing epitomizes the excess of India's super-rich better than Mukesh Ambani's £1 billion, 27-storey home on Mumbai's Altamount Road, which some estimate cost, in relative terms, as much as the Taj Mahal.[13] Known as 'Residence Antilia', the soaring eco-tower, with lush green planting spilling down its sides, is, after Buckingham

Palace, the most expensive home on earth, boasting a six-storey parking garage, a spa and wellness centre, indoor pools, a cinema and, of course, a snow room. 'The reason why that house is so extraordinary is you just don't get that anywhere else,' James explains. 'Your "normal" sort of Indian billionaire still has an enormous mansion or maybe a kind of a tower block, but nothing, nothing quite as prominent as the Ambani house.'

'Why aspire to such a thing?' I asked. It was, James told me, about creating a private world:

> You know, even in hotels, these guys can't sort of walk around without being without being kind of bothered. So in India you need to have your own buildings because public space is so difficult. So, the Ambani house is the sort of ultimate example of this where you just have everything inside the skyscraper, all your sports equipment [through to] an ability to host a wedding. You have places where you can host anybody you want. It's a sort of private affluence in public squalor.

In China, things are a little different. After all, the arrival of the billionaire is a fairly new phenomenon there, and as Desmond Shum explains in his explosive book *Red Roulette*, those who have made serious wealth have required serious friendships with senior Communist Party officials, who in turn require a bucket-load of discretion. The children of the super-rich, on the other hand, are a different story, and for some years, the bad behaviour of the *fuerdai* – the second-generation rich 'born with silver chopsticks in their mouths' – has made headlines around the world.[14]

Take Wang Sicong, the son of China's richest man. He was already infamous for posting pictures on social media of his Alaskan husky, Keke, adorned with two gold Apple watches, before he spent €350,000 in a single night at a Beijing karaoke bar. Or Ling Gu, son of the former general secretary's chief-of-staff, who died after crashing his Ferrari containing two half-naked young women. Or Lu Xiaobao, who claims descent from a Chinese revolutionary hero, and who provoked national outrage by driving her luxury Mercedes around the Forbidden Palace – where cars are banned. This crowd loves Gucci, Louis Vuitton, Chanel and Versace, along with buying homes in New York, Los Angeles, Sydney, London and Tokyo. As Wang Daqi, a *fuerdai* himself, explains, many of these children are in the transition period of taking control of family businesses.[15] Hence, the almost universal requirement to get an overseas education, ideally in business. (Indeed, I have taught *fuerdai* myself, at Oxford's Saïd Business School.)

By contrast, in Russia, the behaviour of the generations is the other way round. The rise of the super-rich in the United States, India and China has been spectacular, but nowhere has it been so transparently dangerous as in Russia. Paul Caruana-Galizia is among the best students of the phenomenon. A handsome, softly spoken journalist, with brown eyes and a stubbly beard, Paul and I met for the first time in Strasbourg, when he was campaigning for justice for his murdered mother Daphne, killed with a car bomb. He has skilfully unpicked the tale of Russian oligarchs' penetration of the British establishment.[16]

'It's funny,' he told me, 'because they accumulated so much wealth and power that people started seeing them as existing in a different world. And so, in an ironic way, we started caring less about them and almost saw them as exotic things.' He continued:

If you look back to the reporting of Roman Abramovich when he first came here, to London, it's amazing if you think about it; it was like someone spotted a rare tiger: 'Oh, look, yes, this billionaire, and look, he's buying a football club.' It's extraordinary… no-one cared, like, where did he get his money?

As *Tatler* magazine – which knows about these things – put it recently, 'Russians bought swathes of property in Knightsbridge, football clubs and yachts; they shopped on Sloane Street with their bodyguards, bombed through Chelsea in blacked-out Range Rovers; they were flashy, gauche and worst of all, nouveau.' Unlike the Chinese, the Russian children – or 'little tsars' – had to learn a little reserve. Of course, they became fixtures of the season in both Britain and Russia, with Instagram feeds full of private planes, Gloucestershire shoots, Chanel handbags and rooftop pools together with 'louche parties in Moscow one week and genteel days out at Goodwood the next'. But, says *Tatler*, they are 'glamorous, wealthy, hard-working... [but] curiously discreet'.[17]

The inequality of wealth in Britain is not as bad as in America, China, India or Russia. It is not as bad as it was in the days of *Downton Abbey*. But it is twice as bad as income inequality, and it is getting worse. Which is why we *should* be getting worried.

The best unofficial data we have can be found in the pages of the *Sunday Times* and the Rich List it produces every year. The list's compiler, Robert Watts, told me that he has definitely noticed a few changes over the nine years he has edited it, but what stands out is the incredible run of the super-rich in recent years. 'The Rich List dataset is not perfect,' Robert acknowledges, 'but yes, it does suggest that the past five years in particular have been a golden age for Britain's super-rich. We had more wealth in the top 250 of the 2022 list than in the entire 1,000 individuals and families we featured in 2017.'

In 2019, just before the pandemic, the Rich List recorded 151 UK billionaires. Despite all the travails of the British economy – what we might call the ABC of recent history (Austerity, Brexit and Covid-19) – the most recent list at the time of writing (2023) shows that the number of billionaires has gone *up*, rising to a hundred and seventy-one.[18] This might be down six on 2022, but the wealth of this lucky few still soared by almost £87 billion in 2021–23, despite overlapping with a surge in interest rates.[19] That is an incredible contrast to the fortunes of the rest of the UK. The most recent estimates are that over the same period, thanks to the same rising interest rates, an extraordinary £2.5 trillion has been wiped off the value of the UK's net household wealth, as house prices dropped and pension pots shrank – creating the largest fall in household wealth on record.[20]

But this story of differing fortunes is what has defined the last decade and more. In fact, House of Commons Library analysis of data provided by the World Inequality Lab reveals that between 2010 and 2021, the average wealth of an individual in the top 1 per cent of the richest in Britain rose by £1,670,121 – that is thirty-one times the increase in the average wealth of the bottom 99 per cent, which rose by just £53,409.

All told, overall wealth in the UK has risen by more than £4 trillion between 2010 and 2021. An incredible one quarter of it (23 per cent) – nearly £1 trillion (£977 billion) – has gone to the top 1 per cent.[21] And it is very unlikely that we have the full picture, because the data we have to help us understand the super-rich in Britain – of any nationality – is not great. No-one could accuse UK Prime Minister Rishi Sunak of being an unknown figure. Yet he and his wife, the heiress and venture capitalist Akshata Murthy, only appeared on the Rich List in 2022, entering the gilded ranks with a fortune of £730 million that, hitherto, no-one appeared to have noticed.

The UK's 'official' *Survey of Wealth and Assets*, undertaken by the Office of National Statistics (ONS), only dates back to 2006. It is updated every couple of years, but the staff who put it together freely admit that collecting data on the super-rich is very hard. Leading the team is statistician Hilary Mainwaring, who explained to me how the census is compiled: 'Our sample size is around 17,000 over a two-year period, [so] trying to pick up enough [wealthy] people to be able to collect that and measure it at a relatively accurate level can be somewhat difficult.'

The *Survey* includes three basic categories of wealth – property, private pensions and financial assets – but unlike in some studies abroad, no information about the value of business assets is collected, so we only have a partial picture of the true wealth of the very rich. Some of the intricate detail around private pension wealth is sometimes tricky to estimate correctly, and data on 'financial assets' may simply be under-collected. In fact, the UK think-tank Resolution Foundation estimates that some £800 billion is missing from the ONS wealth estimates for the very richest.[22]

'What the actual volume of wealth looks like in the country,' Hilary explained, 'is something that we do struggle with.' She admitted that 'we just don't collect enough [data] on those at the very top' and acknowledged that there were issues in knowing where 'wealth is highly skewed'. In essence, 'We struggle with the top of the distribution and we struggle with the bottom.'

Yet this story of differing fortunes for the rich and poor is only half the tale of how Britain has changed this century. Because, almost unheralded, a profound shift has unfolded to push the rich and poor further and further apart. It is what you might call the wealth-to-wages curve. More than a decade of easy money and low interest rates – flattered by almost £1 trillion of 'quantitative easing' (QE) – has transformed the relationship between, on the one hand, the assets that make up our wealth, and on the other, the wages we earn to buy them.

Back in the 1970s, the total wealth of the UK was around four times the nation's national labour income. Because wealth is a reflection of asset prices, we can see that assets were relatively affordable, if people saved up for a bit. Now, however, a combination of booming asset prices and a long-term squeeze on wages means that the wealth-to-wages curve has been transformed. Indeed, in 2021, on the eve of a new spike in interest rates, UK net household wealth had risen to *ten times* the nation's labour income. All told, between 1970 and 2021 the value of UK wealth (the total price of assets) rose by £12 trillion.

Yet over that same arc of my life, the annual income flowing to labour each year rose by just £1.2 trillion – ten times less.

As we will see, this great transformation has shattered the dream of building a wealth-owning democracy in the UK. Rising interest rates will adjust this picture, and this might mean that homes become more affordable and decent pension pots easier to save. But even the estimated £2.5 trillion meltdown in wealth that has been estimated by some will only return the wealth-to-wages ratio to where it was before the 2008 Financial Crash.[23]

These changing realities are transforming our economy, our politics, and our culture. We never used to read much about the super-rich. Not much. And when we did, in the novels of Balzac or Trollope, Dickens or Dostoyevsky, they were cunning or lax or jaded or cynical.[24] They were not bent on world domination or demanding impunity from the laws and norms that bind the rest of us together. Now, on screen, in a flood of dramas and reality shows, we are treated to banquets of bad manners and misbehaviour from the aristocratic to the semi-pornographic, in the most magnificent *mise-en-scènes*.[25] From America we have stages made of country clubs, tennis clubs, yacht clubs, boardrooms and sky-scrapers, around which rampage casts of characters who are nipped, tucked, bleached, botoxed and blow-dried. From Britain, we have country estates, stables, silver service and cut-glass accents, dinner suits, tweed suits, morning suits and cocktail dresses, furs and sparkly jewellery, cut glass and candelabra, horses, dogs, and birds shot to death. The sets and costumes may vary, but the protagonists have in common a rude and condescending snobbery, along with something worse: a sort of 'aspirational impunity'.[26] As the super-rich Tom Wambsgans boasts in HBO's hit show *Succession*, 'Here's the thing about being rich. It's fucking great. It's like being a superhero, only better. You get to do what you want [and] the authorities can't really touch you.'[27]

A world in which Russian oligarchs build a Londongrad to hide their (stolen) fortunes, in which 'Crazy Rich Asians' party like there's no tomorrow, in which a billionaire Raj bestrides the world's largest democracy, in which space barons race each other into space – none of this is normal. We know that something is going badly wrong. Which is what this stream-athon of wealth-porn might be trying to tell us. This feature of our culture is how we cope with a world that is being re-arranged around us. As Julian Fellowes, creator of *Downton Abbey* explains, today's dramas of riches flourish because they connect to 'a subconscious desire in many people to believe that the rich and successful are somehow morally lacking'.[28] We like the reassurance that in their little lands of bling, banality and bitchiness, the super-rich are as vulgar, vapid and value-free as the worst of us; that for everything about them that is extraordinary, in their stately pleasure-domes, they are, well, less than us. After all, choreographed mockery is how humans have dealt with up-startish behaviour for millennia.

I think it is time we listened harder to our inner fears. When our culture is haunted by an unreconciled uneasiness, we know we are worried. In fact, my polling reveals that nearly three-quarters of British people (72 per cent) now think that the gap between those with lots of wealth and those with little wealth is too large. Worse, around 40 per cent now think that the richest 1 per cent have the most power in the country: that is almost twice the proportion who think that national governments have paramount power (24 per cent).

Things are now so bad that the vast majority of UK citizens believe that Britain has become an 'inheritocracy', where inheritance – not hard work – is the only way to get on in life. They believe that the family you're born into, the availability of useful networks, or one's access to a good education are the most important explanations of wealth – and more important than 'hard work' or 'natural talent'.

Yet what you learn in politics is that things can always get worse. And indeed, on current trends things are set to get *much* worse. Because, if the world's luckiest continue to pile up their riches at the pace enjoyed since the Great Financial Crash of 2008–10, by the year 2030, the top 1 per cent will no longer control half of global wealth but *almost two-thirds*.[29] That is an extraordinary £246 trillion, more than triple the wealth of the top 1 per cent today.[30]

What would such a world be like? I can tell you: poor, corrupt and stagnant.

2

The Cost of Affluence

The damage to decency, democracy and meritocracy

I thought he was about to die. It was just after 10 a.m. on a freezing Sunday in January, and I was out with the Community Street Kitchen team in Birmingham, sharing out blankets, clothes, little packets of sandwiches and warm drinks to the city's homeless. And there, on our final run into New Street Station, we turned into an underpass that stank of urine to find Richard, a double amputee. He was ashen grey, crying in pain and lying next to his wheelchair. As we desperately tried to help him, we saw to our horror that Richard was still dressed in his hospital gown with a hospital tag on his wrist. He had been on the pavement for three days.

Since I lost my dad to a lifelong struggle with alcohol in 2015, I have done whatever I can to shine a light on the way a twist of fate can knock someone from a decent life onto the streets, where too many die. Most of the people I have met are ill. On one typical night, I met 'John', who suffered from paranoid schizophrenia and bipolar disorder. Around the corner was 'Patrick', who had just lost his disability benefits and could not read, so he could not follow the instructions on his medication; instead, he self-medicated with crack and heroin to 'block out the bad thoughts'. At the bottom of the ramp by New Street Station was 'Gaynor', a woman in her fifties whom everyone called 'Mom'. Also bipolar, she self-harmed 'to let things out' when things got too much, and she was addicted to alcohol. She showed me her wrists. They were scarred with cuts. Another pair were camping out in the lobby of a bank on Birmingham's most expensive street: one was nursing the other, his friend, who had been 'swilled' – attacked with a cup of boiling water full of sugar, a torture devised because the sugar sticks to the skin, intensifying the pain. One person could not stop to talk, because he was trying to get his friend to hospital: he had just been bitten by a rat while sleeping, and they were panicking in case he might have sepsis.

Everyone I have met on the streets has suffered some hazard of fortune just like my dad. His descent into alcoholism was triggered by the death of my mum, when she was just fifty-two. I could not save my dad from drinking, but at least I could make sure there was a loving family on hand when crisis struck. Most people on the streets do not have anyone to catch them. Yet their stories unfold in the second city of the sixth-richest country on the planet. It is a long way from the Monaco Yacht Show, and the contrast underlines why we should care about inequality. If society's wealth is a pie, when the lucky have lots of it, there is quite literally less for everyone else. And the numbers of those with 'less' are now extraordinary.[1] In the early 2020s, more than *eight million* working-age adults were living in poverty.[2]

These inequalities are bad for people; yet what alarms me is not only what I see on the streets of Birmingham, but what I see in Westminster's corridors of power. Today's media might be starstruck with tales of the super-rich and their conspicuous consumption. But it is their *inconspicuous* consumption – of power – that should really worry us, because it inexorably heightens the risk for countries, even countries like the UK, of becoming corrupt, poor and stagnant.

Corruption begins when wealth seeks power to protect fortune. *Homo economicus* might be a myth of economics, but *homo pecuniosus*, the wealthy man, is very much a fact of political life, a political animal instinctively drawn to the wellheads of power like wasps to jam on a sunny day. The instinct of the rich to seek power is economically rational. But there is powerful psychology at work too.

More than a century ago, the pioneering sociologist Thorstein Veblen noted in his 1899 book, *The Theory of the Leisure Class*, that once individuals had food and shelter in abundance, it was status that then became important. And the way status was acquired was through consumption – and ever grander displays of privilege. One of the best students of this reality today is Brooke Harrington, Professor of Sociology at Dartmouth College in the United States, who specializes in economic anthropology. She went to the lengths of training for two years to become a wealth manager, in order to understand the super-rich a little better. When we met, Brooke explained why Veblen was right: 'The point of earning more money is to buy yourself more social status,' she said, 'because when you have higher status, it triggers these feel-good chemicals in your brain, like dopamine and serotonin. It makes you feel good.'

'How do we know?' I asked. Because, according to Brooke, primate studies reveal a lot. 'It turns out that if you measure the blood levels of the alpha ape, or monkey, their serotonin, testosterone and dopamine levels are higher than those of the other monkeys or apes.' And we know that this is not simply correlation, but causation, as Brooke explains:

Take a monkey who's way down at the bottom, and move [it] to the top, and kaboom, those levels of serotonin and dopamine, and other neurotransmitters that make us feel good, shoot up. So, the assumption is the same thing happens in people. So we're basically status addicts.

Working with wealth managers from around the world, Brooke heard plenty of horror stories of what happens when these instincts unfold, unchecked. 'One of the wealth managers I spoke to said, "I tell my co-workers if I ever become like our clients just shoot me because not only are they horrible people who basically don't want to play by any of society's rules like tax, [but] they want, like, full and complete freedom from all laws and all social norms."' 'This guy told me,' Brooke went on, aghast, 'that "Some of my clients, in all seriousness, believe that they are the descendants of the pharaohs and that they are entitled to inherit the earth. So they behave like pharaohs. That's what you're dealing with here. You're dealing with delusional neo-pharaohs."'

Few men illustrate the hunger of the rich for power better than Mohammed Amersi, as I discovered one January morning in 2023 when I stopped by the Royal Courts of Justice to watch him – or rather his barristers – in action. Just opposite the church of St Clement Danes at the top of London's Strand, the Royal Courts are a magnificent seashell-coloured cathedral to the law, built in Portland stone, replete with soaring gothic arches, stained-glass windows and immaculately polished marble-mosaic floors you can slide across – if the security guards do not catch you. I was heading for Court 13, a compact cubic court about twice the size of a squash court. The lovely brown carved panelling lent the place a Protestant simplicity, reminiscent of the City churches designed by Sir Christopher Wren. It was warm, and the black-gowned clerks yawned and stretched beneath the high bench from which the judge looked down upon us all.

Gathered together behind the barristers' desks was a group of supporters of the former MP, Charlotte Leslie, whom Mr Amersi was trying to sue for defamation, because Ms Leslie had warned the hierarchy of the Conservative Party that Mr Amersi had a past. Indeed, it was quite a past. Mr Amersi was exposed by the BBC's *Panorama* programme as being involved in one of Europe's biggest corruption scandals, which entailed £177 million being paid to a Gibraltar-based company owned by the daughter of the President of Uzbekistan.

Over the years, Mr Amersi had become a very serious donor to the Conservative Party, stumping up £524,000. He always insisted that his political donations came from UK profits, but the *Financial Times* revealed that he had 'received $4 million from a company he knew to be secretly owned by a powerful Russian' – President Putin's then telecoms minister.

Nevertheless, Mr Amersi had suggested that the party might like to make him chair of a new outfit, the Conservative Friends of the Middle East and North Africa, which would of course be a fabulous calling card in places where Mr Amersi had plenty of business interests. Indeed, Mr Amersi had a name for this: 'access capitalism'. 'You get access,' he boasted to *The Times*, 'you get invitations, you get privileged relationships, if you are part of the set up, and where you are financially making a contribution to be a part of that set-up. Absolutely.'[3]

Ms Leslie's warning, however, had proved quite the setback. Not to be defeated, Mr Amersi was now suing in a case that he ultimately lost. But the case underlines the risk we now run: when wealth inequality rises, so does the risk that the wealthy buy into politics to seize the pens that write our laws – and use that influence, bluntly, for their own self-interest.

One of the most astute observers of this risk in recent years is Oliver Bullough. His book *Moneyland* (2018) was among the first to light up the incredible global industry of 'enablers' who help the fortunate minimize their dues. When we met to chat, he was very clear about the risks of unequal countries: 'obviously... the greater the concentration of wealth, the greater the temptation of people with power to accommodate the wishes of that wealth... Because wealth is just stored power, right? It's like the battery that you can charge up'.

Gloom about graft is literally as old as Western literature. 'I would not be an honest man, not now,' lamented Hesiod in the eighth century BC, 'Nor wish it for my son – when I see how/ It's evil to be honest in a land/ Where crooks and schemers have the upper hand.' But what fascinates me is the way that the great British public has an instinctive sense of this. In my most recent polling with the Policy Institute, King's College, London, we asked people what they feared most from a world where the top 1 per cent has the most power. The answer was 'unfair business influence' on governments and a rising risk of corruption.[4] People know that rising wealth inequality risks the emergence of a super-class with the power to lord it over the rest of us.

A world where oligarchs *roam* the earth becomes a world where oligarchs *rule* the earth, while not paying their taxes.

When the luckiest burrow their way into power and use that power to find ways to hoard, not share, the harvest, the result is very simple: the impoverishment of the nation and the defunding of government. So, when we have extremes of wealth inequality, we risk a world where a bigger and bigger share of national product is hidden from the taxman.

Of course, many successful people *are* scrupulous in playing by the rules. Indeed, the wealth of many of Britain's most successful people is critical in paying the bills for Britain's public services. In 2022, for example, the *Sunday Times* Tax List reckoned that Britain's fifty biggest tax contributors from its Rich List chipped in around £3.7 billion.[5] But there are a surprising number of people on the Rich List who do not feature on the Tax List at all, and that helps illustrate the problem: the overall tax take in Britain is not as healthy as it should be for the simple reason that while many of the super-rich do pay their taxes, the problem of what Brooke Harrington calls 'aspirational impunity' means that too many do not. And in the UK, a huge industry has boomed over the last century, devoted to helping the lucky in life keep as much of their wealth as possible. And this puts pressure on everyone else.

As if we needed proof, recent years have given us a snowstorm of 36 million leaked files, showered on journalists like ticker tape on a Broadway parade, and revealing a common thread in scandals with sunny code-names. The great data dumps of the Panama, Paradise and Pandora files have uncovered the sheer scale of wealth disguised, out of sight of the tax authorities, by the most powerful of perpetrators, including 120 politicians and their immediate relatives. When the rich avoid their taxes, as Oliver Bullough explains, 'you end up with a situation whereby to support any basic functioning of the state, taxes have to be levied off an ever smaller share of national wealth, which then degrades ever faster [and] then the incentive for anyone who can afford it to stick their stuff in trust becomes ever larger.'[6]

There are, of course, many philanthropic billionaires. But there are also many with great wealth who venture into politics for the worst of reasons, equipped with very low levels of empathy and a concern to dismantle anything resembling redistribution and, thereby, their tax bills. One US study on the political views and activities of the top 1 per cent of American wealth-holders concluded: 'We find that they [the richest] are extremely active politically and that they are much more conservative than the American public as a whole with respect to important policies concerning taxation, economic regulation, and especially social welfare programs.'[7]

But why do the very rich behave like this? In the worst case, political engagement can resemble Brooke's 'aspirational impunity'. She describes it as 'the rush of being able to use the laws as a weapon against other people to protect your private property and your legal rights... the law is a weapon in your hands, but you are never subject to that weapon'. And where that search for status becomes a quest for political influence it can ruin the public square for the majority. Advances in anthropology and, indeed, neuroscience help explain things, as Brooke described:

> There's neuroscience research that says that when you become wealthy and powerful, one of the things that happens is [that] it sort of decreases the functioning of your mirror neurons. Those are the brain structures which allow us to put ourselves in the shoes of other people. It's literally your ability to understand the consequences of your actions for other people.

Some of this research has been pioneered under Dacher Keltner, a professor of psychology at the University of California, Berkeley. His team's experiments involved giving $10 each to volunteers, of different income levels, which they could share with a stranger. What they found, in 2010, was that those with a lower income level gave more.[8] As Keltner put it later, 'we've done several studies that look at how your wealth, education, and prestige of your career or family predict generosity. And the results are consistent: poorer people assist other people more than wealthy people.'[9] Keltner hypothesizes that poorer people, because they face more risks in life, survive by connecting with others and forming strong social ties. 'Humans,' he goes on 'have this wonderful ability to bond in the face of threat.'[10]

But what is really striking are studies of the vagus nerve, which stretches from brainstem to the abdomen. When it is active, we feel a warm expansion, as when we are moved emotionally. In Keltner's studies, students from lower-class backgrounds had a high vagus-nerve response when shown images of children with cancer. Conversely, 'We didn't get much response at all in upper-class students,' Keltner explains. 'In fact, in every study we've done, poorer people show a stronger vagus nerve response. To me, that's tough proof.'[11]

In fact, as reported in 'seven separate studies', researchers at UC, Berkeley, 'consistently found that upper-class participants were more likely to lie and cheat when gambling or negotiating', more likely to 'cut people off when driving', and more likely to 'endorse unethical behavior in the workplace'.[12] One study found that 'upper-class participants presented with scenarios of unscrupulous behaviour were more likely than the individuals in the other socio-economic classes to report replicating this type of behaviour themselves'.[13]

Dr Paul Piff, who was part of the study team, has gone on to develop the experiment with loaded rounds of the board-game Monopoly.[14] Two hundred volunteers were invited to play, but some players were given twice as much cash as others and were allowed to collect twice as much money when passing Go; they also got to roll the dice twice as often. As the games went on, the 'rich' players 'spoke louder, moved their pieces more aggressively, and even consumed more pretzels from bowls'. 'We had little gradients on the table where you could measure how much space a person is taking up from when they began to when they ended,' Piff told me. 'The richer players began to take up more room. They got bigger as they got richer.'

Yet the risk of the rich behaving badly is not simply a lower tax take to pay for public services. As we can now see all too vividly in Britain, an industry of enablers which flourished to minimize the tax liabilities of the wealthy can all too easily morph into an 'impunity industry' with all the tricks, tradecraft and technology to enable something darker: economic crime.

The story of Britain's impunity industry began a century ago, but it has flourished in the years since the fall of the Berlin Wall and coincided with the collapse of the Soviet Union and the rapid deregulation of London's financial services industry.[15]

While an extraordinary network of enablers may have started by sheltering clean money, it has now helped Britain become one of the world's capitals of dirty money.

Oliver Bullough explains the dynamics like this: the *globalization* of wealth, alongside the *fragmentation* of regulation and legislation, has allowed the very rich to move money anywhere, because the incentives for individual jurisdictions are to try and attract as much of that wealth as they can. What emerges is a 'tragedy of the commons', whereby 'It might be good for the world that this wealth is taxed at a high level to prevent wealth inequality – but what is good for the City of London is different.' And this, Oliver explains, has had terrible consequences for Britain, because 'when you plug a corrupt jurisdiction – with complete inequality of all kinds – into a rule-of-law jurisdiction [as in Britain], then you end up with people being able to, essentially, use their criminal control of power in one place to obtain a legal amount of wealth in another place'.

Your average oligarch now has access to an extraordinary playbook of techniques designed to help the rich get richer. Among Parliament's experts on this dark craft is Dame Margaret Hodge, who used to chair the Public Accounts Committee and who has relentlessly campaigned on the issue. In an explosive report called 'Losing Our Moral Compass: Corrupt Money and Corrupt Politics', which she produced for King's College, London, Dame Margaret summed up the risks of the impunity industry:

> The methods used crop up time and time again. They set up companies in the UK or in our tax havens. They use British banks, accountants, lawyers and advisers to establish the structures that will help them bring their illicit wealth into the legitimate economy. They use the UK courts in litigation about their wealth. They buy expensive properties in the UK, they use their ill-gotten gains to purchase luxuries from

jewellery to art or furs to private schooling for their children. They secure citizenship through golden visas. They grow their influence through philanthropic giving, and through buying into major institutions like football clubs and they contribute towards political parties and politicians.[16]

To date, the report is unpublished, because of threats from one of the oligarchs named. But her conclusion is stark: 'Tax is avoided or evaded through *the very same mechanisms by which money is laundered.*' (My italics.) The problem was so bad, she concluded, that 'the UK is shifting from a facilitator of corruption elsewhere... to a jurisdiction where corrupt behaviours are also beginning to flourish'.

To plumb the depths of this, on one October morning in 2022, I and sixteen other MPs assembled in the elegant blue and concrete-grey Boothroyd Room of the House of Commons for an autopsy – on the filthy, malignant state of Britain's economic crime, or more precisely: for the witness hearings for the Economic Crime Bill that a number of us had pushed so hard for. It was a tragedy that it took Russia's 2022 invasion of Ukraine for UK ministers to get serious about policing economic crime, but nevertheless, here we were, arranged around an oak horseshoe-shaped table to cross-examine an army of experts on the fastest growing crimes in Britain: fraud, corruption and money laundering. Here were police officers and commanders, researchers, barristers, experts in counter-terrorism, activists, financial forensic specialists, bankers and think-tankers. And the picture they painted was appalling.

Like modern-day rot-spreaders, the corrupt scatter the spores of graft like a fungus into the timbers of our national institutions, where they canker. Dirty fortunes will always seek assets – like real estate, reputation, relationships – and thus influence, allowing the truly enterprising to shift up a gear, from breaking the law they do not like to buying the laws they would prefer. And the problem with economic crime, especially for under-funded governments, is that the police cannot afford to stop the sin, while those in public life cannot resist its fruits. In the UK, the proceeds of suspect wealth are now slowly and surely seeping into the royal court and the judicial courts, into charities and universities, and into the property market and the nation's power structures themselves.

In *Moneyland*, Oliver laid out how kleptocrats follow a three-step process: 'steal, hide, spend'. The autopsy that we MPs performed for the Economic Crime Bill suggested a little modification. Today's playbook seems to consist of six steps: stealing, hiding, migrating, followed by spending, dodging and (reputational) cleaning.

Stealing the money is something Duncan Hames, a former MP and now head of policy at Transparency International, knows all about. We got to know each other during his time in Parliament and I have always admired his combination of intelligence and integrity. He explained for me the way corruption and inequality are intrinsically linked. 'We [at Transparency International] define corruption as the abuse of entrusted power for private political gain.' So, in cases of corruption, 'something which is meant to be serving the wider population of the public is instead distorted to serve a private interest'. In the worst cases, this becomes a recipe for inequality:

> Organised systems of extracting wealth from a whole pop-
> ulation put it in the hands of a few. That obviously creates
> inequality. Assets, which are part of a shared wealth, which
> could be providing benefits and services to a whole popula-
> tion, end up in the hands of a very small number of people
> for their own private interests.

So, I asked, once you have got quite pronounced levels of inequality in society, does it simply multiply? Duncan was unequivocal: 'It *is* a vicious cycle,' he replied.

If you have a system of government where those who have the greatest wealth are able to command the greatest influence – and then capture the way the public-interest decisions are made to serve their own interests – then having unequal amounts of money can be a tool to enjoy unequal benefits from the way our society is governed.

The channels by which this happens are various. It might be abuse of government contracts, or expropriating a natural resource. The methods, too, might vary, from bribery to something more subtle, like lobbying. But what is common is that the public good is milked for private gain. And the sheer scale of this nowadays is mind-blowing. The World Bank and World Economic Forum now put the total global cost of corruption at more than 5 per cent of the world economic product. Bribes alone are estimated to cost more than £800 billion a year.[17]

To really understand this phenomenon, I talked with someone who knows an awful lot about it. Arturo Herrera Gutierrez is the softly spoken former Mexican finance minister, who now helms the anti-corruption team at the World Bank in Washington, DC. One balmy September, I sat down with him at World Bank headquarters, together with a group of anti-corruption crusading MPs from across Africa, to ask some basic questions. Is corruption getting worse? If so, why? And if it is getting worse, how much of it can we blame on the rise in inequality?

'I often say, half joking,' he chuckled, 'I have never seen a politician running on a platform to increase corruption.' And yet the scale of corruption today is quite possibly, unprecedented – ironically due to the transition to democracy, as Arturo explained:

Many countries twenty years ago were living under auto-cratic regimes, and then transitioned to democracy which is extremely important, really good. But that also means there's additional electoral competitions and electoral competitions

[that] require financing, and one of the things that we are seeing is corruption which is not necessarily linked to personal enrichment but which has a political intention behind it.

At its most extreme, he concluded:

... if you have very polarized economic power, you may get state capture... some very few powerful people may buy the media, get members of Parliament elected who are close to them, [or] influence the regulatory agencies. So they buy access, and... one of the things that could happen is that they get contracts awarded in a non-competitive manner. So there's a link between inequality and corruption.

The second step for the economic criminal is to hide the money, smuggling it through a variety of trusts, shell companies and bank accounts layered in jurisdictions – say, a Singapore company owned by a company registered in the British Virgin Islands, which is in turn owned by a Liechtenstein trust with nominee proxy owners and directors. The UN's Financial Accountability Transparency and Integrity Panel estimated that criminals launder the equivalent of 2.7 per cent of global GDP each year. That is £1.3 trillion dollars – similar to the GDP of Canada.[18] Much of it flows through London, because every day £1.8 trillion moves through the City's financial institutions. It is the proverbial haystack in which to hide the dirty needle. Ministers have admitted that 'there is a realistic possibility that the scale of money laundering impacting the UK annually is hundreds of billions of pounds'.[19] Even conservative estimates from Ben Wallace, the UK's security minister at the time, suggested that money-laundering alone might total some £90 billion.[20] The National Crime Agency thinks a further £190 billion is lost to fraud. That is a significant chunk of the UK's GDP. Yet the National Crime Agency is so starved of resources that its director general said that it could not take on cases where the legal costs were too high.

To the UK's shame, it is the City of London's financial infrastructure that has oiled some of the world's largest money-laundering scandals. Between 2007 and 2015, €200 billion of suspicious transactions moved silently from Estonia, Russia and Latvia through an Estonian branch of Danske Bank. 'They could have gone anywhere in the world,' a senior NCA officer told me, but 'they chose to launder 40 per cent of it through the UK… It is staggeringly bad.' About 5 per cent of it went through UK banks, but 35 per cent of it went through corporate structures set up through Companies House just to give it that magical 'facade of reasonableness and regularity'.

But the table of crimes in recent times is larger even than this. In fact, Global Witness believes that over the decade to 2016, Britain's impunity industry helped launder some £68 billion out of Russia – through British Overseas Territories alone.[21] The hugely complicated 'Troika laundromat', exposed in March 2019, saw £3.9 billion moved out of Russia, including through shell companies in the British Virgin Islands. The 'Russian laundromat' (2010–14) saw £16.8 billion moved out of Russia, through major banks including HSBC, Bank of Scotland, NatWest and Lloyds, which together helped facilitate £750 million.

Nor is the story exclusively Russian. The scandal of the 'Azerbaijani laundromat' (2012–14) saw £2.3 billion funnelled through UK shell companies. Some of the money was used for lobbying, including the bribing of European politicians. Much of the illicit wealth of Nigerian dictator Sani Abacha ended up in UK banks, including £248 million in accounts based in Jersey.[22] One of the biggest crimes of the lot was revealed in 2020, when US and Malaysian prosecutors froze £266 million in the London accounts of Clyde & Co. as part of its investigation into £3.5 billion siphoned in the Malaysian

'1MDB' scandal. State funds were simply stolen and laundered through an elaborate network of offshore bank accounts and shell companies to pay bribes, buy luxury properties and art – and even fund Hollywood movies, including Martin Scorsese's *The Wolf of Wall Street*; the producers of which eventually agreed to repay $60 million.[23]

Having stolen and hidden their loot abroad, the corrupt oligarch will then often take step three to access it: migration. And what better way than to buy a visa? Many countries, including the UK, have operated so-called Golden Visa schemes, where, in return for the promise of certain investment, citizenship is effectively sold. The UK Parliament's Intelligence and Security Committee noted in July 2020 that, 'It is widely recognised that the key to London's appeal for Russian oligarchs and their money was the exploitation of the UK investor visa scheme.' Transparency International UK declared that substantial sums from China and Russia had been laundered into the UK through the scheme. One half of all the visas issued in the UK were later reviewed for possible national security risks.[24]

With a bank account and a visa, the economic criminal is then free to take step four: spend the cash. Some simply go overboard at Harrod's, where Zamira Hajiyeva, the subject of the UK's first ever Unexplained Wealth Order, spent £16 million.[25] But in London, nothing beats property. Nearly 250,000 UK properties – roughly 1 per cent of the total housing stock in the country – are now owned by people who are based overseas. Global Witness analysis indicates that more than 87,000 properties in England and Wales are owned by anonymous companies, including 10,000 properties in Westminster.[26] Transparency International UK has added to the picture. Their research shows that £4.2 billion has been invested in UK property via suspicious wealth.[27] Meanwhile, the think-tank, Chatham House, has created a database recording ninety-nine purchases by elites involved in Eurasian kleptocracy cases, with a total value in excess of £2 billion. The 'vast majority of these,' they conclude, 'are owned by kleptocrats and their associates in three resource rich-countries – Azerbaijan, Kazakhstan and Russia'.[28]

Once established, however, the economic criminal then has to stay a step beyond the law – in the UK, that means the National Crime Agency. That is not so hard, not least because the portion of the NCA's budget devoted to anti-corruption enforcement is tiny compared to the challenge. And as one very senior official at the NCA confessed to me, the Agency has to juggle the business of going after oligarchs with other threats, like drug gangs: 'it's quite hard to compare the harm caused by an oligarch here to an organized crime gang bringing in tonnes of cocaine'. There are other impediments, too. 'Are we intimidated, financially and legally?' he asked, rhetorically. 'I wouldn't use the word "intimidate". [But] is it a factor in our decision-making, that we could lose an awful lot of money from what is inevitably a stretched budget? Yes. So, do we have to think about which jobs we do? We do.'

Finally, having laundered one's money, there is the business of cleaning one's reputation as well. The UK offers a great opportunity for doing this, for the simple reason that, as Alexis de Tocqueville observed in 1833, 'The English aristocracy has been adroit in more than one respect... it has talked a great deal about liberty. But what distinguished it from all others is the ease with which it has opened its ranks.' In the 1960s, the journalist Anthony Sampson was still able to observe:

> The British aristocracy has survived partly because it has never been very exclusive: it has always been ready to admit outsider sons-in-law, provided they were rich... the English aristocracy is not very aristocratic, and its history has been very mercenary.[29]

These days, reputations can be burnished in all sorts of ways: a charitable donation or a foundation; support for a think-tank or an academic programme at an elite university;

the acquisition of a football club; or maybe a huge political donation. Turkmenistan-born Dmitry Leus, who settled in the UK in 2015, sought to offer the Prince of Wales Foundation some £500,000. It took the money – until discovering that Mr Leus had spent time in a Russian prison for knowingly dealing with laundered funds. The Dmytro Firtash made big donations to the University of Cambridge. 'Opportunities for reputation laundering are placing the integrity of a range of important domestic institutions at risk,' argued Margaret Hodge in her report. 'Philanthropy to UK universities and charities is one method by which post-Soviet elites clean up their reputations. But these donations are processed in secret, and several cases suggest their due diligence has been flawed.'

I do not want to live in a country where rising levels of inequality feed an impunity industry that supplies its services to some of the greatest economic criminals on the planet. The costs are terrible. At their most extreme, 'assets laundered through the UK are financing President Putin's war in Ukraine' and 'illicit finance... spreads corruption across the United Kingdom... [undermining] our national security by supporting corrupt and autocratic regimes around the world'.[30] Those were among the conclusions of the Parliamentary Foreign Affairs Committee on which I sat.

When wealth inequality grows, politics becomes more vulnerable to the rich who seek power. Risks then grow that the state will be defunded of taxes from the luckiest and most successful, and worse, that a permissive environment for corruption is allowed to flourish. This is not just bad for democracy – it is terrible for meritocracy.

Since the 1990s, economists have become fascinated by the way that unequal countries tend to grow more slowly than more equal nations. If we compare the Philippines and South Korea, for example, we can see that in the 1950s the Philippines was the slightly richer of the two but was far more unequal. That difference was in part because inequality led to corruption; and corruption began to deny the talented poor all sorts of opportunities to rise. In other words, meritocracy stalled, and social mobility went into decline.

In the UK, 'social mobility' has been part of the national religion since the Puritans. The Victorians shovelled the ideal like hot coals into the furnace of politics. In 1859, Samuel Smiles published – appropriately at his own expense – his first book, *Self-Help*, as a paean to hard graft and perseverance. 'Riches and rank have no necessary connexion with genuine gentlemanly qualities,' wrote Smiles; indeed, anyone with a bit of gumption could master a 'diligent self-culture, self-discipline and self control – and above all... that honest and upright performance of individual duty which is the glory of manly character'. A year later, Charles Dickens made his hero of *Great Expectations*, Pip, a model for just these virtues; and in 1862 came the first recorded pantomime version of the greatest go-getter in English history, Dick Whittington.

These traditions helped foster what Harvard professor and broadcaster Michael Sandel has called 'the rhetoric of rising' and provided a rich store of ideas for twentieth-century politicians like Margaret Thatcher and Tony Blair.[31] Thatcher famously wanted to give *Self-Help* as a gift to every schoolchild in Britain. 'She instinctively agreed,' wrote one of her biographers, 'with Mr. Vincy in [the novel] *Middlemarch*, who announces that "it's a good British feeling to try and raise your family a little".'[32] And Tony Blair enthusiastically announced that 'New Labour is committed to meritocracy'.[33]

But unequal societies are not good for meritocracy nor social mobility. The basic problem, as Arturo Herrera Gutierrez reminded me, is that 'if you have countries which are really unequal then you may have very talented citizens that are born poor, in poor families, and they don't have the opportunity to educate themselves' – or, indeed, access good healthcare or good jobs. And that is a problem laid bare by a bit of geometry: the Gatsby Curve.

Although he is too modest to admit it, Professor Miles Corack could lay a good claim to having discovered the Gatsby Curve – as many of his peers confirmed. Working with UNICEF in the 2010s, as part of the team writing about child poverty, he felt that research around the world had suddenly advanced to a stage where significant insights were available into the *intergenerational* consequences of poverty and the relationship between a parent's fortunes and a child's destiny. Miles had been part of an international network connecting researchers in the UK, Scandinavia and Germany, which was beginning to explore these ideas. As he told me, by the late 1990s, 'data was becoming available, enough in many countries, to be able to make these comparisons'. Later, through a friendship with Alan B. Krueger, then Chair of President Obama's Council of Economic Advisers (2011–13), Miles was able to disseminate his research directly into the White House, which shared it with the world in 2012.[34] It was Krueger who named the curve after Jay Gatsby, the icon of Fitzgerald's novel of the Jazz Age.

The Gatsby curve plots the inequality of nations and how easy it is for the poor to rise up and become rich; more specifically, it shows, in essence, how the inequality in a country is very closely related to the likelihood of one generation rising to earn more than its parents' generation. The key value of the curve for Miles lies in the questions it provokes about the fortunes of those at the top, in the middle and at the bottom of the labour market. 'When you actually look at the Great Gatsby curve, what we're really interested in is... our long-term measures of people's earnings power, which are correlated more closely to wealth.' And what appears to happen – as we might have guessed – is that wealth generates not simply wealth but *privileges* whereby children of wealth can earn more wealth. For example, as Miles told me, 'In the United States, in Denmark and Canada, if you are a child of someone in the top 1 per cent, your chances of working for the very same employer as your father are upward to 70 per cent.'

So what's getting passed on? Children get an inheritance, which is monetary – and that inheritance is, by definition, through connections. That inheritance provides access to all sorts of helpful social institutions – and it is skewed at the top. If that process of inheritance is allowed to continue, then inequality in society simply gets worse and worse. At the top, Miles went on, 'income is this flow... and if you keep that tap running [at the same pace], with the 1 per cent getting this higher income, year after year, decade after decade, that's going to change wealth'. In sum, in Miles's view, 'inequality breeds entitlement among some and shame among the many'.

The Gatsby Curve has provoked a storm of new thinking, not least in the old home of the neo-liberals, the University of Chicago, where I caught up with one of the most important authors on the topic, Professor Steven Durlauf – a bearded, warm and brilliant thinker, who tells great jokes (and is not a fan of Milton Friedman). I started off by asking Steven why we should care about what the Gatsby Curve tells us. He put the ethics of it very simply.

'Well, what are the inequalities we deserve?' he asked.

If you and I went to a casino tonight and one of us won and one of us lost, I wouldn't have much claim on the winnings. But in a college class, is it fair that some might have opportunities denied to others just because they were born in a poor family? Of course not. And yet, that's what the Gatsby Curve reveals: in more unequal societies, your parents' fortune defines the horizons of your destiny. And most of us would say that simply can't be fair.

'These are easy examples,' explains Steven, 'but the principle is about unjust inequalities, [and] whether people are responsible for them or whether they deserve them.' But Steven's work has convinced him that rising inequality augurs yet further falls in social mobility, because 'broadly defined... inequality begets segregations of various types, and segregation perpetuates inequality across generations'. When, for example, young people grow up in communities where unemployment is high, fewer people go to college. Steven spells out the impact: 'the more inequality, the more segregation there is of neighbourhoods, and the more segregation, the bigger the disparities and experiences'.

The perils of wealth inequality for society and democracy should not surprise us. Indeed, the lesson used to be part of a classical education. In the story of the Catiline Conspiracy (63 BC) that almost destroyed Ancient Rome, we can read how, after years of wealth multiplying in the hands of ambitious men, the adventurer Catiline launched a coup against the Senate. It was only narrowly defeated after the renowned consul and orator, Cicero, exposed the plot in a series of famous speeches. *O tempora, o mores!* he declaimed, 'Oh, what times! Oh, what behaviour!' Standing with him was Marcus Porcius Cato – Cato the Younger – whose attack on the oligarchs of his day rings uncomfortably true today. 'We pile up riches for ourselves while the state is bankrupt,' he raged at the Senate's wealthy, 'all the prizes that merit ought to win are carried off by ambitious intriguers. And no wonder, when each one of you schemes only for himself, when in your private lives you are slaves to pleasure, and here in the Senate House, the tools of money or influence.'

We should avoid this sort of hazard. But unless things change, the risks are set to multiply for Gen Z, which I fear may grow up to live in a world of haves, have-nots and won't haves, with many doomed to never rise.[35] It is time to assess what the British economist John Maynard Keynes once called 'the economic prospects for our grandchildren'.

3

The Lack of Affluence

Gen Z, its prospects and the lottery of inheritance

'I can't breathe!' Three dying words, gasped by George Floyd as he was murdered by a Minneapolis police officer in 2020, sparked a global protest against racial injustice. And in Europe's youngest city – my home town of Birmingham – it brought an extraordinary generation to the streets, filling the city's vast Centenary Square with passionate, articulate, outraged young people. Here was the first mass protest led by those born roughly between 1995 and 2010, better known as Gen Z.

Two and a half billion strong, Gen Z are the planet's first true digital natives. Confidently vulnerable, treasuring kindness, they are storm-born. In their young lives, they have already seen a global War on Terror, the Great Financial Crisis, Covid-19, the invasion of Ukraine, extreme weather and the looming threat of a climate emergency. Conflict, crash and contagion have shaped this diverse generation, which has grown up permanently connected in a multiverse of media. Networked practically from birth, in the digital chat of WhatsApp and Instagram, it is a 'we generation', which came of age asking: 'What do *we* think of this?' Creative and activist, Gen Z is navigating its way in a highly competitive world that it is determined to change. At the cutting edge of modern protest – from Black Lives Matter to #MeToo to climate strikes – Gen Z remonstrates, demonstrates and articulates its views in novel and thoughtful ways. It is a group of people that innovates frugally, shares generously and collaborates naturally. This generation is going to change the world.

As I wandered through the huge crowds in Centenary Square, trying to find the group to which I had promised to lend a sound system, what struck me was the way the protestors had self-divided into smaller groups, like cells, in which everyone had the chance to speak, teach and share. This was no traditional mass rally with 'distinguished' leaders orating from on high in a karaoke of opinion, where only the self-important got to speak. This was a reinvention of a protest. And Gen Z will need these skills. Because Gen Z is set to become the most unequal generation in history.

It is, in the UK, a national religion to patronize the young. Shakespeare gave us Polonius and his pontifications to his son Laertes to 'neither a borrower nor a lender be'. Dickens gave us Mr Micawber's advice to David Copperfield,[1] and Twitter has given us celebrity property-search consultant Kirstie Allsopp, who sparked outrage in 2022 when she seemed to suggest to the *Sunday Times* that it was perfectly possible for young people to buy a house if only they 'find homes up north', move in with their parents, or indeed give up their 'EasyJet, coffee, gym, Netflix lifestyle'.[2]

Some pointed out that if you wanted to move somewhere cheaper it would be best to move to the 1970s. It was left to Ms Allsopp's *Sunday Times* interviewer to remind the gentle reader that Kirstie, daughter of the Eton-educated 6th Baron Hindlip, had had the deposit on her first home paid by her parents. The newspaper subsequently deleted its online article, after Allsopp objected that she had been misquoted. Nevertheless, as the *Sunday Times* explained, with the average deposit for a first-time buyer now at £59,000, the young would need to forego their Starbucks latte, Netflix subscription, gym membership and EasyJet flights for about thirty-seven years.

All this underlines that today's parent-splaining is wholly unfair. It might be a national sport to slag off our young people as work-shy, X Factor-obsessive X-boxers, but in my view, Gen Z is amazing. If anyone can rebuild Britain, they can. They have got guts and grit. They are curious, creative and connected. They understand the twenty-first century like no-one else. And right now, what they need is a little help from politicians who want to back them, not attack them.

To dramatize the point for the *Daily Mirror*, I once took myself off down the A13 from London's East End to Southend, to talk to young people across Estuary England. From boxing clubs in Dagenham to a McDonald's in Pitsea, from factory floors to shopping centres, from schools to colleges, I spent time asking the next generation about how they saw the future. Everywhere I went, I found young people bursting with aspiration, ambition... and anger. They want to make it. They are juggling jobs and gunning for great grades, all at the same time. I met more people who want to start an apprenticeship than be on TV's *The Apprentice*. They are managing A-levels, a Saturday job and two evenings a week on the shop floor at Lakeside shopping centre. One college head in West Ham told me – in reference to London's giant shopping centre on the site of the old Olympic Park – that 'without our young people, there's no way Westfield [Stratford] would open in the morning'.

The young people I met were looking for practical help. They wanted proper careers advice, work experience that might help figure out what they would like to do in life, a real option to earn while they study for their degree, lower college fees and proper help with day-to-day bills so they can study to get the best job they can. They want to be the best they can be, but they have a profound sense of just how tough the world has become. And of course, they are right.

★

The good news for Gen Z is that we *have* escaped the curse of youth unemployment, which sparked riots when I was growing up. But the bad news is that Gen Z is at the sharp end of the boom and doom phenomenon that has transformed the relationship between wealth and wages.

We already know that Millennials – Gen Z's older siblings, born roughly between 1981 and 1995 – are, relatively speaking, paid far less than their parents. And like Millennials, Gen Z are coming of age and graduating still in the shadow of the Great Financial Crisis, Covid-19 and conflict in Ukraine, with high debt, higher taxes, sky-high house prices – and rock-bottom wages.

This phenomenon is global. Every Western generation that went to work after 1980 was competing in a labour market that has grown by almost 70 per cent. When China joined the World Trade Organization it sparked a huge migration from the world's old farms to the world's new factories, and all in all, the world's workforce rose by 1.2 billion to around 2.9 billion between 1980 and 2010.[3] Then, as Bobby Duffy writes in his brilliant book *Generations*, came the combination of the Great Financial Crash and, a decade later, Covid-19. Together these shocks meant that 'the net effect has been that income growth for younger generations in many countries has ground to a halt or reversed'.[4]

The impact has been that, at a comparable age, *every* cohort born after 1960 has been paid less, relatively speaking, than the preceding generation. In the United States, the average baby boomer in middle age enjoyed an income that was 26 per cent higher than that of the pre-war generation, and by the age of thirty-five, they already had their hands on a fifth of the nation's wealth. Since then, it has been downhill. The relative fortune of American Millennials will be *seven* times smaller than their grandparents'. In Italy, things are even worse. While middle-aged

Italians of Generation X – those born 1965–80 – had 11 per cent less income than baby boomers; Italian Millennials between the ages of thirty and thirty-four had 17 per cent less income than Gen-Xers.[5]

Meanwhile, here in the UK, the plight of Gen Z is especially grim. 'Analysis across China, South Korea, Japan, Italy, the US and the UK,' Bobby explains, 'shows that everywhere, except South Korea, the young are much more likely than others to have already experienced a drop in income, with the UK seeing one of the biggest relative declines.'[6]

In the UK, the wage challenge has been especially sharp for young people because a bigger fraction of eighteen- to twenty-nine-year-olds are now working in the sectors with bad pay: in fact, 40 per cent now toil in relatively lower-paying occupations. The net result is that between 2009 and 2014, Gen Z took a 9-per-cent pay cut and is now the *only* group with lower non-housing spending.[7] The over-sixty-fives, by contrast, enjoyed a rise in non-housing spending of 37 per cent.[8]

And this is only half the story. Gen Z is not only *paid less*; it is also now *denied access to assets* its grandparents enjoyed because of – as we saw – a quiet revolution in the wealth-to-wages curve. This means that assets are far more expensive relative to wages than they were in the 1970s. While the price of an average home multiplied sixty-five-fold between 1970 and 2021, average weekly wages only multiplied thirty-six-fold.[9] With disparities like these, it is no wonder that more than two-thirds of people aged between twenty-five and thirty-four cite the problem of raising a deposit as the primary barrier to buying home.[10]

This disparity helps explain why home ownership rates have been falling in general since the early 2000s. But the sharpest falls have been among the youngest. Around six in ten families headed by those born in the early 1950s were homeowners by the age of thirty-three. The proportion fell to just four in ten of those born in the 1980s. As a result, more young people have to rely on the Bank of Mum and Dad for a deposit – or the spare room, or old childhood bedroom, of Mum and Dad for a home. Almost half of those aged under thirty – 48 per cent – now live with their parents. That is 4.5 million people. An incredible 1.9 million *fewer* young families in the UK own their own house than would have been the case had the UK sustained earlier, higher rates of ownership.[11] This is the sharp end of an economy where assets are pricey and wages are low. Rises in interest rates, of the kind we have seen lately, might knock down house prices and make it easier to save a decent pension pot. But the changes in the wealth-to-wages curve are so big that for Gen Z, at the bottom of the wage pyramid, the ideal of a property-owning democracy has collapsed.

One of the people who has thought about this most is the Conservative peer and former minister, Lord (David) Willetts. David has done more than anyone else in Parliament to highlight the challenge of intergenerational fairness, penning a book on the topic in 2010 and today chairing the best think-tank on living standards, the Resolution Foundation.[12] He confesses that he came to the subject through a classic kind of middle-class parental anxiety: 'It was partly the personal experience of living in a house in Shepherd's Bush [West London], and my wife saying to me, "How on earth are kids going to get started on the housing ladder?"' Over the course of holding Opposition political portfolios shadowing the departments of Education and Social Security, he became more interested in the way life-cycles unfold.

When we met to chat, he underlined just why the boom and doom cycle is so important. 'In some ways, the most vivid fact about Britain in the last thirty years is that assets have gone from three times GDP to eight times GDP. Wealth just matters more. So, inheritance matters more, and what you earn matters less.' Ironically, he went on, this is the opposite of what Mrs Thatcher would have hoped for. She wanted a nation where the path to wealth was earned or saved and not inherited. 'I think that is a massive change in the character of society,' David concluded, 'and it's tough for Gen Z... [because] converting your earnings into an asset is much harder.'

The woe of Gen Z, therefore, is to live under the curse of the baby boomers. Today, the wealth of many over-sixty-fives has ballooned. But their own curse is to have grandchildren who cannot afford a place to call their own. How can this have happened? Because, though we do not like to say it, we live in a gerontocracy.

The principal factor in recent British electoral politics is that at the 2019 UK General Election, the Conservative Party won the over-sixty-five vote by more than 3 million. That huge margin guaranteed power. And this Conservative lead was no accident. As the former MP Gregg McClymont once observed, the Conservatives are past masters of building a political economy of winners and losers – and associating themselves with the winners. And since 2010, the British centre-right has ruthlessly built a political economy centred on boosting older voters' spending power and wealth, with an expensive strategy of discounts on council housing, a 'triple lock' on pensions and very, very low interest rates.

The sale of council homes dates back to the 1980s. On the eve of Margaret Thatcher's election as prime minister in 1979, 42 per cent of the British population lived in houses and flats rented from their local council. In the years that followed, 2.6 million council homes were bought by tenants who enjoyed discounts on the price of their home of up to 70 per cent, depending on the length of the tenancy: that was worth anywhere between £80,900 and £108,000. Today, these discounts live on; by 2023, they were worth up to £96,000 – or £128,000 in London.[13]

As house prices rose, those lucky enough to have bought at the time have made a fortune. There is not much data on the profits made by tenants 'flipping' their council homes, but one investigation by the BBC found that homes in Britain bought under the scheme between 2000 and 2019 had been sold on for £6.4 billion in collective profit.[14]

The second great gift to older UK voters was the triple lock – the 'guarantee' ensuring that the state pension is uprated, annually, by the *higher* of the rise in earnings, the rate of inflation or 2.5 per cent. Mrs Thatcher infamously broke the link between pension rises and earnings, and the result, for those who depended on the state pension, was massive pensioner poverty, which took years for the subsequent Labour government to fix. David Cameron, as the incoming Conservative prime minister in 2010, was not going to make the same mistake Margaret Thatcher did. While Labour had declared that it would restore the earnings link in the Pensions Act 2007, the measure was not brought into effect until April 2011. But the new Coalition government's triple lock went further, and it was worth a fortune. In fact, in a decade, the triple lock routed £48 billion extra to pensioners, over and above what would they would have received had state pension uprating unfolded in line with earnings.[15] This massive transfer helped boost pensioners' consumption over and above the percentage rise for non-pensioners – with average weekly consumption among the over seventy-fives rising by 48 per cent in the decade after 2010.[16]

A series of pension reforms were then introduced in 2015 allowing those about to retire to take a quarter of their fattened pension pot in cash. And many used this money to buy a second property to rent out for extra income.[17] An incredible 1.9 million people now own buy-to-let properties,[18] and one-fifth of the entire value of Britain's property market lies in property wealth held by those who own multiple dwellings: a portfolio worth £1.36 trillion in 2021.[19] Most of it is rented out.

Yet among this shower of gifts for older voters, nothing has been as valuable as the decades of easy money, which might account for *most* of the £9 trillion increase in household wealth between 1997 and 2021. Low interest rates are the closest we have come on earth to alchemy – and the long span of low rates has been the key reason for the long-term boom in older people's wealth, because low rates have been good for the pensions and housing that account for almost £4 in every £5 of UK household wealth.[20]

If we look back at the very long run – as far back as the year 1311 – we can see that, on average, interest rates have been falling globally for a very long time.[21] But over that long arc of seven centuries, there have been nine 'real rate depressions', of which the 'secular stagnation' of real rates, beginning in 1984, is the second longest.[22] And interest rates were held down in the years after the Great Financial Crash by a gigantic injection of almost £1 trillion in quantitative easing created digitally in the Bank of England: this had the effect of knocking about 1 per cent off base rates without so much as a vote in Parliament.[23]

A variety of analysts have now shown that the rise in real house prices since 2000 can be explained *almost entirely* by these lower interest rates.[24] The Resolution Foundation concluded that 'four-fifths of the increase in property wealth since the early 1990s has derived from these above-inflation passive effects'. The biggest winners were those born in the 1940s and 1950s. In fact, the Resolution Foundation went on to conclude that 'The rapid pace of property wealth accumulation for older cohorts... is largely due to the windfall effect of the house price boom of the mid-1990s to the mid-2000s' – and that was largely driven by the fall in interest rates.[25]

As it happens, this era of low interest rates has also transformed the value of older peoples' pensions. The UK government's *Wealth and Assets Survey* encompasses around 90 per cent of British pension wealth. The ONS team that calculates national wealth first looks at the income stream promised to the individual by their pension provider.[26] A significant proportion of the over sixty-fives (about one-fifth) have a defined-benefit (occupational) pension scheme, which provides a guaranteed payout each month, and of course, life expectancy is rising, which means the payouts last for longer.[27] The ONS then calculates what size 'bond' would be needed to yield this guaranteed flow of income. As interest rates fall, the size of the bond has to get bigger. As such, between 80 and 90 per cent of the recent increase in total pension wealth is attributable to interest-rate falls rather than to the savings accumulated. That is around £2.2 trillion.

All in all, the strategy of discounts on council house sales, the triple lock on pensions and low interest rates has proved so bold that it has actually changed the structure of the UK economy.

A few years ago, Lucio Baccaro and Jonas Pontusson of the University of Geneva developed a way to understand varieties of capitalism by looking at differences in the different drivers of overall demand in the economy.[28] What they found in Britain was striking. 'Over the period 1994–2007,' they reported, 'the United Kingdom relied on household consumption as the main driver of economic growth.' And as my old colleague Professor Nick Pearce – former head of the Number Ten Policy Unit – spotted, the Conservatives' consumption-driven economy in the decade to 2020 was powered in large part by the baby boomers, over the age of sixty-five.[29] The combined effect of both growing numbers of older households and their rise in spending power – which has risen by an incredible £74 billion – now means that they account for almost a quarter (22 per cent) of UK consumption, up from 17 per cent back in 2010.[30] All told, by 2018–20, half of Britain's wealth was owned by the baby-boomer generation aged between fifty-five and seventy-five, up from 42 per cent in 2006–08.[31] What a contrast to every generation that followed. No cohort born since 1960 has recorded *any* substantial progress in accumulating wealth compared to their forebears.

It is a bleak picture. But to understand the full inequality of economic prospects facing so many of the baby boomers' grandchildren, we have to remember that not everything in life is forever – including the baby boomers.

Their demise will spark the largest transfer of wealth in history as the total value of inheritances is set to double over the next two decades, peaking in 2035.[32] But not all heirs will be equal. Some will receive a sizeable inheritance. More than half of older households now boast wealth worth over half a million pounds, while on paper, a quarter of over-sixty-fives are millionaires, and home ownership is now quite widely diffused, as the baby boomers have ended up with home ownership rates of around 75 per cent.

But there is no getting away from the blunt truth that, as the Resolution Foundation concluded, 'With increasing amounts of wealth not being consumed during lifetimes, intergenerational wealth transfers look set to widen absolute gaps [in equality] further, with the already wealthy most likely to benefit from the coming inheritance boom.'

We can already see significant inequalities in who gets what. For example, in 2012–14, the richest fifth of heirs aged between forty and fifty-nine inherited nearly *three times* as much as the bottom 20 per cent of that age group.[33] And this inequality will just get worse, for not all baby boomers are rich: the poorest 10 per cent of them have just £1,000 of net wealth. Their 'beneficiaries' will only inherit bills from parents and grandparents who have nothing more to pass on than high care costs. Indeed, 25 per cent of adult Gen Zers expect to help their parents financially and to pay for long-term care for a loved one in retirement.[34] And so we are about to see inequality cascade down the generations. In fact, the immediate transfer of all parental property wealth to children would result in a *near-doubling* of the absolute difference between the top fifth and bottom fifth of those aged twenty to thirty-five.[35]

Bobby Duffy is convinced that one of the key stories for the next twenty to thirty years will be how the baby boomers' wealth trickles down. When I called him to talk about his book, he told me that in this 'enormous cohort', and given the 'weaknesses of inheritance and wealth tax generally', baby boomers 'will prefer to be able to protect that wealth they hand on to their children. And the concentration of wealth means it's going to flow down very unevenly.'

These huge differences suggest, as Bobby puts it, that inheritance 'is a key dynamic'. Gen Z 'will be very fractured as a cohort,' Bobby concludes, 'because some of them are going to do really well out of the wealth that their parents have made and others are going to get nothing.' Not least because there is now an industry of advisors paid to ensure that inherited wealth never 'trickles down' to the poorer reaches of society but sticks forever within the family. It is, if you like, the theory of 'trickledown' dammed.

Most societies have some sort of proverb about the creation, enjoyment – and eventual destruction – of wealth: 'shirtsleeves to shirtsleeves in three generations', as Andrew Carnegie put it, or 'sandals to sandals' in China, or the Italian *dalle stelle alle stalle*, 'from the stars to the stables'. In her brilliant book *Capital without Borders*, Brooke Harrington explains how today's wealth-management industry is now working hard to stop this history repeating.[36] Once upon a time, families tried to defend their wealth without the need for professionals, through intermarriage, primogeniture and 'entail' – the laws that keep land inheritance within the family. When someone put their assets at risk – for example the knights of medieval Europe departing for Crusades – some began to adopt the practice of putting assets in trust, that is, administered by one party for the benefit of another. There was a time when the system of trust was held together by a 'web of oaths', which relied on the honour of trustees to do their duties. But as fortunes became more complex, so did wealth management. A century ago, the leisured class who employed people to oversee their wealth might have numbered in the low four figures. Now, wealth management is a global industry. The London-based Society of Trust and Estate Practitioners (STEP), which was only founded in 1990, now has 21,000 members in 96 countries employed in burying wealth inside enigmas inside puzzles.[37]

'Wealth management strategies,' explains Brooke, 'now hinge on scattering assets as far and wide as possible'[38] and so the super-rich employ a complex cast of professionals, trustees, directors and proxies, using a mix of structures like trusts that hold shares in multiple underlying corporations across different countries. The purpose is to exploit the truth that nation states are a patchwork system, which coordinates very poorly. When I rang Brooke to understand this better, she eloquently explained the inner logic of the wealth-management industry:

> One of the things that most struck me about the wealth managers I spoke to – one of the big takeaways from the training programme [to be a wealth manager] – was that your multi-generational client is not the family. It's the family fortune. And your job is not to take care of the family. Your job is to protect the fortune from the family. So that the spendthrift heirs, or the drug addicts or the people who can be blackmailed and extorted don't destroy the whole thing, because in the natural course of events, fortunes don't last.

All sorts of perversities flow from this, including the icy grip of the founders on the fortune down the generations. 'One of the things that leaving a fortune to your descendants gives you,' Brooke went on, 'is a kind of immortality' in being able to control the behaviour of the heirs by the conditions imposed on any inheritance. 'Some of my students,' Brooke explains, 'say, "Yeah, I'm a trust baby. I will inherit a pile of money, but there are strings and one of the strings is I have to get married and have biological children, but guess what? I'm gay. So I don't know what to tell my family."'

*

While wealth sticks within lucky families, the sort of pressure we see driving down wages for young people may well get worse, as what we used to call the Fourth Industrial Revolution gathers steam.

Ask experts about artificial intelligence (AI) and 'the rise of the robots' and you hear contending views. On the more positive side, it is true that, down the centuries and over time, new technology always tends to create many more jobs than it destroys. Thinkers like Alec Ross (who used to advise Hillary Clinton on innovation) tell me that, whereas entire industries were once built on oil, new industries will be built on data.[39]

But ask a voter and you get a very different answer. When I ran polling on the subject a few years ago, I found that 55 per cent of working-class voters in Britain thought that automation would make it harder for them to earn a decent wage or land a secure job in the years to come.

People are right to worry, for the simple reason that a new wave of AI-led automation – like Chat GPT – is going to hit some jobs harder than others. The forces driving us into the Data Age – quantum computing, 5G networks, smart devices, the 'blockchain' ledgers that underlie cryptocurrencies and AI – will, together, transform our ability to collect data, transmit it, trust it, process it, interpret it *and* profit from it. And the disruption to current jobs that will follow will dwarf the industrial dislocation of the last thirty years. It is a revolution that will wipe out jobs like never before. Globally, it could cost the jobs of up to 1.2 billion of the world's 3.5 billion workers, destroying livelihoods for hundreds of millions of people in the process. In 2018, Professor Carl Frey at Oxford University's Martin School estimated that as many as 47 per cent of jobs in the economy could be on the road to automation.[40] And the working-class jobs dominated by retail, transportation and routine manufacturing are going to get hit hardest of all. In fact, in the UK, more than five times more jobs might be lost in these sectors than in the demise of the coal and steel industries put together.[41] In the jobs that are left, wages will be under pressure, as Carl explained to the BBC in 2023:

> Consider the introduction of GPS technology and platforms like Uber. Suddenly, knowing all the streets in London had much less value – and so incumbent drivers experienced large wage cuts in response, of around 10 per cent according to our research. The result was lower wages, not fewer drivers. Over the next few years, generative AI is likely to have similar effects on a broader set of creative tasks.[42]

Those who are fortunate enough to win in the lottery of life and get into good schools and good universities will be able to take the high road in the years to come. But for those in work at risk of automation, the years ahead will be tough. Those hit the hardest might well be black or women, or both. As it is, black graduates earn a quarter less than white graduates and experience unemployment that's twice as high; and people defined as being of 'Black African ethnicity' hold the lowest amount of wealth in the country (median £24,000) – around eight times less than the typical wealth held by a person of white British ethnicity (£197,000).[43] This gap of £173,000 grew between 2006 and 2008, and 2016 to 2018. Meanwhile, although the gender pay gap remains stubbornly high at around 9 per cent for full-time workers, the gender *wealth* gap is much bigger, totalling an extraordinary £15 billion: investments held by women are half the value of male-held investments (2020 figures).[44]

To forecast where these trends might take us, we need look no further than the United States, where there are now serious concerns expressed by writers like Robert Putnam that the forces fuelling inequality are moving the country 'toward *a caste society*, where your fate in life is determined by the one decision that you never did make: who your parents are going to be'.[45] (My italics.)

I have long admired Robert's thoughtful sociology and we first met when I invited him into the Treasury to brief us on his famous book *Bowling Alone*. But his later book, *The American Dream in Crisis* (2015), is a horror story. Here, he offers a paean to his 1950s' hometown of Port Clinton, Ohio, 'a passable embodiment of the American Dream, a place that offered decent opportunity for all the kids in town, whatever their background'.[46] No more. As inequality in accumulated wealth has grown, so some children have done far better than others, for the simple reason that '[p]arental wealth is especially important for social mobility, because it can provide informal insurance that allows kids to take more risks in search of more reward'.[47] What Robert saw was that 'a child who can borrow living expenses from Mom and Dad can be more selective when looking for a job, whereas a child without a parent-provided life preserver has to grab the first job that comes along'.

This creates a situation, he warns, where '[p]oor kids, through no fault of their own, are less prepared by their families, their schools, and their communities to develop their God-given talents as fully as rich kids'.[48] That opportunity gap for children obviously creates a huge opportunity cost for society. We can already see signs of the same thing happening in Britain. Even though levels of wealth inequality are much lower than in the United States, we already know that those young people blessed with prosperous or well-educated parents do better. Recent ONS data revealed that the average wealth of someone whose parents have a degree is more than £117,000 greater than the offspring of parents with no qualifications – and that gap has almost doubled.

It would be naive to assume that these sorts of changes, left unchecked, will not have a political impact. To understand where this divergence of wealth and wages might leave us, I spoke to two people who have transformed our understanding of inequality: Kate Pickett and Richard Wilkinson, the co-writers of two best-selling books, *The Spirit Level* (2009) and *The Inner Level* (2018), which help explain why inequality is so bad for society.

Key to their insights is the reality that inequality jeopardizes the social relationships that sustain us, and this 'is fundamental to the other effects', as Richard told me, 'from life expectancy to domestic violence, to the quality of your mental health'. The quintessence of happiness is the quality of our social relationships, and so our lives are twisted if we live in societies that are very unequal and we grow up with a hunted sense that everyone is a rival, out for themselves. 'It's not a frivolous thing,' Richard concluded, 'to be able to participate in society, to have relationships with other people. And… if you live in a more unequal society versus a more equal society, it frames how you get socialized, it frames how you are parented and nurtured and what kind of society you're prepared for.'

So what happens, I wanted to know, if inequality gets worse? 'All of the things that we show, in *Spirit Level*, related to inequality will get worse,' replied Kate, 'all of those health indicators, all of those indicators of our human capital development [and] social mobility will decline.'

Richard added:

Trust will decline, civic participation will decline, cultural participation will decline; there'll be much cross-class suspicion, and the rich trying to protect their position and their status and their goods; there'll be more gated communities; there'll be more people wanting to have their children in private education, and you'll end up with a more polarized society and more polarized politics, playing to those different interests; you'll get a harder right, and, you know, you will get unrest, ultimately civil unrest and riots and those sorts of things.

It sounds like the kind of caste society Robert Putnam is warning us about. And politically, it may prove to be a country where populists flourish, democrats fade, and in the void, separatists prevail.

Let us look at the populists first. In a remarkable bit of political science, Professor Ben Ansell and his colleagues revealed how, in the UK, those left out of the wealth boom are far more likely to vote for populists. Unhappy citizens are scrappy citizens, offering rich pickings for populists, keen to milk the bitter wrath. Studying the Brexit vote, Ben's research found that 'Poorer, traditionally Labour, areas had stagnating housing markets, reinforcing community support for leaving the European Union.'[49] In more detailed, recent studies, looking at Scandinavian trends, Ben and his colleagues found that when house prices rose, people were driven away from populist parties – but equally, 'when prices decline, they're driven towards them'. That creates the possibility, he told me, 'that rising housing inequality is also pushing regions apart. And it is associated with growing populism. But it's not now because of the winners. It's because of the losers'.

In so many countries, that pessimism has now been hijacked, ruthlessly exploited and methodically radicalized by a new generation of populists, who are not so much nationalist as tribalist.

Nationalists tend to be bad for their neighbours. But tribalists are bad for nations. They are populists who insist that legitimate power rests only with 'the people not the elites', but this means that they are almost all authoritarian. They insist on the importance of security against risks of instability and disorder (such as, for example, foreigners stealing our jobs, immigrants attacking our women, terrorists threatening our safety); they demand group conformity to 'guard our way of life' and demand homage to the strong leader who protects all others. But they do not seek to unite a nation behind a national story, because they are sectarians, defending a supremacist project. They don't seek to inspire a nation's people; they deliberately set out to radicalize and divide. They are what we might call, Cadmeans.

On his journey to found Thebes, the very first Ancient Greek hero, Cadmus, had to first slay a dragon. Victorious, he was then instructed by the Goddess Athena to sow the dragon's teeth in the field. Up sprang a race of fierce armed men, the Spartoi, ready to do battle. But the quick-thinking Cadmus flung a precious stone among them, and the soldiers fell upon each other, until almost all were dead. Today's sectarian politics is the equivalent of sowing dragons' teeth; and today's Cadmean preachers know their craft and the power of anger. Clever tacticians once sought to prevail by divide and rule. Today's new populists have risen to power by adapting this. Their playbook is not 'divide and rule' but 'enrage and rule'. Theirs is the art of the 'amygdala hijack', a deliberate attempt to trigger the instinctive fight-and-flight instincts of the brain.[50] And the cocktail they prefer is a toxic mix of identity politics and a 'dark social playbook' of digital tricks – hacking material, pushing talking points with alternative news sites that infect the more mainstream media, and importing the outrage into social media, where 'dark money' or bots can amplify them almost infinitely. [51]

Having divided a people in order to gain office, populists noisily set off shouting and tweeting towards dystopia by launching a culture war on the institutions that hold nations together: the mainstream media, elections, other politicians and political parties, public servants, judges, the intelligence services, intellectuals, scientists, the constitution and international organizations, each in their own way condemned as fake news, fraudulent, a swamp, dysfunctional, the deep state, enemies of the people, liars and leakers, arrogant liberals, experts we don't need, get-rich-quick lobbyists, a rigged system, bureaucrats or a talking club. It is quite a list.

Much of this profoundly and properly offends and angers Gen Z. But there are two risky reactions. The first is disengagement, creating a challenge for the political class of 'ruling the void' in a country where voter turnout rates collapse. [52] Lots of studies now confirm how young people's confidence in politics is falling. Cambridge University's Dr Roberto Foa recently reported that Millennials are 'the first generation in living memory to have a global majority who are dissatisfied with the way democracy works while in their twenties and thirties'. [53] Satisfaction with democracy is in steepest decline among those aged between eighteen and thirty-four almost everywhere, but young people are most positive about democracy when a populist leader (of either Left or Right) is in charge.

Is anyone surprised? 'Since the advent of the welfare state,' says Mark Franks, Director of Welfare at the Nuffield Foundation, 'what could be described as an implicit social contract has existed between generations. Younger people would work and pay taxes, which would help to support the older population, with the expectation that they themselves would experience… the prospect of a comfortable later life.'

That contract is under threat. If matters get worse, the second risk emerges: that it is the *separatists* who eventually prevail, as frustration foments an acid so potent that it melts the joints holding a nation together. After all, revolutions are not one-off events; they are processes that unfold over many years. The historian Steven Pincus once perceptively observed that 'revolutions occur only when states have embarked on ambitious state modernization programs… [in a] self-conscious effort by the regime to transform itself in fundamental ways'. [54] But in weakened states, a moment arrives when reform is so rapid that either the centre fails or fledgling opposition movements flourish. [55]

Revolutions do not pit modernizers against defenders of the

past. Powerful interests tend to agree on the need for a change, but they disagree fundamentally about the direction in which change should move. And today, some of the most powerful 'modernizers' in politics are not seeking to defend the states that exist today. They are seeking to break them up and create new nations. Around the world, there are plenty of places where movements for sovereignty or independence are serious.[56]

Once upon a time I thought this was impossible in Britain. A week knocking on doors in Glasgow during the 2014 Scottish independence referendum changed my mind. Not much united those who were voting for independence. Some harked back to the economic destruction of Thatcher's time and argued that life had not improved under Tony Blair. Others talked of losing jobs, living on food-banks and looking for hope – any hope – that things might get better. Surely another path was worth trying? A buzzy, optimistic, patriotic party offering a ray of hope was appealing. Everywhere, voters were saying 'give me a radical reset that gets me out of here', while traditional leaders offered either tiny gestures or more of the same.

In a world where a fear of the future, like the smell of smoke, alarms us, there are real risks of a doom-loop of disengagement, populism and separatism. Is there another way? I think there is. But if we want to build a great wealth-owning democracy this century, we will have to rewrite the rules of our economy so that a fair share of the wealth is no longer beyond reach, and a fair share of wages are no longer beyond hope.

But that requires us some honest self-assessment. We have to first understand why it was that politicians got their economics so wrong.

PART II

4

All Hail the Market!

A brief history of market supremacism

Not far from Los Angeles, in the steep San Simi hills that fringe the city, is one of the most extraordinary political monuments I have ever seen: the Ronald Reagan Presidential Library. Henry Kissinger once said:

> When you talk to Reagan you sometimes wonder why it occurred to anyone that he should be president, or even governor. But what you historians have to explain is how so unintellectual a man could have dominated California for eight years and Washington already for nearly seven.[1]

The Reagan Library, hacienda-style as befits the Cowboy President, explains precisely why. It is quite simply one of the greatest political museums in the world, a veritable showcase of Reagan's appeal and the way he melded the values and iconography of the American West to his own image – with the optimism, the self-reliance, the strong faith, the smile, the jokes – to become the culture hero of America's national story, rich in its pioneering spirit and sense of manifest destiny. But Reagan's power was not simply cultural. In the orbit of his smile were philosophical, economic and ideological concepts revolving in rude harmony. What Reagan helmed in the 1980s was a coherent shift of world-view.

Of course, he did not invent it. It is commonplace to begin chapters on political economy with John Maynard Keynes's famous observation that 'Madmen in authority, who hear voices in the air, are distilling their frenzy from some academic scribbler of a few years back.' In my experience this is not quite right. Far more dangerous is the reality that worldviews in political life are not the product of lone scribblers but packs of them, who create symphonies of compatible, sympathetic ideas sculpted together like the great edifice of a cathedral. They are in their own way magnificent, intimidating and seemingly inevitable. Until they collapse.

'Market supremacism' is precisely such a symphony, an extraordinary harmony of intellectual effort, its intricacies woven and crafted over the course of a century. It is as daunting, alluring, enchanting – and as dangerous – as the Siren's song, tempting us onto the rocks. Born almost a century ago, it took hold at the beginning of the 1980s, after which inequality – in both income and wealth – really began to rise.

The story of 'market supremacy' began on the beautiful Swiss Plateau in the charming lakeside resort near the bottom of Mont Pèlerin, where, in 1947 a group of intellectuals and academics met to discuss the birth of a new movement with a simple ideal: the roll-back of the state and the roll forward of the market. It became known as neoliberalism.

For more than a decade, Republican alarm at the ambitions of Franklin D. Roosevelt's New Deal, and (in the UK) Conservative alarm at the Labour Party's aspirations for a 'New Jerusalem', had been rising like a flood-tide. Throughout the 1930s, Roosevelt's administration drove through a revolution in American government, creating social security, union rights, minimum wages, public works, public housing and public support for farming.[2] Meanwhile, the British Labour Party, in the wake of its disastrous 1931 election defeat, had fallen in love with planning. By 1934, 'full and rapid socialist planning' was Labour policy. In 1935, the co-founders of the Fabian Society, Sidney and Beatrice Webb, were lauding the economic planning methods of the Soviet Union; in the same year, the former Labour minister Hugh Dalton published *Practical Socialism for Britain*, including a long paean to planning, and a year later, in 1936, Keynes produced his landmark *General Theory of Employment, Interest and Money*.

The backlash was not long in coming. Within a year of Keynes's book, the American journalist Walter Lippmann replied. Once described as a 'Manhatted Zeus' and 'a child of the Enlightenment, with a Gallic mind and a Gallic passion for reason', Lippmann was, by the time of his death (1974), lauded as 'the dean of American political journalism'.[3] In his book *The Good Society*, Lippmann drew strength and inspiration from a generation of academics opposed to New Deal policies but found a language and line of argument that were far more potent. True, some of Lippmann's phrases were ludicrous: 'We belong to a generation that has lost its way... [and] returned to the heresies of absolutism, authority, and the domination of men by men.' But the nub of Lippmann's argument became a cornerstone of the neoliberal case: 'a prosperous and peaceable society must be free'. Political liberty required economic liberty.

During the next year, 1938, the Colloque Walter Lippmann convened in Paris, and on Lippmann's foundations, three Austrians – Karl Popper (1902–94), Friedrich Hayek (1899–1992) and Ludwig von Mises (1881–1973) – began hauling into place a world-view with a distinctive perspective on history, on the vices of the state and on the virtues of the market. At the core of it was the observation that markets were more effective at diffusing information and knowledge than a few planners in an office, for, as Lippmann wrote, 'no human mind has ever understood the whole scheme of a society'.[4]

Karl Popper agreed. Born in Vienna to an academic and a pianist, Popper left Austria as the Second World War approached and eventually settled in London, where he penned what some have called one of the most influential books of the twentieth century, *The Open Society and Its Enemies* (1945). Popper argued that designing collectivist societies was a fool's errand because of the first, fundamental challenge of getting the blueprint right. 'The holistic planner,' argued Popper, 'overlooks the fact that it is easy to centralize power but impossible to centralize all the knowledge... necessary for the wise wielding of centralized power.'[5] He added: 'Utopian engineering... claims to plan rationally for the whole of society, [but] we do not possess anything like the factual knowledge to make good such an ambitious claim.'[6] Worse, the complexity of steering a society towards a final blueprint, warned Popper, risked planners taking shortcuts, simplifying and eliminating individual differences along with the messy business of trial and error that is so essential to discovering mistakes and then correcting course.

Friedrich Hayek, in his surprise bestseller *The Road to Serfdom* (1944), made a similar point, emphasising that 'it would be impossible for any mind to comprehend the infinite variety of different needs of different people which compete for the available resources and to attach a definite weight to each'.[7] Once described as 'articulate, austere and infinitely urbane', Hayek, like Popper, was also Viennese.[8] He had served as a gunner in the First World War before earning doctorates in law and economics. To neoliberal thinking, he supplied the insight that coordination in any society is very hard if what economists call the 'price system' – the process by which prices emerge in a marketplace – is demolished by the setting of prices centrally. 'Once centralisation is necessary,' wrote Hayek, 'the problem of coordination arises.' 'Coordination,' he went on, 'is precisely what the price system does... and which no other system even promises to accomplish. It enables entrepreneurs, by watching the movement of comparatively few prices, as an engineer watches the hands of a few dials, to adjust their activities to those of their fellows.'[9] The myriad intricacies of decisions facing the centrally planned society, according to Hayek, would soon entail outsourcing decisions to unaccountable experts; and this risked an inexorable slide to dictatorship as simply the most efficient way of implementing the plans in question.

Ludwig von Mises concurred. Known for the brilliance of his teaching at the University of Vienna, Mises had also escaped the advance of fascism in his Austrian homeland. He went on to be considered by some as the intellectual godfather of the German post-war 'economic miracle'.[10] No fan of collectivist societies, he wrote that the complexity of decisions taken by a central planner was impossible to reconcile with effective democratic oversight, and nor could he see how bureaucracies could innovate, in the absence of a profit motive; after all, he noted, 'in public administration there is no market price for achievements'. This risked a dull monotony, which Mises projected was contrary to human nature: 'If primitive men had adopted the principle of stability, they would long since have been wiped out by beasts of prey and microbes.'[11]

No-one could accuse the Austrians of under-selling the risks they foresaw for either society or the soul. The 'drift towards collectivism' in the West, a trend they dated to a turn of opinion away from individualism and towards collectivism in the 1870s, was a step towards the totalitarianism of National Socialism and Soviet Russia.[12] 'Mankind is manifestly moving toward totalitarianism,' lamented Mises in 1944, 'and the rising generation yearns for full government control of every sphere of life.'[13] Hayek went further. He was 'increasingly convinced that that at least some of the forces which have destroyed freedom in Germany are also at work here'.[14]

For all the alarm, these arguments were left lying in the wings of public life in the smoking aftermath of the Second World War. Nevertheless, the Austrians had supplied a powerful epistemology, which was now animated by the emergence of a new economics that combined both good models and good mathematics. And as the 1950s gave way to the 1960s, market supremacism slowly began to flourish as epistemology and economics were woven together – and decked in a new political flag.

The gift of second sight has been sought by rulers since the pharaohs. As a politician, I can testify that much of the economists' power is baptized by the promise to reveal 'laws' for human behaviour as simple and elegant as Newton's laws of nature and so foretell the future. By the 1950s, 'market supremacists' began to promise exactly this kind of foresight by mixing together a brew of arguments from ingredients that dated back a century. It became known as the 'neo-classical synthesis' and could trace its roots back to economists of the nineteenth century who had taken basic ideas about diminishing marginal returns on production and the diminishing marginal utility of consumption, and begun the invention of economics as a mathematical science.

The basic concept is simple: in any production process there comes a point where the yield from extra resources put into the process is not as great as the first move. If I am growing coffee beans, I might make a tidy profit on the first and most fertile acres I plant. But as I reach the less fertile 'margins' of my field, my yields decline until there comes a point where, frankly, the profit from planting is simply not worth the effort. Equally, if I am buying coffee, the first cup of the morning might be almost priceless. But by my third cup, I am over-caffeinated, and experience tells me to pay nothing for any more.

Léon Walras (1834–1910) was among the first to begin formalizing these ideas with mathematics. After a brief career as a bank manager, journalist and romantic novelist, the Frenchman from Normandy turned to economics. In his *Éléments d'économie politique pure* (1872; *Elements of Pure Economics*), he began pilfering from physics to create mathematical models that sought to predict the 'natural' point of equilibrium that might emerge in a marketplace where lots of different (rational) people with lots of different preferences bought many different things.

Like Walras, the Liverpudlian William Jevons (1835–82) sought to translate the maxims of the moral philosophers into mathematical precision. Jevons added both the notion of trade and the concept that individuals seek to maximize their happiness within the limits of their resources by trading their way to the happiest possible mix of things – a concept un-romantically known as an 'optimized personal utility'.

The ideas of Walras and Jevons were then combined by one of the greatest economists of all time, Alfred Marshall (1842–1924), into an analysis of a general equilibrium. The son of a cashier at the Bank of England – and the great-great-grandson of 'a half-legendary herculean parson of Devonshire', who reputedly twisted horseshoes with his hands – Marshall was the man who bequeathed to millions of economics students the first graphs with crossed lines representing supply and demand. To this work, the Italian engineer Vilfredo Pareto (1848–1923) added the insight that people in this market would continue trading until every win–win bargain – or at least every win–no-lose bargain – had been exhausted, so that any further trades would make them worse off. This 'Pareto optimal' point was 'the best that one could do in a free society', and crucially it appeared to offer the reassurance that free trading in a market was the best means of ensuring a sort of maximum happiness for the maximum number of people.[15] So, 'the theory of economic science', boasted Pareto, 'acquires the rigour of rational mechanics'.

It was the United States' first Nobel Prize-winner in Economics who supplied the next leap forward. Born in Gary, Indiana, Paul Samuelson (1915–2009) once said of himself that 'in this age of specialization, I sometimes think of myself as the last "generalist" in economics'.[16] In the early 1950s, Samuelson had melded the two ideals of 'constrained optimization' and 'equilibrium' in competitive markets (where prices fluctuated in a way that ensured supply equalled demand) together with the insight of Keynes that full employment was not inevitable under laissez-faire policies. He went on to modernize the theory of demand to do away with the nineteenth-century conception of 'utility' and replaced it with logical rules, which ordered or ranked consumer preferences based on consumers' rational, observed behaviour. Samuelson's *Foundations of Economic Analysis* (1947), based on earlier work for his Harvard PhD thesis, went on to become one of the biggest selling books in economic history.[17] To this, Ken Arrow (1921–2017) and Gérard Debreu (1921–2004) added work on the key role of prices in allowing a 'general equilibrium' to emerge in complicated markets, even where there was much uncertainty, for the simple reason that because people either substitute things or buy complementary things, markets for one thing are generally linked to markets for something else. Self-interested people, went the argument, react to price signals, and as they rationally seek to maximize personal utility, they drive not just a market but an entire market *system* to an equilibrium point that is socially optimal.

So emerged, from the hands of many weavers, an extraordinary tapestry of ideas. 'To simplify somewhat,' wrote Richard Thaler (b.1945), 'we can say that Optimization + Equilibrium = Economics. This is a powerful combination, nothing that other social sciences can match.'[18] It was a model of such exquisite elegance that it inspired thinkers to begin asserting the supreme rationality of the market with what was christened the 'Efficient Market Hypothesis' (EMH). And that, in turn, encouraged the spread of markets everywhere.

In essence, EMH combined two basic ideas: that in free markets prices are rational, and that 'beating the market' is impossible. In a free market, so the argument goes, any asset will sell for its true 'intrinsic value'. So, if the rational value of a company is £1 million, then its shares will trade at a price such that its market capitalization will total £1 million. More specifically, because all publicly available information is reflected in current share prices, it is impossible to predict, reliably, future prices, and therefore impossible to speculate successfully on the share price to make a profit. As Richard Thaler explained: 'Suppose a stock is selling for $30 a share, and I know for certain that it will soon sell for $35 a share. It would then be easy for me to become fabulously wealthy by buying up shares at prices below $35 and later selling them when my prediction comes true.' But of course, if the information used to make this prediction is public, then you are unlikely to be the only one in the know.

By 1970, the theory and evidence for EMH was robust enough for US economist Eugene Fama's comprehensive literature review around it, published that year, to stand for many years as 'the efficient market bible'. There was no shortage of confidence in its nostrums. 'I believe there is no other proposition in economics,' argued Michael Jensen, a professor at the University of Rochester business school, 'which has more solid empirical evidence supporting it than the Efficient Market Hypothesis.'[19] It was, as Alan Greenspan, former Chairman of the US Federal Reserve believed, 'the critical functioning structure that defines how the world works'.[20]

Over the course of the 1960s and 1970s, these new axioms and arithmetic, like muses, helped inspire not only a new politics, which aspired to 'rolling forward the market', but an ideology hell-bent on rolling back the state. As markets came to be seen as superior to planning for allocating the resources in an economy, so politicians came to be persuaded to build markets left, right and centre. Michel Foucault summed it up nicely: neoliberalism 'is not a question of freeing an empty space,' he wrote, 'but of taking the formal principles of a market economy and... projecting them on to a general art of government'.[21]

However, as Machiavelli so wisely observed, 'There is

nothing more difficult to take in hand, more perilous to conduct, or more uncertain in its success, than to take the lead in the introduction of a new order of things.' Which is why in politics it *always* takes a crisis to move new thinking from the fringes to the mainstream to supply fresh answers to what seem like intractable problems, ideally presented as a 'return to common sense'. This is precisely what happened during the 1970s, in the wake of the Vietnam War, as the costs of the conflict coupled with that era's 'oil shock' broke, first, the settled, international post-1945 system of monetary management (the Bretton Woods system) and then triggered a combination of stagnation and inflation, dubbed 'stagflation'. The stage was set for one of the twentieth century's most influential economists: Milton Friedman.

The fourth child of parents who worked in New York sweatshops and who later opened a New Jersey clothes store, Friedman (1912–2006) lost his father young and waited tables to help fund a scholarship at Rutgers University, where he started in 1929, the year of the Wall Street Crash.[22] Like the founding fathers of neoliberalism, Friedman firmly believed in the interdependence of economic and political liberty: 'economic freedom,' he wrote, 'is... [a]n indispensable means towards the achievement of political freedom'.[23] He embraced the price mechanism as the means of securing 'coordination without coercion'.[24] He also criticized at length the limits placed on economic freedom by the modern state – like exchange controls, compulsory old age insurance, licences, fair trade laws, and even prohibitions on illegal drugs.

Friedman burst onto the economics scene in 1957, with a book that went on to help transform macro-economics: *The Theory of the Consumption Function*. In contrast to Keynes's 'loose psychological theorising', Friedman presented an approach to economics that characterized humans as rational individuals making rational plans about spending over the course of their lives. Six years later, his monumental *Monetary History of the*

United States, written with Anna Schwartz, fundamentally reassessed the role of the US Federal government during the Great Depression, arguing that it was the Federal Reserve's failure to prevent the collapse of the American money supply after 1933 that turned a recession into the Great Depression.

Friedman's insights into the importance of monetary policy, along with his belief in the way individuals developed rational expectations about the future, provided the theme for his 1967 lecture to the American Economic Association. There, against the tide of contemporary thinking, Friedman took apart the notion that governments could use spending to foster demand and thereby reduce unemployment. As an economy runs out of capacity and prices rise, Friedman argued, workers begin to factor the higher levels of inflation into their wage bargaining, thereby ratcheting up wage demands, and so increasing prices ever further. The solution, argued Friedman, was to do away with the politics of 'fine-tuning' demand with extra spending and to roll back government largesse in order to lower the overall demand for money. This would, the theory went, lower interest rates, which would in turn encourage businesses to borrow to invest in productive capacity. 'There is,' argued Friedman famously, 'always a temporary trade-off between inflation and unemployment; [but] there is no permanent trade-off.'

Milton Friedman's approach represented a radical translation of the market supremacists' philosophy into practical politics. It met its unlikely poet in Barry Goldwater.

Every political movement has its John the Baptist, the voice in the wilderness who appears, in retrospect, to have been some sort of prophet. For the market supremacists, it was Senator Barry Goldwater, who published his short book, *The Conscience of a Conservative*, in 1960, and who battled against Lyndon Johnson for the US presidency in 1964. Here, for the first time in a long while, was a Republican Party candidate who set himself against his party's establishment as a defender of the Constitution, a champion of the people and a fighter for the free. '[F]or the American Conservative,' he wrote, 'there is no difficulty in identifying the day's overriding political challenge: it is to preserve and extend freedom.' The chief enemy was the state:

Throughout history, wrote Goldwater, government has proved to be the chief instrument for thwarting man's liberty. Government represents power in the hands of some men to control and regulate the lives of other men. And power, as Lord Acton said, corrupts men. 'Absolute power,' he added, 'corrupts absolutely.'

The hour, said Goldwater, was growing dark: 'Our defences against the accumulation of unlimited power in Washington are in poorer shape, I fear, than our defences against the aggressive designs of Moscow.'

Goldwater was comprehensively defeated in 1964. But the election was the moment when America first got to see the man who would prove to be the neoliberals' pin-up, for, introducing Goldwater with a text that became known simply as 'The Speech', Ronald Reagan shot to national prominence.[25] Reagan avoided the shrill divisiveness of Goldwater, a man who – let us remember – declared: 'Extremism in defence of liberty is no vice.' Reagan offered the same urgency but with silk and honey. '[F]reedom has never been so fragile, so close to slipping from our grasp as it is at this moment,' he declared. Like Goldwater, Reagan counterpoised government and freedom: 'This is the issue of this election: whether we believe in our capacity for self-government, or whether we abandon the American Revolution and confess that a little intellectual elite in a far-distant capitol can plan our lives for us better than we can plan them ourselves.' With his invocation of a 'rendezvous with destiny', Reagan brought the house down.

British politics did not have telegenic former movie stars to draw on, but in the 1960s, the Conservative Party could supply caustic sceptics like Enoch Powell to provide an English chorus to the new American expostulations. Yet it was not until 1974 that the Conservative Party's neoliberal-in-chief emerged, when the rather un-telegenic Sir Keith Joseph declared that he had been converted to 'true Conservatism' by the ideas of Milton Friedman.[26] With the election of Margaret Thatcher as prime minister, this new thinking became the party's credo. It was preached with such strict exactitude that one minister, Sir Ian Gilmour, later lamented that 'Belief in monetarism... was now a prerequisite not only for controlling inflation but for being a real Conservative... Those who resisted conversion and clung instead to traditional Tory principles were soon regarded as, at best, suspect infidels or, at worst, the enemy within.'[27]

By now, the market supremacists' ideas machine was pulled by a troop of think-tanks – early leaders like the American Enterprise Institute (founded 1943), the Foundation for Economic Education (founded 1946) and the London-based Institute for Economic Affairs (established 1955) were now joined in the stable by a newer, vigorous herd of public intellectuals in Heritage (1973), Cato (1977) and, in the UK, the Centre for Policy Studies (1974), founded by Joseph and Thatcher.

Together, these helped supply both Thatcher and Reagan with the practical policy that became the basic canons of the 'Washington consensus': a roll back of the state and roll forward of privatization; the expansion and deregulation of markets; the deregulation of labour markets; cuts to tax and a celebration of the enterprise culture; and efforts (in the UK rather than the United States) to slash government deficits in order to reduce public debt as a way of underpinning lower interest rates. Unions were now fought, and social security was cut back. In the United States, the Federal minimum wage was allowed to stagnate, while in the UK, the introduction of a minimum wage was resisted altogether. State-owned assets were privatized. Mocking the 'Left's proclivity to spend taxpayers' money', Ronald Reagan's argument was not Keynesian, but classical: 'if a national economy is to soar,' he told the US Chamber of Commerce, 'first the inventive, enterprising, pioneering, dreaming entrepreneurial spirit of the Nation's people must soar'. That meant 'not more regulations but fewer. Not more government direction, but less; and yes, not higher taxes, but lower taxes'.[28]

Of course, the fastest way to shrink a state is to defund it. And both Reagan and Thatcher were backed by the ranks of a small-state chorus now swelled by those who counselled that economic growth was imperilled when countries devoured too large a share of their nations' resources. Far better, argued the so-called supply-siders, to cut back the state and use the savings to fund tax cuts, to arouse the nation's animal spirits and stir innovators to grow new businesses and create new jobs. This was not a new set of ideas. '[M]uch of our supply-side economics,' wrote the economist Marty Feldstein in later life, 'was a return to basic ideas about creating capacity and removing government impediments to individual initiative that were central to Adam Smith's *Wealth of Nations* and in the writings of the classical economics of the 19th century'.[29] But it made for very happy party donors.

The story is almost complete. But not quite. For the true power of market supremacism was not simply its political sway but its unprecedented scope. For market supremacism was not – and is not – simply a philosophy for political manifestos. It is a playbook for private-sector management.

Down the ages, modern capitalism has been shaped by demons, but by plenty of angels too, like George Cadbury (of chocolate fame), William Lever (of soap fame) and John Spedan Lewis (of department-store fame) – ethical entrepreneurs who sought not just to build a business but change the world by investing in schools, libraries and 'model communities'. But from the early 1970s, this sort of virtue was made anathema. And once again, it was Milton Friedman who led the charge.

In 'The Social Responsibility of Business is to Increase its Profits', Friedman argued that business had no social responsibility save for any specific purpose specified by the shareholders.[30] 'Only people can have responsibilities,' he argued, '"business" as a whole cannot be said to have responsibilities even in this vague sense.' The 'business-man' must therefore guard against 'spending someone else's money for a general social interest' or stand guilty of effectively imposing a tax on workers, on shareholders, on customers in deciding how the proceeds should be spent. And how could the business leader know what best to do with it? The conclusion was simple: 'There is one and only one social responsibility of business – to use its resources and engage in activities to increase its profits.'

By the 1980s, this epistle had become a pseudo-scientific method of maximizing business returns taught to hundreds of thousands of business-school students, myself included, complete with toolkits to calculate the adequacy of the return to equity holders who needed, in turn, to cover their cost of capital and the risks they took investing in one business rather than another. The 'value' of a firm was calculated as the total of forecast future net cash flows, summed and discounted to crystallize a value – a little like a bond. Maximizing these future cashflows was, it was argued, an all-round win–win scenario. As one of the textbooks handed to me at the Harvard Business School, called *Valuation*, put it:

> … shareholder wealth creation does not come at the expense of other [shareholders]. Quite the opposite. Winning companies when compared to their competitors have greater productivity, greater increases in shareholder wealth and higher unemployment.[31]

And so, the argument went, what was good for companies was good for entire economies, because 'countries whose economic systems are not based on maximizing shareholder value... will slowly be starved of capital as capital markets continue to globalize'.[32] Comparing economies over the years between

1950 and 1990, *Valuation*'s authors correlated American GDP growth and shareholder focus to arrive at the conclusion that 'the US with [its] shareholder value focus, remains the GDP leader'.

The question left unanswered, of course, was: 'Whose GDP?'

It was Winston Churchill who once said: 'However beautiful the strategy, you should occasionally look at the results.' And the truth is that forty years of market supremacism has created, in the UK, a country that produces peaks of inequality so high that our systems of redistribution find it hard to flatten them. Market supremacy inexorably drives up returns to capital – and in practice, drives down returns to labour, otherwise known as your pay packet.

Perhaps the best illustration of the long-run effect is the following snapshot. Back in 1955, the 'labour share' of national income – the national income that went to workers as opposed to 'capital' – was around 70 per cent. Today, it is 60 per cent.[33] Had workers today enjoyed the same share of national earnings that characterized life in the 1950s, then £243 billion extra would have flowed in peoples' pay packets in 2021.

Or take a second illustration. In the years between 2000 and 2020, labour productivity grew by 19 per cent. In that same period, real median hourly wages increased by less – 15 per cent – for all employees, and by *even less* – 13 per cent – for full-time workers.[34] In other words, over those two decades, workers were producing more each hour while not getting paid in full for the extra they produced.

How can we explain this? In large part, the answer is provided by a recent revolution in economics. While we have nothing that quite matches the impact of Keynes's *General Theory* of 1936, we do have a wave of new thinking that has laid bare a *political* economy of privilege, rent-seeking, monopoly and oligopoly in markets that malfunction by producing bubbles which then burst. This new thinking is what you might call 'Reality Economics'. It explains what happens when the abstract symphony of a perfectly behaving market collides with flaws and imperfections of human nature and human society. And it provides a much better explanation of the extreme wealth inequality we experience today.

But unpicking this story begins with a history lesson.

5

A Licence to Profit

Politics and the privilege cycle

Some of the nation's most precious jewels are guarded not in a palace, but in a Brutalist peach-and-yellow, concrete-and-glass edifice. You could mistake it for a multi-storey car park. Britain's National Archives, just around the corner from Kew Gardens, are the vaults for the national memory, home to 11 million documents, from the Domesday Book to the Cabinet minutes. And there, in a big, bare room flooded with autumn sunlight pouring in through glass walls, archivists Amanda Bevan and Oliver Finnegan had laid out for me our oldest records that explain the origins of English capitalism. Carefully inked on animal skins were state-sponsored permission slips for pirates.

We do not admit this very often, but most of Britain's first great companies were part-founded not simply with spit, grit and elbow grease, but with fortunes stolen from the Spanish, Portuguese and Dutch. Buccaneering Britain was founded by, well, buccaneers. But being British, they followed rules, and here they were, neatly written out on sheepskin parchment smaller than an iPad.

By the seventeenth century, England's buccaneers already had a long and blood-curdling history. In medieval days, an enterprising sea captain could sail forth and steal what he could from the enemy with impunity, so long as the nation was at war. But as war became so frequent in Tudor and Stuart times, English piracy became organized. Elizabeth I never issued a *formal* declaration of war against Spain, but she did shower 'letters of reprisal' on her nation's sea captains, authorizing them to steal from her enemies. As Oliver put it to me that afternoon, 'in the sixteenth century, there's this drive... to try and bring some kind of order, create systems of documentation, that control where ships go and what they're doing'. It is what you might call very early red tape.

Our oldest letter of reprisal dates from 1601, dispatched to the good ship *Hopewell* for Captain Anthony Nokes, gentleman, of Portsmouth. It confirms permission 'to sail forth to the seas' with full authority for 'the apprehending and taking of ships, goods and merchandises of the King of Spain, and any of his subjects'. It goes on to constrain any stealing to the coast of Spain or the Canary Islands but urges theft of sugar, which was among the most valuable drugs of the seventeenth century and a favourite of the queen.

When such 'prizes' were landed, the queen's officials made a comprehensive list of the cargo, its worth, and when to sell it. And some prizes were worth a fortune, as I gleaned from another parchment laid out on the table that afternoon. It was a receipt for the prize landed by John Hawkins, son of the infamous Caribbean pirate, from his ship *Neptune*, for sugar landed off Madeira worth £2,407 – more than £400,000 in current sums.[1] These sorts of windfalls were vital for 6,000 people of Elizabethan London who went on to found a host of new companies with exotic names – like the Company of Merchant Adventurers to New Lands, the Muscovy Company and the Spanish Company, or the East Land Company, the Turkey Company and the Venice Company, not forgetting the Levant Company, the East India Company and the Virginia Company.[2] Those at the top led by example: James Watts, for example, was not only a member of the Spanish, Levant, Virginia and East

India companies, he was also, in 1607, Lord Mayor of London and, as the Spanish ambassador, Pedro de Zuniga, observed, 'the greatest pirate that there has been in this kingdom'.

The story of the nation's pirates helps highlight how the evolution of English capitalism is rather less salubrious than we are taught in textbooks. It is a tale of two paths. One trail is blazed by the good. As I set out when I wrote *Dragons*, a history of Britain's greatest entrepreneurs, the possibilities of this world have been transformed by generation after generation of inventors and innovators, entrepreneurs and world-beaters.[3] Entrepreneurs see new ways of doing things. They create jobs. They create wealth. They innovate in ways that improve our lives. Entrepreneurs make history by inventing the future. And by creating new possibilities, they grow the economy, diffusing wealth, employing people and expanding the boundaries of our freedom. It is a virtuous way to live, as I was reminded by the Archbishop of Canterbury: 'Even Jesus Christ,' said His Grace, 'was a wealth creator who worked for 90 per cent of his life.'[4] In economics, this faithful work is known as the 'Schumpeterian paradigm', inspired by yet another Austrian economist, Joseph Schumpeter (1883–1950), and described by Philippe Aghion and colleagues rather nicely: 'innovation and the diffusion of knowledge are at the heart of the growth process. Long-term growth results from cumulative innovation in that each new innovator stands on the shoulders of Giants who preceded him'.[5]

But not all entrepreneurs create value for society. Yet they too can thrive because markets are human institutions and so prone to failures that the market supremacists did not foresee. We understand this far better now thanks to the work of the 'Reality Economists'; the new institutional economists, the neo-Schumpeterians and the behavioural economists who have helped us understand why it is that markets inevitably channel a wealth of riches to some and not others.

Reality Economics begins with a privilege cycle, favours or prizes that include rules for the marketplace, which allows some to extract wealth without creating any particular social good. With both privileges and invention, elites can build oligopolies to maximize their gains, but over time, in unstable markets, there is inevitably the odd crash, which almost always hurts the poorest most, but from which the wealthiest tend to recover fastest. And so, a system emerges that funnels fortunes to the few – and with that, inequality grows.

Privilege is the original sin of Reality Economics, and it dates back millennia. Its operation is inextricable from the development of human societies, because – as they multiply and population density rises – the risks of violence grow exponentially.[6] So, as rulers seek to keep the peace – or more often than not, divide and rule – they reward or license elites with some kind of economic privilege.

As it happens, Adam Smith well understood this, as did his intellectual heir David Ricardo. In Book III of *The Wealth of Nations*, Smith explained how, after the fall of the Roman Empire, 'The princes who lived upon the worst terms with their barons seem accordingly to have been the most liberal in grants... to their burghs.'[7] David Ricardo (1772–1823), however, developed the idea to bequeath us the modern notion of 'rent-seeking' with his explanation of the ways in which a landlord is able to raise rents for fixed economic factors, like land in ways that do not create new wealth, but rather simply transfer wealth from tenant to landowner. But it was not until the late 1960s that the American economists Gordon Tullock (1922–2014) and then Anne Krueger (b. 1934) transformed the concept to explain why modern-day rent-seekers spend so much time and effort acquiring a different sort of privilege: the kind controlled by governments.[8]

As we saw, in an ideal economy, entrepreneurs are busy inventing new things, making them and selling in a market, where lots of firms compete to drive down prices and produce enough to satisfy demand. Profits are sought and made by creating value for customers. 'Rent-seeking', by contrast, is different to this sort of profit-seeking. It is the business not only of extracting more in profit than is strictly needed to mobilise effort to achieve some objective, but also an attempt to maximize rewards by securing privileges through the political arena; and it allows this sort of entrepreneur to cut himself, or herself, 'a bigger slice of the cake rather than making the cake bigger'.

Gordon Tullock's great insight was that it is well worth the individual entrepreneur spending huge amounts of money on lobbying for these sorts of privileges, because the potential gains will dwarf the costs of lobbying. From society's point of view, this is all a giant waste. The money spent on lobbying has not been spent on researching some great new breakthrough. Nothing new has been created; supply is lower, and typically, prices are higher than they would have been, because competition has been damaged. 'Tullock's Paradox' exposed the truth that rent-seekers wanting political favours can bribe politicians at a cost much lower than the value of the favour to the rent-seeker.

The Nobel Prize-winner Robert J. Shiller provides a great example. Imagine, he writes, 'a feudal lord who installs a chain across a river that flows through his land and then hires a collector to charge passing boats a fee... to lower the chain'. There is nothing productive about the chain or the collector. He goes on: 'The lord has made no improvements to the river and is helping nobody in any way, directly or indirectly, except himself.'[9]

Over the last two decades, the revolution in 'New Institutional Economics' has helped throw light on how the process works in practice.[10] Few have explained it better than the great American economic historian Douglass C. North (1920–2015). He showed how, over time, elites of all societies strike bargains with leaders to shape the rules of institutions in their own favour, in ways that magnify and multiply further wealth, and which therefore increase inequalities. '[N]atural states,' wrote

North and his collaborator Barry Weingast, 'do not deal with violence by consolidating control over it. Instead... They create a pattern of interlocking economic, religious, political, and social interests to provide powerful individuals with incentives not to use violence.'[11] Rulers therefore develop institutions or 'pacts', which reward potentially violent elites with extravagant shares of the fruits of peace – and therefore create incentives to keep the peace. 'Throughout recorded history,' write North and Weingast, 'the cessation of violence is not achieved when violence specialists put down their arms, but rather peace occurs when the violent devise arrangements to reduce the level of violence.' The cost, otherwise, is that 'elite rents are reduced if violence breaks out'.[12]

Over time, therefore, elites of all societies strike bargains with leaders to shape the rules of institutions in their own favour, in ways that magnify and multiply further wealth, and hence increase inequalities. But the price of peace – of minimizing the potential violence of growing societies – is therefore a licence for inequality, as the lucky elites are granted rights to carry off the fruits of progress.

The process is at least as old as the first empires founded twenty-six centuries ago, in societies as diverse as those of Hawaii, the Cuzco, Ancient Egypt, Ancient China, medieval Europe and the New World, as historian Walter Scheidel explains in *The Great Leveller*.[13] Here, the 'delegational nature of rule in premodern states *required* rulers to share gains with their agents and supporters as well as with preexisting elites'. (My italics.) The same process was there at the foundation of Norman England, as William the Conqueror divided his new dominions between his barons, while his heirs issued liberties to trade to early towns and trading companies.

To get a better handle on this, I had the honour of sitting down with North's co-author, Barry Weingast, at the House of Commons to chat through the argument. Barry, still recovering from a recent traumatic brain injury, was modesty itself, insisting that it was North who was always the visionary. But he agreed that the notion of a privilege cycle made sense. For one thing, Barry helped me see that we cannot understand political economy, historically, in England without appreciating the almost permanent state of war that fostered rulers' huge need for money. The privilege cycle was not simply driven like a merry-go-round by ambitious privilege-seekers; it was equally powered by cunning rulers creating the privileges to sell internally, in order to finance war externally. 'You can think about the rent-seeking,' explained Barry, in relation to the way elites strive to secure privileges, 'as the demand side... But rent creation is the supply side [where] rulers create the rents. And rulers create the rents because they need to create the glue that holds [their] coalitions.'

Today, our economies are riddled with rent-seeking, like a form of dry rot. All sorts of businesses make fortunes by controlling what Michael Hudson calls 'essential choke points in the economy'. It is as true of age-old industries, like mining, and brand-new industries where there are powerful network effects benefitting monopolistic behaviour – the kind of behaviour that has been attributed to firms like Microsoft, Amazon, Google or Facebook/Meta. My very rough analysis shows that as much as 40 per cent of corporate profits made in the UK are made in sectors prone to rent-seeking behaviour.* 'Instead of providing basic infrastructure services at cost or subsidized rates to lower the national cost structure and thus make it more affordable,' argues Hudson, 'the economy is being turned into a collection of tollbooths.'[14]

Unsurprisingly, rent-seeking is very, very bad for the economy.

---

* Calculation based on HMRC, Corporation Tax Statistics 2023, combining the declared corporate profits in the following industry sectors: Financial and Insurance; Information and Communication; Real Estate; Mining and Quarrying; Electricity, Gas, Steam and Air Conditioning and Water, Sewage and Waste.

Not least because, as Philippe Aghion and colleagues explain, in many industries, new and old, incumbents rely heavily on lobbying to protect their rents by limiting the entry of new firms. In fact, 'the largest firms as measured by sales are those that utilize lobbying the most intensively'. Yet, as Philippe goes on:

> ... the firms that spend more on lobbying are less productive and have higher profit margins than other firms... [but] as a firm grows greater market power and moves toward market dominance, it focuses its efforts less and less on innovation and more and more on political connections and lobbying.[15]

Investing in lobbying comes at the expense of innovation, and collusion between firms and politicians increases the cost of entry into the market. The higher the proportion of politically connected firms in an industry, therefore, the less dynamic that industry becomes. In Aghion's view, the effect may also be to 'reduce social mobility'.

This simple bit of economics helps explain the allure of the powerful to the wealthy, which we can now see play out around the world, and crucially, it helps us understand just why we have experienced the sorts of inequalities that scar societies today.

Nowadays, the extraction of rents from politics can be truly staggering. In many countries, the sheer scale of the corruption designed to capture economic privileges, from which to harvest economic rents, has come close to collapsing the political system. In countries like South Africa, Egypt, Peru, Bolivia or Sierra Leone, we witness states damaged by 'extractive' institutions that 'destroy incentives, discourage innovation, and sapped the talent of their citizens by creating a tilted playing field and robbing them of opportunities'.[16] But we cannot avoid the simple truth that at the last count, 60 per cent of the world's billionaires live in just four countries: the United States, India,

China and Russia. And while it is surely true that the explosion in trade and tech has helped create much of the wealth in the last thirty years, rent-seeking has helped explain just who benefits from that wealth.

There are few countries that illustrate the transparent danger of rent-seeking as well as Russia, which also provides a salutary lesson in being careful what you wish for. As Paul Caruana Galizia reminded me, Russia's oligarchs were actually responsible for the rise of President Putin in the first place. Explaining his ascent to power, Paul told me that 'it was the oligarchs who sort of got together and said, "We need a sort of technocrat who won't bother us." We just keep things ticking along smoothly. And so Boris Berezovsky said, "Well there's this man Putin, and I think his is the man we're looking for."'

Post-Soviet Russia was a country rich in resources, but liberalization did not bring what the West expected. 'Instead,' Paul goes on:

> ... you just got people who are initially privileged and powerful, becoming even more so. And the institutional framework that should have developed and acted as a check on their behaviour never came. In fact, it was weakened, because once in power, the oligarchs constantly undermined it.

So, those that did well were either part of the security services, or high up in important ministries, or worked for state-owned enterprises in sectors like mining, oil and gas. When these firms were privatized in the first wave of 'shock therapy', citizens were given tokens in the firms. Yet living standards – and education levels – were so poor that the average person had no idea what to do with these certificates.

'But those privileged people did,' Paul continues, 'including Oleg Deripaska or Abramovich. They were right off the mark.

They started going around people's houses saying, "Give us your shares, and we'll give you some vodka. Give us your shares, and we'll give you a few buns," and slowly they accumulated massive shareholdings.' In this way, a lucky few ended up with great fortunes – even if the power relations between the oligarchs and Putin have now tipped in the latter's favour.

Few people know this story better than the *Washington Post*'s Catherine Belton. Author of the best-selling *Putin's People*, she spent much of 2021 in court defending her research against a crude gagging effort by Roman Abramovich. So I called her as a witness to Parliament, to ask about the oligarchs' relationship to Putin now. She did not hold back. 'Basically, Russian businesses very often have to act as arms of the Kremlin,' she told our committee. 'Russian businessmen have to follow Kremlin orders in order to hold on to their wealth. It is not just money that is coming into our system and making everyone rich; it is money with an agenda, and that agenda can be to undermine our democracy.'

In China, things are a little different, and the entrepreneur Desmond Shum has given us a vivid inside story of how rent-seeking works there. His book, *Red Roulette*, is a tragedy that tells the story of the disappearance of his ex-wife Whitney Duan (also known as Duan Weihong), with whom he made a fortune, with a lot of hard work, buckets of *guanxi* – social connections – and a very special relationship.

Whitney began her career in the province of Shandong as a deputy county chief, which served as an early education in how to make friends and influence people. She hated it. Sexual harassment was common and 'she was forced to drink so much that she broke out in hives'. Whitney graduated to a leadership position in a real-estate development company run by China's military. But her breakthrough came with meeting and impressing Zhang Peili, the wife of a man who would become one of China's premiers: Wen Jiabao. By the end of the evening, '[t]he pair had exchanged cell-phone numbers' and Zhang told

Whitney 'to call her "Auntie," a sign she was willing to consider a more personal relationship'.

Over the years that followed, 'We turned the Grand Hyatt's Yue Ting Restaurant into our private canteen,' explained Desmond. 'Sea bass at $500 a pop was a favorite dish of ours, as was a $1,000 soup made out of fish maw.' Before long, an opportunity came along to snap up a stake in insurance giant Ping An, owned by a troubled shipping firm. When Ping An was later listed on the Hong Kong Stock Exchange, in January 2004, the share price jumped eight times and the partners' stake was worth £81 million. With these sorts of profits and connections, Desmond and Whitney were able to go and make a fortune in real estate. 'People had learned that Whitney was close with Auntie Zhang,' recounts Desmond, 'so we were often presented [with] deals.'

However, things unravelled after the *New York Times* published a huge exposé in October 2012, estimating the Wen family's wealth as close to £2.4 billion. Whitney was named in the piece, and five years later, in 2017, she disappeared from the streets of Beijing.

In India, the principles of rent-seeking are similar, but it manifests itself differently. In *Billionaire Raj*, James Crabtree lays bare how 'scarce assets worth billions in sectors like telecoms and mining were gifted to big tycoons, in a series of scandals known as the "season of scams"'. 'Back in the nineties,' James told me:

> it wasn't really worth your bother trying to buy off politicians in order to get your hands on one of these assets. But if you fast forward ten years, when India reopened and became much more globalized and its economy was larger, and the technology was growing, then suddenly getting your hands on a mobile phone licence – or licence to dig coal out the ground, or iron, or simply land – is incredibly valuable.

The Indian economist and former governor of India's central bank (the Reserve Bank of India), Raghuram Rajan, coined a term for this: the 'Resource Raj'. As James set out in his book, this meant 'a Russian-style system in which politicians, bureaucrats and industrialists colluded to carve up access to valuable natural resources and shared the proceeds among themselves'.

Enquiries later revealed a series of corruption scandals that had taken place over the course of Manmohan Singh's prime ministership (2004–14). In them, assets like land and coal were found to have been doled out to special friends. Public resources were being gifted to industrialists in increasingly vast quantities, Raghu argued, allowing them to rake in outsized and undeserved profits. 'Three factors – land, natural resources, and government contracts or licences – are the predominant sources of the wealth of our billionaires,' he argued. 'The numbers are alarming – too many people have gotten too rich based on their proximity to the government.'

The lure of rent-seeking encouraged Indian tycoons to build sophisticated influence machines in Delhi. James notes that many created modern versions of 'the old Reliance Industries' "intelligence agency"' in New Delhi, referring to the sophisticated lobbying operation built up over the decades by Mukesh Ambani's father. A variation on the theme was to open hospitals, schools, hotels and, crucially, newspapers. After all, even those who regard cash bribes as wrong might be tempted to take a gift in kind, whether that is free medical treatment, schooling, a hotel banquet for some a family wedding, or a decent write-up in the press.

Democracies create all sorts of rent-seeking opportunities, because politicians need the money to fight ever more expensive elections (not least the costs of social media advertising). One estimate costed the 2014 Indian General Election in the region of £4 billion. That money has to come from somewhere. And this, explains James, is the mother of some Indian invention:

The classic way of [rent-seeking] is that you are looking to get state resources or resources that are controlled by the state on the cheap. And there was a very unsophisticated model of corruption; you turn up and give a politician some money and there's literally a suitcase full of money to get a decision that goes your way. And that happens a lot in India as it does in many countries. Including rich ones.

But the really smart way of doing this is that... you're on both sides of the deal. So, you're an entrepreneur, you have a cousin who's in politics, you kind of cook up the idea that you're going to do a particular project that's going to have such and such an upside, and we decide to share the wealth... the really smart politicians are the ones who went from taking bribes to taking equity.

As you know, entrepreneurs are creating value, not by being better or more innovative, but just simply by being cleverer in, getting access to the telecoms spectrum or mobile licences or whatever it might be.

Lest we like to think that this sort of bad behaviour is confined only to countries on the rise, outside the First World, we need only gaze for a few moments at the United States. When I pushed Bernie Sanders on just how the world's greatest democracy had ended up in a position where the richest three Americans owned the same wealth as 160 million other Americans, he did not pull his punches. 'Look, there is a reason why the rich are getting richer,' he exclaimed:

You asked me about the growth of billionaires... That has a lot to do with the policies established by Congress. And those policies are largely influenced by big money interests. They have their policies, [and] they literally in some cases, write the bills.

Ever since the Supreme Court's 'Citizens United' ruling, which granted corporations unfettered freedoms of free speech, and hence the right to supply billions in election campaign contributions, we now have the very rich spending a fortune to get the candidates they want.

'If I were running for office,' explains Bernie, 'it would be totally legal for some group of billionaires to spend tens and tens of millions of dollars, hundreds of millions of dollars, against me, running TV ads, brochures and whatever they choose to do.' The so-called 'super PACs' – political action committees that draw donations together – will spend more money on a campaign than the candidate.

'What does that do to politics?' I asked. 'The candidates become puppets to the puppeteer,' he answered. But what, I asked, are they buying? 'The answer is obvious,' Bernie replied:

Number one: you keep from office, people who will threaten you in one way or another. So, if you are in the fossil fuel industry, you will keep from office somebody who is concerned about climate change. You will keep from office – if you are the pharmaceutical industry or the insurance companies – somebody who wants a national healthcare system. Just recently, in the last couple of months, the microchip industry... received $76 billion (£61 billion) in corporate welfare and tax breaks. Lobbyists who make huge campaign contributions make a tremendously good investment. So, if you spent $50 million in campaign contributions and lobbying to get $76 billion, well your return on your investment is pretty good.

But the list is longer than this. Indeed, Bernie Sanders cited 'disastrous trade policies, which have resulted in the loss of millions of good paying jobs', 'attacks on trade unionism making it harder for workers to form unions', and 'minimum wages that don't keep up with inflation'. Oh, and 'massive tax breaks for the people on top'. It is quite the package.

In the United States, lobbying represents approximately £2.4 billion each year, and industries like pharmaceuticals now have some 1,700 well-paid lobbyists in Washington, DC – all for just 535 members of Congress.[17] But the multiplier on this is the revolution of dark money in American politics.

In her spellbinding book, *Dark Money,* the *New York Times* journalist Jane Mayer lays bare the influence of players like the Koch brothers who, back in 2009, were worth an estimated £11 billion. In their circle was Richard Mellon Scaife, heir to the Mellon banking and Gulf Oil fortunes; Harry and Lynde Bradley, who made fortunes from defence contracts; John M. Olin, a chemical and munitions company titan; the Coors brewing family of Colorado; and the DeVos family of Michigan, which founded the Amway marketing empire. From the late 1970s, these individuals began to create what was described in a 2016 study by two Harvard University scholars as an unprecedented and unparalleled permanent, private political machine. By 2016, Mayer explains, 'the Kochs' private network of political groups had a bigger payroll than the Republican National Committee... with 1,600 paid staffers in thirty-five states and boasted that its operation covered 80 per cent of the population'. But this was only part of an operation that encompassed 'investment' in intellectuals whose ideas would serve as the 'raw products', investment in think-tanks to turn ideas into marketable policies, and the subsidizing of 'citizens' groups to pressure elected officials to implement the policies.

'A small number of people with massive resources,' Mayer concludes, 'orchestrated, manipulated, and exploited the economic unrest for their own purposes [using] tax-deductible donations to fund a movement to slash taxes on the rich and cut regulations on their own businesses.'

'So you know,' Sanders wearily concluded, 'when you use the word "democracy", you should put quotations around it.' 'We used to call this oligarchy,' I said. 'Well,' responded Bernie, 'I think that's what we're looking at, an oligarchy. So you got to have elections and all that stuff, but the real power is rested with moneyed interests.'

Now, as it happens, I do not think UK politics is quite this bad. It is certainly not as bad as it used to be. But if you cast your eyes over how some of England's leading history-makers made their fortunes, as I did in *Dragons*, you discover that a relationship with power lies at the heart of what I would call the seven deadly sins by which they tried to make their fortunes: speculation (Nathan Rothschild, who, with some advance information about the Battle of Waterloo, turned gold into government bonds and never looked back); attempted tax-dodging (the medieval wool baron Sir William de la Pole, who tried to corner the market); fraud (George Hudson, the railway baron who manipulated share prices); invasion (Cecil Rhodes, his ambitions manifested in no-holds-barred imperialism in southern Africa); war mongering (William Jardine, who lobbied government to launch the Opium War against China as a way of protecting his interests in opium dealing); and perhaps most egregious of all, slavery (Caribbean pirate and tobacco baron Lord Robert Rich, 2nd Earl of Warwick).

All of these six sins were made possible by the seventh: that the very rich find politics irresistible. William de la Pole effectively became the king's finance minister; Lord Robert Rich was a leading force in the English Civil War before becoming a key adviser to Oliver Cromwell; Nathan Rothschild was an intimate of king and Cabinet; Cecil Rhodes was actually prime minister of the Cape Colony; William Jardine and George Hudson were already very rich men when elected to the House of Commons, but both were masters of manipulating both Parliament and ministers.

Today, however, the UK – a small, open country with a vast financial-services system and a world-leading 'impunity industry' – is naturally vulnerable to rent-seeking fortune-hunters wanting to make it their home, as Robert Watts of the *Sunday Times* Rich List confirmed: 'The UK has become this magnet to the world's super-rich for lots of reasons. The City, the private schools, the universities, stunning properties, country estates, but where's the bang for the buck? You know, what does this deliver for millions of British people?'

But what is worse is that many of the most dangerous trends that we see driving rent-seeking elsewhere are now obvious in the UK – especially the unholy alliance between politics, finance and business. In his interviews with those on the Rich List, Robert has certainly noticed a fascination with politics. 'I think it's a combination of different things with different people,' Robert observed. 'With some, it's just, "Why can't these people get it right? Why can't they understand that we're the good guys... we create finance for public services. So why don't they make it easier for us to do business?"' However, for others, as Robert explained, engaging in politics is a vanity trip: 'it is simply about power' and ambition to project a story. As Robert put it, it's a case of 'I want you to know what I've accumulated, and this is a way of being more comfortable with that rather than genuinely trying to effect change and help.'

In my experience, the influence of wealth on power in Westminster operates at three basic levels. At its simplest is good old-fashioned lobbying. In a typical week as an MP, I might receive a couple of emails like the following from the UK Cryptoasset Business Council (UKCBC). 'I am contacting you,' it opens, 'regarding a cross-party joint letter (enclosed) organised by [an MP] to update current financial legislation that would signal a huge step for the growth of the UK's digital economy.' Then we might have a bit of public interest argument; in this case, 'it is vital the regulatory environment keeps pace with technological developments and ensures the UK's digital economy continues to thrive'. And then comes the ask: 'We would welcome your support in signing this letter' calling for 'a simple Statutory Instrument' to delete a current legal requirement to be a 'recognised stock exchange'. It concludes with a reassurance that the former Treasury minister 'noted that such a change could be implemented quite swiftly'.

Or take the missive I got from Novavax, asking me to meet the Senior Vice President, Government Affairs, Market Access and Alliances, 'to discuss the ongoing threat of COVID-19 and the role of [its] COVID-19 vaccine in the UK'. The company's problem becomes clear in the penultimate paragraph. Its Covid-19 vaccine 'achieved overall efficacy of 89.7 per cent and demonstrated a reassuring safety profile [but] Despite Novavax's investment into the UK and the positive outcome for their COVID-19 vaccine, the JCVI has provided a very limited recommendation for the use of Novavax's vaccine in the Autumn 2022 booster programme.' So, Novavax was demanding that the JCVI (Joint Committee on Vaccination and Immunisation) recommendation 'must be revised' to help them sell their drugs.

This kind of influence operation is not only aimed at UK politicians. The civil service is, if anything, a more important target. And here, the influence operations are more insidious. Take, for instance, the Wealthy Stakeholder Forum. It was set up in 2009 to discuss 'the operational processes and technical tax issues that impact "wealthy" customers'. It consists entirely of lobbyists and professional representatives of the accountancy profession.[18]

At the second level of what Mohammed Amersi called 'access capitalism' comes the think-tank, which is closely related to the newer phenomenon of the All Party Parliamentary Group. Lots of these do an excellent job helping Parliamentarians understand issues better. But as openDemocracy recently revealed, there are now 755 of them – more than there are Members of Parliament – and they are funded to the tune of some £25 million a year, half of which comes from 'private firms including healthcare bodies, arms companies and tech giants'.[19]

A group of these think-tanks shot to fame when the BBC finally ran a story about the special right-of-centre collection based at 55 Tufton Street, London. This was home to, among others, the Tax Payers' Alliance and the Global Warming Policy Foundation, as well as being the former 'Brexit Central' – the base for the Vote Leave campaign in the 2016 referendum on EU membership.[20] Of course, there are other think-tanks on the Left – less well funded, I might add – and I have worked with many of them over the years. But it troubles me that the sources of think-tank funding are opaque, because think-tanks have a huge influence on training politicians' special advisers, setting news agendas and incubating new ideas. And a think-tank is an important nexus for wealth and power to mix.

One well-connected journalist described to me how the process worked in relation to a wealthy individual who went on to become a Conservative Party Treasurer. The relationship starts with someone from a think-tank meeting politicians at a charity event. That person might say, 'Well, if you really want to influence… get someone to write a report for us suggesting perhaps a policy change.' But then they're told, 'You know, if you *really* want to change things you've got to put in multiple funds. After all, it's those scruffy people in Westminster who write the laws.'

It is, however, the third level of 'access capitalism' that worries me most. As in the United States and India, politics in Britain is now very, very expensive, not least because of the total absence of spending limits on social media and other advertising in between the tightly defined election periods. And that creates the most potentially dangerous space for wealth and power to combine, for in a truth that should be universally acknowledged, a titan in possession of a good fortune generally wants a powerful lawyer – and a pliant law-maker. And frankly, the UK's political parties have never been so vulnerable to temptation.

Since the Electoral Commission's database was set up, logging donations since 2001, it has recorded around £1.3 billion sloshing into UK political parties. The General Election year of

2019 was the most expensive to date, clocking up an incredible £149 million in donations. And when we look at where the money came from, one piece of information stands out: almost 40 per cent of the cash was donated by just thirty individuals and organizations, who, together, routed £44 million into British politics.[21] This is part of a long-term pattern; in fact, in 2021, we discovered that a fifth of political donations over twenty years had been made by just ten men – all white, with an average age of seventy. Together, they had shovelled an incredible £106 million into British political parties and campaigns, and they included plenty with links to Putin's Russia.[22] Where does it all lead for an energetic donor with deep pockets? Potentially to a seat in the House of Lords, replete with a vote on the nation's laws. Indeed, one in ten Conservative members of the House of Lords has donated more than £100,000 each to their party, a total of almost £50 million.[23] This is not a sensible road for us to take.

Rent-seeking, or the acquisition of economic privilege, has been true across history, true across the world, and it is true in the UK today. It is bad for democracy and it is terrible for economies. But to understand its full power, we need to examine how the common good is undermined not only by the ambitious seeking rents, but also by governments all too happy to write the 'rules of the game' in favour of those with plenty.

6

The Feathering of Fortune

From rules to rents

My favourite moment in the House of Commons is when we meet each morning. MPs stand before the famous green leather benches and face the wood-panelled walls, on which hang the little shields bearing coats of arms for colleagues who died in service. Then the chaplain offers a little prayer to focus minds:

> May they never lead the nation wrongly through love of power, desire to please, or unworthy ideals but laying aside all private interests and prejudices keep in mind their responsibility to seek to improve the condition of all mankind; so may your kingdom come and your name be hallowed.

It is a reminder that MPs are there to serve the *common* good, 'a requirement of justice and charity', as Pope Benedict XVI put it, a good 'that is sought not for its own sake, but for the people who belong to the social community'.[1]

In my experience, that is exactly how the vast majority of MPs see the task each day: to deliver for the many and not the few. Yet for all those good intentions, the UK today is not a fair and happy nation in which our condition is improving much at all. The free marketeers, like searchers for unicorns, have led us to a most unhappy place.

The 'free market' might sound like a liberating and benign 'return to nature'. But it is simply a persuasive conceit, a smooth evasion offered to disguise a fantasy. Look up the definition for 'free market' and you will read it is defined as 'an unregulated system of economic exchange, in which taxes, quality controls, quotas, tariffs, and other forms of centralized economic interventions by government either do not exist or are minimal'.[2] In other words, it is a mirage, not a market, because real markets everywhere, and always, are spaces full of institutions bound by rules that effectively ordain who gets what.

None of the market's institutions – whether they be property rights, companies, labour rules, capital markets (replete with banks), central banks or currencies – are found in nature or any 'natural state'. Which is why we need *political economy* to help us understand that there is no celestial marketplace that exists like some Platonic ideal. *Political* economists know that, in reality, markets and their institutions are imperfect because they are *social* creations, designed by flawed human beings who wield the factor missing in the market supremacist's equations: power. As the economist Samuel Bowles explains, 'the exercise of power is an essential aspect of the working capitalist economy even in its idealised, perfectly competitive state'.[3] And it has always been this way: 'The consistent theme across the millennia of political analysis,' writes Brooke Harrington, 'is of the inextricability of commerce and politics, as embodied in the elites who rule democratic states.'[4]

Few people have thought as hard about these matters as the Nobel Prize-winning economist Joseph Stiglitz.[5] We got to know each other a few years ago at some events I organized in London to promote a brilliant analysis of the ways in which the rules of our market institutions allow a lucky minority to make their profits and hold down earnings compared to the income that flows to shareholders. And this minority did it not through good old-fashioned competition in the marketplace, but through manipulating the rules of the game on trade, on cheap labour, on complementary science, and with the aid of lax competition rules and light regulation, easy money and bailouts, large contracts and, of course, low taxes. This sort of rent-seeking, Stiglitz explains, 'takes many forms: hidden and open transfers and subsidies from the government, laws that make the marketplace less competitive, [and] lax enforcement of existing competition laws'.[6] Together these rules help keep sales high and costs low. They are all rule sets designed after millions of hours of debate about how to foster growth. But without doubt, they reward some more than others, and it is workers who come off poorest.

In fact, if we look back at the globalized world we have built in the decades since the fall of the Berlin Wall and the admission of China to the World Trade Organization, a great contrast stands out in the way we have *fostered* rent-seeking for those blessed with property or capital, but *flattened* rents for labour and those trying to earn a decent crust. Often with the best intentions, we have conspired to create a set of economic institutions that help our wealthy but hurt our workers. To help us fully grasp what has happened, as Joe Stiglitz, explains, 'we must... examine the array of laws and policies that lie beneath the surface – the rules that determine the balance of power between public and private, employers and workers, innovation and shared growth, and all the other interests that make up the modern economy'.[7]

I have now been in politics long enough to watch the process become all too familiar. The persuasive reformer offers a plan with a promise of faster progress, some incantations of the common good, and generally some sort of appeal of a 'return to common sense'. The newspapers applaud. The proposals then get very technical very quickly, and the attention of legislators wanders. The laws are passed, and lo and behold, they produce a little common good for the many and a remarkable amount of private gain for the few. And the risks of this happening only grow when, as today, big money is allowed to stride through the small chambers of our democracy. When the gravitational pull of wealth grows stronger, we become too susceptible to writing laws, which, though they might be invoked for the common good, actually fail genuinely to create new wealth or innovation; rather, they simply funnel a greater share of the national economic product to a lucky few.

In order to appreciate the scale of this privilege cycle today, it is worth taking a look at the way we have fostered rent-seeking when it comes to property and capital but have flattened rents for labour.

Let us start with land in its broadest sense, or more specifically, property rights of three kinds: physical, 'positive' and intellectual. Britain's land and property rights were the inspiration for the first analysis of rent-seeking by David Ricardo, who noted in 1817 that as the economy grew and the demand for land rose, the bargaining power of landowners got ever stronger.[8] They could charge more without actually adding anything to what the nation produced, and as their share of national income rose, so the share of income left to everyone else reduced. And what made this economic process possible was command of power.

After the Norman Conquest of 1066, all English land was effectively nationalized, whereupon began a slow process, centuries long, of transferring acres first to the aristocracy and then to the gentry. '[T]ransforming oligarchs into aristocrats is something that Britain has been doing forever,' explained Oliver Bullough to me when we met. '[In fact] the father of the current Duke of Westminster [once] had to fill in one of those forms and put "source of wealth". He used to write "pillage", which is terribly witty because obviously his ancestors came over with William the Conqueror and stole all the stuff.'

Down the centuries, the power of Parliament was systematically used to expand these interests. The size of landed estates was multiplied by the acquisition of monastic land, during the Dissolution of the Monasteries and beyond in the sixteenth and seventeenth centuries. That process allowed the gentry to acquire around a third of England's agricultural land, and it was followed by enclosure, whereby Parliament was used to privatize thousands of acres that were once held in common: between 1750 and 1820, enclosure dispossessed largely poorer agricultural workers of some 30 per cent of England's green and pleasant land.[9]

The value of this land was then multiplied again by the nation's gentry, who once again turned to Parliament to create 'positive' rights to build valuable infrastructure. In the century after the Glorious Revolution (1688) turfed out Catholic King James II, Parliament was flooded with almost 7,000 'private bills', advanced by 'projectors' to build everything from turnpike roads to canals and railways. It was a communications revolution that helped the country become a single marketplace.[10]

Naturally, when the laws to make these things possible were debated, it was the *common good* rather than the private interest that was deployed for persuasive force. The sanctity of private property in Britain is part of our national religion, long enshrined in common law by the notion that, as the sixteenth-century lawyer and politician Sir Edward Coke put it, 'a man's house is his castle, *et domus sua cuique est tutissimum refugium* [and each man's home is his safest refuge]'.[11] The arguments for enclosure were always rooted in the case for 'improvement' of the inefficient open-field system, with its bare-worn wastelands and common pastures full of scrub. Equally, a typical turnpike bill proposed in Parliament to improve the roads might lament the 'very ruinous and bad' state of a track in winter and make provision for a toll to raise funds to maintain it, 'so as that *all* persons may travel through the same with safety'. (My italics.)

From some of the earliest bills to build canals – such as

the Cromford Canal Act (1789) – the projector's report would make much of the canal's benefit to 'the lower reaches of people which form the great bulk of society'.[12] A typical Parliamentary debate on a railway line would generally invoke some appeal to the greater good. In the Liverpool to Manchester railway bill, for example, Robert Peel argued that the railway was 'calculated to serve the commerce of the country *generally*'. (My italics.) The Secretary of Trade Mr Huskinson agreed, declaring that the backers of the railway were to be praised, and the subscribers, he said, 'seem to have a higher object in view, than the mere accumulation of wealth... They would certainly render a great commercial benefit *to the country*'.[13] (My italics.)

This long history of property rights still has profound consequences for the shape of inequality today, and indeed the property sector is very susceptible to lobbying, as Duncan Hames explained to me:

> We did some research in the UK on public policy on housing and [the] lobbying around it. And you know, it was clear that there was quite a lot of money that was going into building relationships with politicians from those with interests in property development. And that they were benefiting from the public policies.

Among the worst examples was the tale of media mogul and property developer Richard Desmond. At a series of events later described as 'inadvertent', a Cabinet minister, Robert Jenrick, found himself in 2019 sitting next to Mr Desmond at a Conservative Party General Election fundraiser, where Mr Desmond had the opportunity to show on his phone a promotional video of his huge property development in the London borough of Tower Hamlets. Mr Desmond was given the green light to develop his scheme so quickly that he avoided a £40 million liability to the local council to build roads and schools. After a High Court challenge, the government eventually rescinded the decision.[14]

Today, the structure of land in Britain still plays a significant role in fostering inequality. In fact, an investigation by Guy Shrubsole and the *Guardian* newspaper found that half of England is owned by around 25,000 landowners, which is less than 1 per cent of the population.[15] And all in all, a very small minority of people – around 2.7 million people – enjoy £41 billion in rental income.[16] There are, too, plenty of other rules that reward property owners simply through the owning or selling of property. Tax breaks on capital gains (Private Residence Relief) are worth another £35 billion a year.[17] But these prizes are dwarfed by the gift of low interest rates, sustained by £850 billion of quantitative easing, which helped deliver an almost £2 trillion increase in the value of property wealth between 2006–08 and 2018–20. Just for good measure, deregulation of the banking sector freed banks to expand rapidly their lending for mortgages, in turn contributing to rising house prices. As Adair Turner noted after the 2008 Financial Crash, most bank lending involves lending against property rather than financing the creation of new businesses.[18]

So there we have it: a philosophy evincing the common good became riddled with rules that benefitted a few rather more than others. This pattern of power to create rents is even clearer when it comes to property of a more abstract kind. The oldest patent protecting intellectual property in Britain dates back to 1449, when King Henry VI granted the Flemish-born John of Utynam a twenty-year patent to make coloured glass – for the windows of Eton College. Three centuries later, the wealth of Britain's Georgian gentry was a vital catalyst for Britain's new industrial age, which above all needed power. And entrepreneurs and engineers were soon perfecting and selling steam engines to provide it. But after James Watt and Matthew Boulton perfected their designs, they too needed patents to protect them. On the eve of the American War of Independence, and after intensive lobbying and petitioning by Boulton, Parliament provided these patents, creating a lifeline that helped keep their business afloat.[19] And so, not only did England protect property rights; it protected *intellectual* property rights.

Traditionally, we defend intellectual property rights as part of the common good. And in order to encourage firms to innovate, we need to allow them a period of profit through exclusive ownership of the secrets behind their discoveries. But these profits are now gigantic, and they flow disproportionately to the few.

Stroll around some of the UK's leading research labs, such as British Telecom's new facility in Suffolk at Adastral Park (now home to fifty-plus companies) or GlaxoSmithKline's Catalyst Park in Stevenage, and you notice how the UK's model of research and development (R&D) has now shifted from 'the cathedral to the campus'. Once upon a time, large companies like GSK or BT piled a load of research scientists into a big building and prayed for the best. Now, they're building landscaped business parks that look like university campuses, with many small labs and small firms of just a few people, experimenting away with hi-tech kit. Once breakthroughs are made, the small firms sell out to the global giants. This is an enormous industry. Britain's Intellectual Property Office does not publish many facts and figures, but in 2014, it estimated that the global trade in intellectual property licences was worth £220 billion, and over half of UK knowledge investment, worth £70 billion, was protected by IPR – intellectual property rights.[20] By 2021, the World Bank estimated that the UK's annual intellectual property receipts totalled $20 billion a year, which was around three times more than at the turn of the twenty-first century.[21]

This wealth is flattered by the gigantic scale of *public* investment, on behalf of you and me, into the science business, especially technology and pharmaceutical firms. The UK government's net expenditure on R&D totalled £15.3 billion in 2021.[22] Some of this goes on in the realm of 'pure science', too. But much of it creates the breakthroughs that the private sector can then monetize. Think about the phone in your pocket and all the apps on it: 'Where did the smart tech behind those gizmos come from?' asks economist Marianna Mazzucato. 'Public funds. The Internet, GPS, touchscreen, SIRI and the algorithm behind Google – all were funded by public institutions.'[23] This sort of research was especially important for Apple and Alphabet/Google, which within sixteen years of its birth, became more valuable than Exxon/Mobil. Thereafter, Alphabet/Google and Apple were the first and second most valuable companies in the world for some years.[24] From the advent of the civil aviation industry to today's tech industry to the drugs that make billions for pharma, the fountainhead of research was funded by government.

That is not all. Many new businesses benefit from the way we choose to write the rules for how new firms do business. Shoshana Zuboff highlighted the impact of Section 230 of America's Communications Decency Act of 1996. It is a little clause with a big effect. Because, as she writes, it 'shields website owners from lawsuits and state prosecution for user-generated content'. In the UK, Section 5 of the 2013 Defamation Act provides a similar defence.[25] The law says that 'It is a defence for the operator [i.e., the platform provider] to show that it was not the operator who posted the statement on the website.' It is this legal immunity that allows both Google and Facebook/Meta to build businesses that, in 2021, accounted for half of global spending on digital advertising.[26]

When all is said and done, property rights – whatever the type – form merely one of the social inventions that make a modern market. You cannot have capitalism without capital, and once again, down the ages, we created institutions with rules – like the Royal Mint, the Royal Exchange and the Bank of England – which create not only value for society but rents for a lucky few.

The Royal Mint's first great reform of the currency, advised by Sir Thomas Gresham in 1560, was especially concerned with defending the exchange rate enjoyed by England's textile traders.[27] Gresham was also the driving force behind London's Royal Exchange. Opened by Queen Elizabeth I on 23 January 1571, it was the core of what later became the Stock Exchange, a hub of financial innovation and a nexus of projectors – of men 'joining their heads to understand the useful things in life', not least how to finance the huge costs of war.[28] And among these traders after 1688, King William III found plenty of London merchants ready to help create a Bank of England. A bank had been discussed for a good forty years. It finally opened in 1694 as a great 'Conveniency', drawing income from the state in return for a loan, allowing the Bank to buy government debt with a guaranteed return, and then sell shares to the public.[29]

At the very core of the first arguments for these reforms and institutions was a case for the common good, which had to be especially strong to defeat the old objections to usury. So, when Thomas Gresham made the case for the Royal Exchange, he argued to Elizabeth's secretary, Sir William Cecil (Lord Burghley), that a domestic capital market would free the monarch from dependence on foreigners: 'I would wish that the Queen's majesty in this time should not use any strangers but her own subjects whereby... all other princes may see what a prince of power she is,' he wrote. When the Bank of England was established in 1694, it was 'to promote the public good and benefit of our people'.[30] Two hundred years later, a similar sentiment was extolled by George Rae in his influential 1885 reflections on 'the rights and duties of shareholders', whereby 'when a man becomes a shareholder in a bank, he... is only one partner amongst a thousand others in your Bank; but that does not release him from the obligation of doing what he can for the common good.'

Yet centuries later, can we say that the common good shapes the way we write the rules for capital markets? Today, the UK's financial services industry creates millions of jobs and billions in wealth, but it also fuels our national inequality, as Oxfam recently noted.[31] A fifth of the top 1 per cent of earners in Europe work in financial services – even though they make up just 4 per cent of the entire workforce. High street banks tend to charge the poorest most for access to credit. Clever new products like High Frequency Trading (HFT), where high-powered computers run algorithms to profit from pure price arbitrage, create little value for the real economy yet fortunes for some.

This freedom to build such fortunes is firmly underwritten by taxpayers. When the financial services crashed in 2008, the subsequent bailout in the UK cost the public around £23 billion.[32] As the Bank of England's Marilyne Tolle pointed out, this implicit funding subsidy allowed banks to take more risks than they should have, creating an unwarranted competitive advantage along with the moral hazard of encouraging reckless risk-taking for ever greater financial gain. That greater risk-taking was effectively 'a wealth transfer from taxpayers to the financial industry'.[33]

However, in recent years the value of this privilege has been dwarfed by the value of easy money in the shape of quantitative easing (QE). As we have seen, during the Great Financial Crisis and then during Covid-19, the Bank of England pumped an incredible £850 billion into the UK money supply, creating new money electronically as central bank reserves, and then using it to buy mostly government bonds, indirectly, from investors such as insurance companies, banks and pension funds who already owned the gilts. These institutions then had the cash they did not have before to invest in assets like shares, providing a higher rate of return. The Bank of England explains that this process 'tends to push up on the value of shares, making households and businesses holding those shares wealthier. That makes them likely to spend more, boosting economic activity.'[34]

In order to understand all this better, I accompanied some fellow Parliamentarians one frosty January morning to the

Bank, to speak with its leaders and put it to its chief economist, Huw Pill, that given the impact of QE on knocking down interest rates, it probably also had a pretty seismic impact on today's level of wealth inequality. He did not demur, but being a good central banker, he somewhat hedged his bets. 'I think you're right to point out that there has been a debate about whether QE had an impact on inequality,' he told us, and 'QE *is* intended to work on the economy by influencing asset prices. So, in a sense, it would be a problem in transmission if it didn't have an effect on asset prices.'

Before Covid-19, the Bank of England had a look at whether the QE injected into the system between 2008 and 2014 had made wealth inequality worse. It admitted that, overall, those people higher up the wealth distribution did much better in absolute terms than those lower down: 'a 10 per cent increase in net wealth for all households would be worth only £200 to the 10 per cent of least wealthy households, but £195,000 to the top 10 per cent of the distribution'.[35] The Bank concluded that because QE had helped sustain employment among poorer households, the *relative* levels of inequality had not changed. That was not how Parliament saw it, as the House of Lords Economic Affairs Committee made clear in its July 2021 report on QE: 'There is a body of evidence,' it thundered, 'that perceives this [rising asset prices due to QE] to have increased wealth inequalities.'[36]

The way we write the rules of our marketplace does not simply create 'rents' for property owners and capital markets. It has a crucial impact on the rewards for workers, and while we have systematically enhanced privileges for the owners of property and capital, we have wrecked the rents for labour, which once helped secure what was called a 'just wage'.

Technically, any sort of wage protection is a form of rent, because it ensures that the worker is paid more than the bare minimum that might be required for the worker to do a particular job. For a long time, such a protection was recognized as a vital part in a philosophy of moral economy that shaped economic thought for centuries. In the fourth century BC, Aristotle first proposed the theory of 'just reciprocation' in the *Nicomachean Ethics*. Since goods exchanged will be of different values, he explained, societies must arrive at a certain equalization of value – an exchange rate of one good for another. And unless this exchange rate were *just*, it would be very hard for a society to continue in a way that allowed every citizen to specialize in their vocation, and therefore difficult to hold a city-state together.[37] His student, Plato, developed the point: the division of labour allowed specialization, which in turn allowed men to live true to their nature. 'I am myself reminded,' Plato wrote, 'that we are not all alike; there are diversities of natures among us which are adapted to different occupations.'[38]

Justice in the process of exchange was the key to sustaining the advantage. Without reciprocal justice of exchange, arts and crafts would be destroyed, because craftsmen would lack the means to support themselves, and the city – the basic unit of economic life, based on a division of labour – could no longer flourish. So, without just compensation, a city would soon become enslaved – because a slave is one who is not rightly rewarded for his work.[39]

It was this tradition that the Greeks bequeathed to the Romans, and which in turn underpinned centuries of European thought. The Roman notion of *recta ratio* – that a good exchange was both 'free and fair' – was enshrined in Emperor Justinian's magnificent sixth-century legal code, the Corpus Juris Civilis',[40] and it chimed with Cicero's ideal of justice as 'a habit of mind which gives every man his desert while preserving the common advantage'.[41] Roman lawyers viewed the law of wages as a division of the law of rents; a payment in exchange for an agreed service. Parties were supposed to negotiate in good faith, reaching a middle ground 'between the extremes of hope on both sides'.[42] A 'just wage' was therefore 'the natural result of bargaining, *supported where necessary by the common opinion of fair-minded people*'.[43] (My italics.)

Onto this theme of Greco-Roman thought, the Christian Church grafted the biblical injunction of Matthew – that 'a labourer is worthy of his hire' – and Luke, 'for the labourer is worthy of his meat'.[44] And so Christian Fathers like Abelard, in the twelfth century, went on to argue that 'justice is that through which the harmony of the community is held together, and which does not deny to each his merits', while Thomas Aquinas spelt out that fair compensation for labour was 'one of the positive acts of justice'.[45]

It fell to Adam Smith, nearly two and a half thousand years after Aristotle, to bring the theory into the modern age. Most market supremacists like to put much weight on Smith's beautiful description of the 'invisible hand', happily and magically reconciling the plethora of interests in the marketplace, but Smith knew his Greek.[46] He understood that bargains struck were not exchanges between self-maximizing players but a bargain between beneficent people who each cared about the well-being of their counter-party. Smith was a firm believer that the rails of justice should keep us on the straight and narrow in all exchanges, as the grand edict of *Wealth of Nations* makes clear: 'Every man, *as long as he does not violate the laws of justice*, is left perfectly free to pursue his own interest his own way.' (My italics).

The nineteenth century was not kind to this tradition. But from the 1830s, a coalition for decency, from Christian reformers to the new Cooperative societies, from trade unionists to – eventually – Labour governments, helped deliver, over the course of a hundred years, new laws, from the Factory Acts of the 1830s to the Wages Council Act of 1945, which meant that workers might enjoy safe working conditions and decent rates of pay. By 1945, 80 per cent of British workers were covered by some sort of collective wage bargaining, and in the years after 1945, this ambition for just wages was buttressed by a consensus that cross-border capital flows need controlling to avoid currency volatility.

By the 1990s, however, this consensus was turned on its head as international organizations – the IMF, OECD and the European Union – all pushed for full 'capital account convertibility', which gave employers a credible threat: either workers would have to accept lower wages, or the work would move abroad. As it happened, at the same time a billion people were joining the global labour force, as a massive movement of people – from 'farm to factory' – began in developing economies, creating a huge oversupply of unskilled workers.[47] And we changed the rules of the global trading system, so that the companies in which these new workers sweated could trade freely with us. Indeed, since 2010, our trade with dictatorships has increased by over £136 billion, and is growing almost twice as fast as our trade with the free world. Almost a quarter of our trade is now with countries classed as 'not free' or only 'partly free'.

Where firms could not, or did not want to, offshore their operations – for example in the services industries – there were new freedoms to import workers. The proportion of foreign-born workers in the UK doubled between 1997 and 2015, part of a global trend as the world went on the move. Together with the opportunity of deploying new technology, this *mobility* of capital has destroyed what J. K. Galbraith once called the 'countervailing power' of workers to argue for fairer wages against the power of the biggest businesses.[48] It should not therefore surprise us that between 2004 and 2017, the International Labour Organization found that labour's share of global income presented 'a substantial downward trend' especially in Europe and America.

All in all, a short survey of property, capital and labour underlines one simple point. While market supremacists might extol 'free markets', in reality the notions of free markets are a well-practised dissembling. Throughout history, markets have always been spaces with rules, and the rules help decide who walks home with what.

Alongside rules for property, labour and capital come other prizes, too, like contracts for public procurement, or loan guarantees in times of crisis. All governments regulate and subsidize private production, sometimes through laws and sometimes through subsidies and taxes, direct or indirect. For example, to take one year, the data for 2019/20 shows that the UK government placed contracts of £295.5 billion – about one-third of public sector spending – which went on everything from missiles to street cleaners.[49] And government loan guarantees were especially important for business during the Covid-19 pandemic, costing £20.9 billion in 2020–21.[50] Tax subsidies are another form of support, though they are often quite hard to trace.

These various factors, contributing to the privilege cycle, are extremely valuable for those who want to profit not merely by winning out in the marketplace, but by moulding the rules of the game, and they help explain why, down the ages, markets produce such high levels of inequality. And yet, they are but the first part of the story. To understand the inequality of wealth today, we have to look at two further twists: the emergence of monopolies, by the boom and bust of bubbles, a feature of the immutable fact that human beings are, well, human.

7

Malfunctioning Markets

Monopoly, bubble and the death of Homo economicus

Set amid mint-green manicured lawns, the Harvard Business School is perhaps the high church of capitalism. Twenty-five years ago, and thanks to a Fulbright Scholarship, I shuffled in nervously, through its flag-decked, dazzling white porticos that made you want to salute, as the only comprehensive-school kid from Britain to join the Class of 2000. For the next two years, I got to study and debate with an extraordinary mix of former military officers, advertising executives, UN workers, consultants, bankers and engineers. But together, we were not trained to protect competition. We were trained to destroy it.

That year, we counted ourselves lucky to be taught personally by one of the greatest business academics of modern times. Our strategy guru, Professor Michael Porter, had literally written the book on competition. But Michael's starting point was pretty arresting. As he put it in his bestseller *On Competition*, '[t]he perfectly competitive industry offers the *worst* prospects for long-run profitability'.[1] (My italics.) Hence the need to conquer the competition, if not by beating it, then by buying it.

That simple logic, taught to generations of business students, helps explain why – whether from a foundation of earned privilege or unearned privilege – the most successful entrepreneurs build power positions in the marketplace, from which they can seek to maximise 'rents', which in the modern world may take many shapes. And the fastest way to do this is by building a monopoly or even an 'oligopoly', which the OECD defines as a market 'dominated by a small number of suppliers'.[2] And of course this is hardly a secret, much less a novelty.

'People of the same trade,' wrote Adam Smith in 1776, 'seldom meet together, even for merriment and diversion, but the conversation ends in a conspiracy against the public, or in some contrivance to raise prices.'[3] Oligopoly is, as the American political theorist Herb Simon (1916–2001) once counselled, 'the permanent and ineradicable scandal of economic theory'. And over the last thirty-odd years, the point has been proved, as firms acquired the freedom to combine in amalgamations that grew bigger and bigger, just as Joseph Schumpeter would have predicted.[4]

Thanks to the new work of French economist Philippe Aghion and the 'Neo-Schumpeterians', Schumpeter is back in fashion.[5] He would be pleased. His ambitions as a young man were to become the greatest economist in the world, the greatest horseman in all of Austria and the greatest lover in all of Vienna. For more than seventy-five years, the great man without doubt suffered an eclipse. Today, he reads like a prophet. For it was Schumpeter who explained how, in a modern economy, 'creative destruction' ultimately leads to the destruction of competition and the emergence of oligopoly.

When Schumpeter was writing his masterpiece, *Capitalism, Socialism and Democracy* (1942), the economic theory of perfect competition, where atomistic firms competed in markets in which each was too small to command market power, was under sustained attack. The story no longer explained the observed reality, in which large, powerful firms dominated the economy – and still managed to create historically unprecedented levels of growth. The secret, argued Schumpeter, was the basic tendency within capitalism towards 'creative destruction':

The opening up of new markets, foreign or domestic, and the organisational development from the craft shop and factory to such concerns as US Steel illustrate the same process of industrial mutation... that incessantly revolutionises the economic structure from within, incessantly destroying the old one, incessantly creating a new one. This process of Creative Destruction is the essential fact about capitalism.[6]

'Creative destruction' is what most remember about Schumpeter's work. But what is less recalled is Schumpeter's insight that the flip side of creative destruction is the destruction of competition. Firms pursue innovation in order to create advantages they can crystallise, to dominate new markets and extract rents. 'Enterprise would in most cases be impossible,' Schumpeter wrote 'if it were not known from the outset that exceptionally favorable situations are likely to arise which if exploited by price, quality and quantity manipulation will produce profits adequate to tide over exceptionally unfavorable situations.'[7] The prospect of large profit is therefore the bait that lures capital onto untried trails. Philippe Aghion summarised the dynamics very well: 'Innovation,' he explains, 'comes from the decision to invest especially in research and development by entrepreneurs motivated by potential returns – innovation rents.'[8]

Schumpeter thought that most monopolies were temporary but that ultimately capitalism would be undone by those monopolies that became unbeatable: 'Pure cases of long-run monopoly,' he wrote, 'must be of the rarest occurrence... [because] the power to exploit at pleasure a given pattern of demand... can, under the conditions of intact capitalism, hardly persist for a period long enough to matter.'[9] But in the long run, Schumpeter went on, 'capitalism was condemned to fail precisely because it was impossible to prevent incumbent firms from obstructing new innovations'.[10] In other words, incumbent forces *can* and do become strong enough to defeat the competition that is necessary for creative destruction to continue.

Schumpeter's focus on incessant innovation and the conflict it created between industries old and new was quite different to the classical economic models of the day and the neoclassical fashion that was to follow. But as a description of the basic dynamics of a capitalist economy, it is as important as Adam Smith's famous enunciation of the division of labour, and when we look at the economy today, frankly, Schumpeter looks like a soothsayer. He foresaw exactly what has been unfolding around us for forty years.

Since the fall of the Berlin Wall, some 1.2 million merger and acquisition deals worth over £70 trillion have helped create a global super-league of companies bigger than countries, capable of placing work with the cheapest of the 3.2 billion workers who now make up the global workforce, while pumping trillions of dollars into technology to create machines that are cheaper than humans.

In the United States, for example, an £8 trillion merger and acquisition wave transformed business between 2008 and 2016, as large firms built market share and cut costs.[11] Industry after industry has become dominated by oligopolies that have emerged in sectors as diverse as dog food, batteries, telecoms, pharmacies and credit cards. Corporate chieftains have taken to heart the advice of American venture capitalist Peter Thiel: '[c]ompetition is for losers', he declared in his book *Zero to One*. A handful of firms now monopolize the aircraft industry, the world's auto business, the world's mobile telecoms infrastructure, pharmaceuticals, beer, cigarettes, aero-engines, computer chips, industrial gasses and canned soft drinks. Between 1997 and 2012, two-thirds of American industrial sectors became more concentrated.[12] In three-quarters of sectors in 1997–2007, the fifty largest firms gained revenue share.[13] 'Consolidation,' noted President Obama's former economic adviser, Peter Orszag, 'may be contributing to… the increased share of firms with apparently super-normal returns.' He was right. In 2018, the *Economist* calculated global 'excess' profits at an extraordinary $660 billion, of which some 72 per cent was down to US firms.[14]

In the UK, though, the story is even worse. The British economy has been transformed by a merger wave that is proportionally 50 per cent *greater* than that of the United States. Among 250 different UK industries, the *Economist* found that more than half (55 per cent) became more concentrated in 2007–14, and that rates of new entrants had fallen in 70 per cent of industries. Such findings confirmed the trend uncovered by the Resolution Foundation, which reported that concentration 'has increased in the majority of sub-sectors (accounting for the majority of revenue) in the UK economy'.[15] Eight out of ten consumer industries surveyed in 2018 by the Social Market Foundation think-tank were found to be 'concentrated'.[16]

Technology means that today's oligopolies are, though, different to the giants of the past. What have emerged are *technopolies*, which use big tech, big brand and big data spend to dominate their markets and lock in customers, and they have big balance sheets and cash piles to buy out the competition.[17] They have created the sort of barriers to new competition that would make Michael Porter proud.

Technology spend is key to the advantage of these modern behemoths. Nowadays, global spending on research and development (R&D) is in the region of £2 trillion a year.[18] But the world's top 2,500 R&D investors account for almost a trillion of that – £943 billion, to be precise, in 2021.[19] It is what Peter Nolan calls 'the core of global innovation in the early 21st-century'.

Brand spending multiplies the advantage. To take one year – 2019 – the world's firms spent around £500 billion on advertising.[20] But the world's largest 200 companies spend £131 billion of it – that is more than a quarter. In 2021, Google's parent, Alphabet, spent a combined total of £26 billion on advertising plus R&D.[21] Microsoft spent a combined total of £20 billion on brand and tech. Apple spends £19 billion. Volkswagen spends £15 billion. How can any firm compete with that?

The evidence suggests that they cannot, especially as technopolies have been given a free hand to use their market power to 'kill in the crib' startup competitors, which threaten the data monopolies that the big firms aspire to build. Competition might be the mother of invention, as the European Union Commissioner for Competition Margrethe Vestager once noted, but today, technopolies simply *buy* small firms that threaten their monopolies. Thanks to outdated legislation, merger control laws do not kick in – because the deals are judged by *turnover* rather than by value or the quantity of data now controlled. To date, Google/Alphabet, for example, has bought 224 businesses since it was founded. Facebook/Meta has bought almost 100 companies.[22] Many of these acquisitions, like the notorious Facebook/Meta purchase of WhatsApp in 2014, were all about building monopolies in personal data. But despite the £15 billion price paid, the WhatsApp deal was too small in *revenue* terms to trigger merger control. Yet the acquisition of WhatsApp allowed Facebook/Meta to add a treasure trove of data on the app's 1 billion users to its pile.

Technopolies are very, very bad for equality of wealth, because they reward their captains in capital but drive down the earnings of workers. Within their huge global value chains – which account for about two-thirds of world trade – technopolies use outsourcing or automation to keep down the costs of wages.[23] And in many places, their power is tantamount to what economists call 'monopsony': the ability to dictate wages while workers lose all power to 'vote with their feet' and move to different firms paying better – because those alternative opportunities simply do not exist.[24]

Monopsony is less understood than monopoly, but it is a similar concept. A firm with monopsony power 'can pay a lower wage than would prevail in a competitive market without losing all its workers to competition employers'.[25] Again, there is nothing novel about the sin. When many sellers of labour face far fewer buyers of labour, 'the imperfection of competition' tells in favour of the buyers, as Adam Smith understood well. 'Masters are always and everywhere in a sort of tacit, but constant and uniform, combination, not to raise the wages of labour above the actual rate,' he wrote.[26] Friedrich Engels arrived at the same conclusion. 'While capitalist sellers,' wrote Engels, are free to add their cut along the production chain, 'labour alone is unable to raise the price of his commodity'.[27] During Barack Obama's presidency, his Council of Economic Advisers concluded that the problem was back. Increasingly, they noted, 'among economists and policy makers', there was a realization 'that employers often have some degree of monopsony power in labour markets'.

In some cases, monopsony might result from the poverty of options. If you live in a town with few employers and poor transport links to places with jobs, then your pay-bargaining options are limited. But what Obama's team discovered was a growing use of new methods to stop the free movement of labour. Non-compete agreements, often forced on employees, hinder the traffic of workers between jobs.[28] Employers often offer ostensibly beneficial sweeteners such as (private) healthcare or pensions that act as 'job-lock' measures, effectively raising the cost for an employee wanting to shift firms, and the sponsorship of licences or work visas creates a dependency of worker on employer.

But technopolies multiply the problem. The American economist David Autor and his colleagues looked closely at the phenomenon of 'superstar firms' driving down workers' share of the national pie.[29] They concluded that 'winner takes all firms', with high profits and low wage shares, hoovered up the revenue in a particular industry. The dynamic they describe is remorseless; technology and innovation are used to extract higher profits which in turn squeezes wages lower and allows 'superstar firms' to become more competitive creating the 'winner-takes-most' features of these new markets.[30] Worse, the innovation that creates high wages was not diffusing throughout the marketplace in the way it once did. Big firms were making sure it did not, with the result that good ideas were being hoarded by what the OECD has called 'frontier firms' – high-tech behemoths like Apple or Boeing or GE, which dominate all around them. If you are lucky enough to work there, you might do well. But if you don't, you don't.

Low wages are bad enough. But more recent evidence suggests that high prices add insult to injury. Even before the recent resurgence of inflation, evidence was growing that technopolies were imperilling low prices, because of the freedom enjoyed by these gargantuan corporations to extract economic rents. In an extraordinary study published in 2019, the International Monetary Fund concluded that prices, or mark-ups – which, it says, are a good proxy for the rising market power of leading firms – had risen on average 38 per cent across advanced economies.[31] I was so surprised by this that I reached out to the IMF and asked their economists to unbundle what was an international study to provide the 'mark-ups' for prices in the UK. Lo and behold, the story was even worse than the global average. 'Mark-ups' to prices in the UK since 1980 were nearly 60 per cent.[32]

So, it is not clear at all whether *consumers*, let alone workers, are reaping quite the benefits promised by globalization. Instead, as we can see around the world, the sort of technopolies we were taught to build have proved remarkably effective in maximizing their earned and unearned privilege, and in turn this has driven inequality relentlessly forward.

But there is one final piece of the puzzle that helps us see that inequality is not simply the consequence of privilege and technopoly: the dreaded bubble. It is an inevitable feature of economic life, created by the truth that we are not the perfectly rational actors that some economists would like us to be.

The market supremacists did not predict bubbles – those moments when traders salivate at the lure of quick profits, and the mirage of one-way bets excite the markets to a frenzy and drive asset prices to soar to beyond the bounds of rational thinking. Until they burst, showering down loss instead of profits, and at their worst, sending whole economies into a tailspin. Thanks to a revolution in behavioural economics, we now understand this better, along with perhaps something that was rather obvious: that while *Homo economicus* is (mythically) rational, *Homo sapiens*, despite the name, is not. Our limitations as human beings mean that markets are not perfect. Rather, they inevitably malfunction.

As Vernon Smith and Bart Wilson explain in their book *Humanomics* (2019), the experimental evidence that began to emerge from game theory in the 1980s and 1990s 'had a falsifying confrontation with economics… from which economic theory had not recovered by the early 2000's'.[33] Contrary to the beliefs of Efficient Market Hypothesis scholars, prices of stocks, shares and other assets *do not* always reflect the sum total of available human knowledge at any one particular time. In fact, prices are riddled with our hopes, fears and delusions, which can be completely divorced from 'objective' reality. In the extraordinary work of several scholars, we see why – as Richard Thaler summarized it – 'the price is often wrong, and sometimes very wrong… [and] when prices diverge from fundamental value by such wide margins, the misallocation of resources can be quite big'.[34]

Economics, put simply, is essentially the study of how we make choices in conditions of scarcity. As we saw, the foundational beliefs of neoclassical economics involved an assumption that we choose by 'optimizing' – we look for the best goods and services that we can afford, and so we approach the business of choosing rationally, fully informed and with our eyes wide open. This 'constrained optimisation' is coupled with a second article of faith: that in competitive markets, where prices are free to move up and down, prices fluctuate so that supply equals demand. The problem is that both these tenets are wrong, because it turns out that human beings are not prophets; neither are they sociopaths.

'The agent of economic theory,' as the Swiss economist Bruno Frey once put it, 'is rational, selfish, and his tastes do not change.'[35] But humans are not omniscient, nor do we have infinite time, memory banks or computational power to calculate the truth of something. 'To a psychologist,' writes Daniel Kahneman in *Thinking, Fast and Slow* (2011), 'it is self-evident that people are neither fully rational nor completely selfish, and that their tastes are anything but stable.' We face a world that is far too complex to calculate the best available options, rationally. Most human beings, adds Thaler, 'do not have the brains of Einstein... nor do they have the self-control of an ascetic Buddhist monk'. And so, because we have both limited time and brainpower, and because we face a world of infinite complexity, we invent shortcuts to help us weave our way through life's maze, creating, as Gerd Gigerenzer put it, 'simple rules of thumb – heuristics – to help make judgments'.[36] This helps us make sense of the world and take decisions at the speed our lives require. Which at times means instantly. This approach to life is very sensible. It typically produces decisions that are 'good enough', especially when problems are intractable or where lots more information will not make much difference, or where searching for all that information is costly.

This being so, traditional economic theories not only simplify the world we live in, they simplify us. They either assume we possess an 'unbounded rationality' or, at the very least, that we optimize given the constraints we might face. But neither assumption is true. Omniscience, omnipotence and optimization are 'beautiful fictions'. 'Logic and probability are mathematically beautiful and elegant systems,' writes Gigerenzer. 'But they do not always describe how actual people... solve problems.'[37]

As humans, we tend to have multiple goals, so optimizing for any single decision is computationally very hard. Moreover, the way we take decisions is often *not* to 'maximize our own utility'. 'The purely economic man is indeed close to being a social moron,' as the Indian economic thinker Amartya Sen once put it. He continued: 'Economic theory has been much preoccupied with this rational fool,' a mythical character now buried by a host of 'cooperation games' which all illustrate our generous, not our selfish, instincts. The 'public good' game is a good illustration. In it, ten strangers are invited together and given five £1 coins. Each must decide how many coins to pop into a blank envelope as a contribution to the 'public good', and once everyone has decided, the envelopes are put in, and the donations doubled. The money is then divided equally among the players. The purely *rational* thing to do in these circumstances is to contribute nothing. But in practice, on average, people 'donate' about half their pot.[38]

As it happens, Adam Smith also understood this. Far from expecting everyone to maximize their own pay-offs – as many of his devotees believe – Smith argued that 'sentiments' change everything. 'Adam Smith's answer,' wrote Vernon Smith, 'could not be simpler, but you have to get past utility theory as a theory of everything.'[39] The reason is that 'fundamentally it is the human capacity for *sentiment*, fellow feeling, and a sense of propriety that is the stuff of which human relationships and the general rules-to-be-followed are made'.[40] As children, we learn the value of both beneficence and justice. As adults, most of us take those values to market. Indeed, we have very little conscious choice, because 'sentiments' are deeply rooted in brain chemistry, evolved over human history, which is why neuro-economics has become so important.

The neurophysician Sir Edward Rolls has argued that our

brains are designed around reward-and-punishment evaluation systems, because this is the way that genes can build a complex system that delivers appropriate, but flexible, behaviour to increase their fitness; genes influence behaviour in ways that are good for gene survival.[41] Decisions are shaped by that part of the brain that Rolls describes as 'an evolutionarily older emotional system with gene specified rewards'. Often, such decisions are deemed 'ethical'. But 'many principles that humans accept as ethical may be closely related to strategies that are useful heuristics for promoting social cooperation, and emotional feelings associated with ethical behaviour may be at least partly related to the adaptive value of such gene specified strategies'.[42]

The inescapable conclusion, put simply, is that the way we take decisions is often not 'logical'. And this has profound implications for whether or not markets are shaped by the cold logic of exchange, self-correcting as new information is brought to the table.

Take, for example, the host of different ways we think about gains and losses. 'Prospect theory', developed by Thaler and Kahneman, revealed that far from calculating rationally, human beings are driven more strongly to avoid losses than to achieve gains. As Thaler explains, '[W]e quickly reached two conclusions... people attach values to gains and losses rather than to wealth, and the decision weights that they assign to outcomes are different from probabilities.' Losses hurt more than gains that we might never harvest. After a range of experiments, Daniel Kahneman concluded that '[r]oughly speaking, losses hurt about twice as much as gains make you feel good', or, there is the insight that people do not actually behave as if gains in wealth have a 'diminishing marginal utility', which as we saw, has been the theory for a long time. In fact, Kahneman and the Israeli scholar Amos Tversky discovered that far more influential than the overall level of wealth were *changes* to actual wealth. Or there is what is called the 'endowment effect'. Suppose you buy a £100 ticket to see your favourite band in a concert than has sold out. You love them and in fact would have paid up to £500 for that ticket. Now, you discover that prospective purchasers on the Internet are willing to pay up to £3,000 for the scarce tickets. The traditional neoclassical theory says you should not hesitate to sell. In practice, however, many ticket-holders prefer to hang on to their tickets. Even economics professors.

All told, the basic instincts revealed by the Reality Economists help explain at least a dozen facts about how we *really* make choices between risky options, 'in flat contradiction to expected utility theory' – and these also include the truth that humans appear to have a tendency towards overconfidence. Indeed, Robert Swiller, yet another Nobel Prize-winner in Economics, once observed that 'some basic tendency toward overconfidence appears to be a robust character trait'.[43]

Together, these challenges to rationality add up to one fundamental conclusion: that our limitations as humans mean that markets *malfunction*. And that is exactly what we discovered during the Great Financial Crisis of 2008–10, for which I had a front-row seat.

When I was ushered into the prime minister's den, overlooking Horse Guards Parade, to talk to Gordon Brown about my new job – helping coordinate his Downing Street operation – he was on the phone, patiently insisting to the chief executive of one of the UK's great banks that it needed to merge with its rival to stave off a collapse. The months that followed, as the world's banking system went into cardiac arrest, were beyond doubt the most difficult, stressful days of my years in public life. If markets were 'self-correcting', how could this have possibly happened?

There has always been such a strong link between financial globalization and financial crises. While many nations have graduated from a troubled past repaying national debts, 'so far', as Ken Rogoff and Carmen Reinhart elegantly put it, 'graduation from banking crisis has proven elusive'.[44] In their masterful book *This Time is Different* (2011), a study of sixty-six countries since the Napoleonic Wars, the pair point out that the world's great finance hubs – the United States, UK and France – have experienced some forty banking crises since 1800, and just four of the nations they studied had avoided a banking crisis between 1945 and 2007. In eighteen of the twenty-six banking crises since 1970, the financial sector was liberalized in the preceding five years, sparking faster mobility of international capital.

In 2008, it was no different, as we watched some very familiar patterns repeat: financial liberalization, faster international capital flows and an asset price bubble. But the scale now was staggering. At the beginning of the twenty-first century, the world was awash with huge cash piles, building up in countries that ran significant export surpluses, such as China and Germany. This abundance helped fuel an extraordinary asset price boom. By 2005, the *Economist* was warning of 'the biggest bubble in history'.[45] These shifts had helped create a gargantuan global industry. By 2010, the British financial services sector had doubled in size to around 10 per cent of GDP.[46] In the United States, Bill Clinton's reversal of Roosevelt's Glass-Steagall Act (1933) had allowed investment banks and regular banks to combine once again, creating huge new risks.

Financial-sector deregulation then multiplied the risk as loans were offered to those who could ill afford them, creating a vast 'sub-prime market', which the US Federal Reserve failed to stem.[47] The US Financial Crisis Inquiry Commission later castigated the Fed for this pervasive permissiveness, pointing to its 'pivotal failure to stem the flow of toxic mortgages'.[48] As a result, 'trillions of dollars in risky mortgages had become embedded throughout the financial system as mortgage-related securities were packaged, repackaged, and sold to investors around the world'. When the housing bubble collapsed, noted the US investigators, 'a string of events... led to a full blown crisis'. 'The sentries,' concluded the Commission, 'were not at their posts, *in no small part due to the widely accepted faith in the self-correcting nature of the markets* and the ability of financial institutions to effectively police themselves.' (My italics.)

When sub-prime lenders began going bust, many of them were simply bought by bigger banks, concentrating the risk in the arms of fewer and fewer banks. And these arms were weak themselves, because safeguards had been relaxed after 2004, allowing banks to reduce their regulatory capital by around £177 billion. 'Banks could [now] either expand their portfolios and take on more risk,' say Adam Blundell-Wignall and Paul Atkinson in 'The Sub-Prime Crisis', 'or return the money to shareholders via dividends and buy-backs.'[49] Worse, the relaxation of regulation on investment banks allowed them to operate with capital ratios that were half the level of commercial banks – yet many were building funds composed of sub-prime problems.

The cost of any financial crisis is severe, because it triggers secondary crises. The US Commission concluded that 'nearly $11 trillion [£9 trillion] in household wealth' vanished.[50] In the UK, a million jobs and £400 billion of UK net wealth – most of it household wealth – would be destroyed, along with God knows how many dreams. Yet when he reflected on the Great Financial Crash, Alan Greenspan, Chairman of the US Federal Reserve at the time, later confessed to the US Congress that 'I made a mistake in presuming that the self-interests of organisations, specifically banks and others, were such that they were best capable of protecting their own shareholders and their equity in the firms.'[51] The behavioural economists help explain why Greenspan got it so wrong.

But bubbles are not only a disaster for the economy. They are a disaster for society. Because when bubbles go bang, it is the poorest who lose most and the richest who recover fastest.[52]

Back in 2010, there were perhaps 1000-odd billionaires

around the world with a total wealth of £2.9 trillion. Within just four years of the Financial Crash, the number of the world's billionaires had increased by more than 60 per cent, to 1,645, and their net wealth had almost doubled, to £5.2 trillion. A similar pattern unfolded after the Covid-19 pandemic. Indeed, Oxfam calculated that it took only nine months for the thousand richest people on the planet to recoup their losses, while it would take more than a decade for the world's poorest to recover.[53] In the aftermath of each great crash, inequality tends to increase. In the UK, at the time of writing, *average* earnings have *still* not recovered to their pre-Financial Crisis level.

When we put together the story of privilege, technopoly and bubble, it is far easier to understand the dynamics behind the insights of Thomas Piketty in his 2014 book *Capital in the Twenty-First Century*. Piketty's much debated work was a heroic effort to assemble a galaxy of data about the evolution of wealth in different countries, and to show the patterns of inequality that can be discerned, like constellations in the sky. Much of Piketty's data is historical and therefore imperfect, and it underestimates the more recent windfalls triggered by the revolution in easy money and low interest rates. But Piketty largely succeeded in creating a long-run picture revealing how annual returns on wealth, predominantly owned by the few, outstrip the average rises in income earned by everyone else – and which is roughly set by the overall growth rate in the economy.

Piketty's contention was that 'r' (the return on capital) averages 5 per cent, while 'g' (the growth rate enjoyed by most in the economy) sets a ceiling on wage growth of much less than 5 per cent. And so, the wealth of the already wealthy always grows faster than the economy as a whole. 'Because r > g,' Piketty concluded, 'the rich will get richer.' The poor do not necessarily get poorer, but the gap between the earnings power of people who own lots of buildings and shares and the earnings power of people working for a living looks set to grow and grow. Inequality increases.

A decade after Piketty's great book, we still lack a consensus in politics about the sorts of changes that electors will actually vote for that might put our economy on a new course – the changes that might create real freedoms for the twenty-first century and help build a wealth-owning democracy. The work of James Meade (1907–97), however, helps us parse the key changes that we need to make.

In 1964, Meade explained how the growth in anyone's wealth is driven by the savings mustered from two basic sources: earnings, plus the returns on any capital they might have hoarded. From this combined income of earnings and returns, people save a certain fraction, and they pile it onto their proverbial pile of gold, earning a return on this capital base for future years. And so, the cycle rolls on.

This means that just four factors basically drive the growth in our wealth:

- our annual income, and the savings we can squirrel away;
- the stock of assets in our name;
- the rate of return we secure on our assets; and,
- the tax we pay – or avoid.

As it happens, this also helps explain why wealth inequality grows inexorably. Because the *incomes* of the rich are much higher than those of the poor, they can afford to save more each year; the *capital pots* of the wealthy are bigger; the rich enjoy *far higher rates of return* on their riches; and those who take their income from capital *pay lower tax*, even before any clever tax avoidance. Thus, we have what Meade called the principle of circular and cumulative causation, otherwise known as the principle of 'to him that hath shall be given'.[54]

This framework, in my humble opinion, helps us pin down

the policy shifts we need to make to rebuild the wealth-owning democracy:

- We need to raise the earnings of all by improving the rate of economic growth and widen access to better paying jobs throughout the country. We need a new growth model, inspired by the lessons of fast-growing nations around the world, to replace the growth muddle we have today.
- To help raise earnings further, we need to ease the market supremacy of the last fifty years into history and replace it with a *civic capitalism* – where we transform the power of pension savers to invest in good work that pays well, and change company law to put purpose and a long-term focus on the board-room.
- We need a *new social contract* that helps *all* citizens build new wealth and grow the kinds of capital they need to thrive: a home of their own, their skills and a decent pension for their golden years. Democracies of opportunity must be republics of wealth, by creating what we could call 'universal basic capital'.
- We need to democratize access to the best returns available. Learning lessons from our history and around the world, we need to build a *national, social wealth fund*, that pays a dividend to every young person to help them get a foot on the housing ladder.
- Finally – and there is no escaping this – in order to finance it all, we need a *tax code that actually reflects a moral code*. We do not have that today, and frankly, it is well past time for some fairness to return to the tax system.

These ideas are not complex. Neither are they untried – they can be found in countries around the world. And if we are to build a democracy of wealth in our country for the twenty-first century, we need to bring them to the UK.

PART III

8

Empowering the People

Creative states in the twenty-first century

Harold Wilson met President John F. Kennedy just the one time. Six weeks into the job as Labour Party leader (and leader of Her Majesty's Opposition), Wilson made for Washington, and at noon on Wednesday, 3 April 1963, he was ushered into the White House. It was not an intimate relationship, but their political strategies rhymed beautifully. 'They live – though so differently – in the same world,' wrote *The Times*, adding: 'Their psychological approach is similar. They will understand each other and feel alike on basic issues.' Like Kennedy, Wilson was eager to tackle his nation's problems, 'with the stress on science, new technology, fresh ideas, youth, batteries of task forces and heavy government stimulants', as the *Wall Street Journal* opined.

Just a year older than the president, but shorter, greyer and more stooped, Wilson wanted to project a Kennedy-esque air of youthful optimism and dynamism. He wanted to get the UK 'moving ahead again' with a 'new spirit of hope and adventure' and, above all, a 'new sense of purpose'; in his own way, he reached for the challenge of what Kennedy billed as a 'New Frontier', a mission to awe the hearts of voters. In Kennedy's case, that New Frontier was the moonshot.[1]

Quite when Kennedy decided to put a man on the moon is not clear. He met NASA's chief scientist – and the Nazis' ex-rocket scientist – Wernher von Braun as early as 1953. The Soviet Union blasted its first satellite into orbit four years later, and a palpable smell of American panic wafted up the noses of Democratic strategists. 'People will soon imagine some Russian sitting in *Sputnik* with a pair of binoculars and reading their mail over their shoulders,' wrote the White House press secretary, George Reedy, to Lyndon Johnson in late 1957. Kennedy spent much of his time as a senator lambasting President Eisenhower for allowing a so-called 'missile gap' to emerge with the Soviet Union, and just a few months into his own presidency, on 12 April 1961, Kennedy had to stand and watch as Moscow launched Yuri Gagarin to become the first man in space.

It was not long before Kennedy was asked at a news conference: 'Mr. President, don't you think we should try to get to the moon before the Russians, if we can?'[2] Sure enough, on 25 May 1961, Kennedy declared to Congress that 'this nation should commit itself to achieving the goal, before the decade is out, of landing a man on the moon and returning him safely to earth'. Eighteen months later, in an extraordinary speech at Rice University in Houston, Kennedy announced: 'We choose to go to the moon in this decade,' not because the challenges would be easy, but 'because they are hard; because that goal will serve to organize and measure the best of our energies and skills'.

Throughout the 1960s, the moon mission remained controversial – and very, very expensive. At no point before the actual landing did an American majority actually support it. At a cost of £21 billion (£145 billion in today's money), it was a bigger line item in the US government's budget than any other programme apart from the war in Vietnam. But what was christened the 'moondoggle' by its critics, in fact came to transform American industry. The day before his assassination, Kennedy talked about how space medicine was changing public health through 'spinoff technology'. He spoke with pride about 'how we had created kidney dialysis machines, heart defibrillators, CAT Scans, MRIs; that biomed miracles were happening because of the funding for Apollo'.[3] 'The technology,' argues Douglas Brinkley, 'that America reaped from the federal investment in space hardware (satellite reconnaissance, biomedical equipment, lightweight materials, water-purification systems, improved computing systems and a global search-and-rescue system) has earned its worth multiple times over.'[4] But the moon mission's impact was greater than that. It broke new ground in the development of integrated circuits and real-time computing and brought into the mainstream of popular culture the concept of 'technology'. As Charles Fishman explained, '[t]he race to the moon didn't usher in the Space Age, it ushered in the Digital Age'.

When Wilson arrived home from Washington, he had less than eighteen months to prepare for a General Election. And he was determined to mimic the Kennedy magic. Wilson was fascinated by the 'freshness' of Kennedy's 'New Frontier' slogan, and he wanted to bring something similar to Britain. He was to set it out with political sizzle and a palpable sense of change in a remarkable speech in Scarborough that September, when, in the words of his biographer, he arrived as the 'herald of a coming age'.[5]

As I know from personal experience, the day before a party leader's conference speech is often tense, fraught and a bit bad-tempered. And at 9 p.m. that evening, Wilson's paper was still blank. He and his political secretary, Marcia Williams, worked through until dawn, finally finishing typing at 6 a.m. as the press officers banged at the doors, asking for the drafts.

Conference triumphs are awfully rare in political history. But this was one of them. 'He spoke beautifully... carrying the whole Conference with him,' wrote the MP and diarist Richard Crossman, adding: 'He had provided the revision of Socialism and its application to modern times which Gaitskell and Crosland had tried and completely failed to do.'[6] Another political diarist, Tony Benn, recorded that 'Wilson opened brilliantly', and the next day it was 'hard not to sniff the scent of electoral victory in the air'.[7] In the press gallery, journalists had to be restrained from applauding.

There, by the seaside, Wilson had offered Britain the electrifying prospect of harnessing the 'white heat of the technological revolution' to create a different kind of country. 'This scientific revolution,' he said, 'is making it physically possible, for the first time in human history, to conquer poverty and disease, to move towards universal literacy, and to achieve for the whole people better living standards than those enjoyed by tiny privileged classes in previous epochs.'[8] His agenda was bold: a new ministry of science; a university of the air; a revolution in education and apprenticeships; radical expansion of the further and higher education sectors; action to stop the 'brain drain'; and the appointment of the first government chief scientist. The election campaign that followed in 1964 opened when the Profumo sex-and-spies scandal was still fresh in the public's mind, tarnishing Macmillan's Conservative government. By contrast, Wilson's vision of 'white heat' was so brimful of hope, so evocative of a different set of possibilities, that I remember my parents still quoting it years later. Although Wilson's electoral victory was slim, it was the triumph of the bold and optimistic story he told about how Britain could face the future – and master what it saw.

Harold Wilson's vision helped transform the social mobility of post-war Britain. More than forty years later, much of my time as Chancellor of the Duchy of Lancaster was spent trying to understand how he did it. Sitting in our war-room-style mission control in No. 12 Downing Street, three seats away from the prime minister, I was tasked with helping to bring together an agenda that would bring definition to Gordon Brown's new prime ministership. We hit upon social mobility as the theme, because it reflected the common thread of much of Gordon's lifetime of work, to create a country where everyone could develop their potential to the full.

In order to craft a framework for new ideas, we published a groundbreaking review of Britain's post-war social mobility, which revealed that those entering the labour market after the Second World War were indeed more socially mobile than those who went to work before the conflict.[9] Two basic explanations stood out: a huge expansion in better-paid, higher-skilled jobs; and a revolution in building the ladders towards those jobs, allowing almost anyone to reach them, no matter where and when they were born. Critical to this was the long boom in higher education over which Harold Wilson presided. The result was the creation of millions of opportunities for a new middle class, including, I might add, for my parents.

If we are to rebuild a *wealth-owning democracy* in the UK today, we have to learn this lesson once again.

On the one hand, we need better ladders, taking us on and up in life. But crucially, we *have* to raise the earnings from which everyone can save, and if we want to build a country of wealthier people, we need to build a country with a bigger supply of better-paid jobs – not just in some places but in every part of Britain. The key to this is fostering more jobs in knowledge-intensive sectors. The mathematics is pretty simple: in 2021, earnings in the knowledge-intensive sectors were £163 a week higher than the national average – 30 per cent bigger than the average pay cheque.

This requires a decisive break with the economic philosophy of the last thirteen years. Unfortunately, from 2010, the nation's Coalition and then Conservative government pursued a strategy straight out of the market supremacists' playbook. It tried to fan the flickering flames of growth with demand-side incentives, like low taxes and cheap money. But this has proved a disaster for earnings. In the decade after the Great Financial Crash, the average disposable income of a UK household did not move. It was no higher in 2018–19 than it was in 2007–08.[10] Those at the bottom of the pile have been hardest hit; the poorest fifth of the UK population are now much poorer, relatively, than the poorest in countries of Central and Eastern Europe.

We need a different approach. And as both Kennedy and Wilson knew, economic growth is powered by both the demand side and, importantly, the supply side of people, their skills and ideas. Ultimately, to boost the supply of better-paid jobs, as Kennedy and Wilson understood, we need to build a more skill- and science-powered economy and adopt what US Treasury Secretary Janet Yellen has christened 'modern supply side economics'[11] with a policy mix designed 'to boost economic growth by increasing labor supply, raising productivity, and reducing inequality and environmental damage'.[12]

The economic logic for this is simple: technology is the power in 'super-power'.[13] It supplies as much as an incredible 85 per cent of economic growth.[14] The IMF has put it like this: 'technology has been key to productivity growth since the first industrial revolution, which, in turn, has underpinned strong per-capita GDP growth'. In 2005, America's scientists came together to warn, in *The Gathering Storm*, that '[w]ithout high-quality, knowledge-intensive jobs and the innovative enterprises that lead to discovery and new technology, our economy will suffer and our people will face a lower standard of living'. The UK's Royal Society has underlined the point. Introducing its brilliant paper, 'The Scientific Century' (2010), Martin Rees left us with the fine phrase 'unless we grow smarter, we will grow poorer'.[15]

The bad news for the UK is that the country has been falling further and further behind its peers. With the return of Great Power competition to the world and the decoupling of high-tech supply chains between the West and China, global competition is fast becoming a 'science race'. Between 2000 and 2020, total global R&D expenditure more than tripled to £1.9 trillion.[16] By contrast, R&D in the UK increased by just 40 per cent.

The UK spends less than half what is spent in South Korea, and just 40 per cent of what is spent in Germany, leaving us in danger of being left behind. In the years since President Biden's election in 2020, the United States and the European Union have passed legislation designed to pour around £1.2 trillion into the US CHIPS Acts and Inflation Reduction Act and the EU's Green New Deal. Yet, Brexit shut the UK out of the US-EU Trade and Technology Council, and we are denied access to the overwhelming majority of US and EU subsidies for industry, research and development. But the story is not simply about America, Europe or China. Spend time in, say, Israel, South Korea, Singapore or Estonia and you see countries racing to put in place the infrastructure of the future: 5G networks, public e-identity schemes, ubiquitous ePayment technology, and smart public-private partnerships to foster new innovation driven businesses.

By contrast, demand for R&D is especially poor among British small and medium-sized enterprises (SMEs),[17] and the UK is bedevilled by large parts of the country being trapped in a low-skill, low-pay equilibrium, where both demand for skills, and supply of skills, is low.[18] This helps explain a gap in productivity per hour between the UK economy and the average among G7 nations, which now looms at 13 per cent.[19] In the long term, the key to a country's wealth is its productivity, and the UK's has recently been poor; indeed, it is worse than at the end of the 1970s, when it was called the 'British disease'.

This failure to invest in science has big implications for our economy. In 2021, knowledge-intensive industries in the UK accounted for around a quarter of economic output (£489 billion) and around a quarter of businesses (1.3 million) but employed less than a fifth of workers (around 5 million). If the knowledge economy made up a *quarter* of British jobs, there would be 2.3 million extra better-paid jobs to go round.[20] Unfortunately, the UK is currently creating knowledge-intensive jobs so slowly that it will take forty-five years to deliver that sort of increase; indeed, between 2015 and 2021, the British economy has only created just over 100,000 such jobs a year for a workforce of 29 million. And three-quarters of these valuable new opportunities are in just twenty-two local council areas, of which six are in London.

We cannot reverse the rise in wealth inequality until we radically improve on this performance. So how do we build a bigger workforce of better-paid, more knowledge-intensive workers who enjoy higher wages? There is only really one way: to ditch the tired old arguments of the market supremacists, who counsel that the best way to grow an economy is to defund the state, and instead to recognize that what we need is a *creative state* where the capital surrenders not tax – but power.

Happily, both new economics and new economic history now help us see with clarity the role of creative states in fostering fast shifts in innovation and in mobilizing investment in people, ideas and industry. To fully appreciate this, we have to recognize the error of old cartoons of the lone genius, muttering like a shaman in his hut, misunderstood and alone until the Eureka moment when a polished bolt of lightning strikes and brings enlightenment. At the very core of the belief in 'Western exceptionalism' is the chimera of this type of free-thinking, free-ranging 'heroic' individual who unlocks progress. As most scientists will tell you, this is not how progress happens. Great scientists, as Isaac Newton astutely noted, stand on the shoulders of giants, and the giants stand in towers built by creative states. Not so long ago, historians like David Landes were able to write: 'If we learn anything from the history of economic development, it is that culture makes all the difference.'[21] Better and more recent history has revised this view, so we can argue that, in fact, institutions are the key to innovation –especially those that mobilize tax and pour it into new industries that break new technological frontiers. New historical research lays bare the reality that it was not the 'culture' of individualism but the invention of creative states that powered progress – states that mobilized the forces of both intellectual discovery and diffusion.[22]

These state-backed institutions are vital because a host of market failures tend to stop innovation before it gets off the ground if left purely to entrepreneurs.[23] Because individual firms and entrepreneurs can never capture all the benefits of their brilliant innovation, 'rationally' they will always produce less innovation than a society needs. And due to high levels of risk and very long-term time horizons, 'rational' companies are especially reluctant to invest in next-generation technologies. It would, for example, have been very difficult for a typical company's shareholders to justify the speculative investment required to create the Internet. The same would be true today for investment in major pure-science programmes like the European Space Agency's 'billion star surveyor' Gaia, or the Large Hadron Collider in Switzerland.

As it happens, private-sector investors are also quite bad at allocating capital to the right opportunities in new firms, as successive boom and bust in the dotcom market proves. This is especially true because there is never a guarantee that breakthroughs have a market, for the simple reason that societies – and markets – do not always welcome innovation when it arrives.[24]

Furthermore, because innovation is complex, the private sector can be prone to coordination failures. Successful innovation depends on a wealth of allied systems, so it is often difficult for the private sector to deliver a game-changing shift in the way things are done. Worse, many industries and firms simply lag behind in adopting proven technologies, which is why we have such a long tail of less productive firms, and why some markets are blighted by free-rider problems: these can cause whole industries to under-invest in skills, because managers fear the talent they develop will be poached by rivals. 'These multiple and systemic failures in the process of innovation,' conclude the authors of *Innovation Economics*, 'should make it clear that, left to themselves, markets will produce significantly less innovation, productivity, and competitiveness than nations need.'

The countries that prosper are therefore those that mobilize investment into innovation. '[W]e observed a very clear correlation,' writes Philippe Aghion and his colleagues, 'between the intensity of innovation and the growth of per capita GDP: states that innovate more grow quickly.'[25] Growth theorists who argue that 'internal' factors (like human capital) drive economic growth have long shown that when one country begins with a greater stock of knowledge capital, it can accumulate knowledge more quickly than its trade partners, 'perpetuating and even adding to its productivity lead',[26] and more recently, a galaxy of data has been assembled by economists like Mariana Mazzucato and others who have shown how public finance tends to 'crowd in' private investment.

Of course, what is now called 'industrial policy' can go wrong. But, as Aghion argues, 'Industrial policy is not a yes or no issue... the question is rather to redesign the governance of industrial policy to make it more compatible with competition and more generally with innovation-led growth.'[27] And the prize is new, innovative firms, which are shown to be good for social mobility. In fact, British data for the period 2004 to 2015 shows innovative firms act as a social ladder above all for low- and middle-skilled employees.

Neither research and development nor systems for educating and retraining workers are free. They are expensive. Which is why defunding the state is the wrong thing to do if we want to foster high-quality, innovation-driven growth. Former prime minister, Liz Truss, had a favourite retort in the House of Commons, that 'you cannot tax your way to growth'. In fact you can, as long as you tax carefully and spend wisely. Indeed, evidence now suggests that taxing wisely is fundamental to mobilizing the resources needed to invest in building up creative states strong enough to foster a bigger supply of knowledge-intensive jobs.

Much of the market supremacists' early work, arguing for pure and simple tax cuts, rested on traditional neoclassical growth theory and used cross-country studies to suggest that bigger governments slowed economic growth.[28] The problem with these studies was that, on closer inspection, it was very hard to see what was correlation and what was causation.[29] In fact, the economist Gareth Myles, in his monumental study of 'Economic Growth and the Role of Taxation' (2009) for the OECD, was moved to conclude: 'There is no empirical evidence in the aggregate data that the rate of economic growth is related to the level of taxation.'[30] His colleague Asa Johannsson arrived at a similar conclusion in 2016: 'The lack of good instruments for government size implies that it is difficult to settle the issue of causality.'[31]

What has emerged, however, is that the key question is less about the *level* of tax and far more about who is taxing, what they are taxing, and crucially, what they are spending the money on. The importance of virtuous government spending the proceeds wisely has now been underlined in study after study. So, even for those like Jean-Marc Fournier and Asa Johansson who found some evidence that 'too large governments reduce potential [economic] growth', the conclusion was: 'In the countries with the most effective governments, the large size of the government promotes equity with no adverse effect on growth.'[32]

There are two key reasons for this, as Fournier and Johansson put it: first, 'larger governments tend to redistribute more, and... better functioning governments tend to better target transfer programmes to disadvantaged groups'; and second, 'most spending reforms, including a spending shift to investment, are associated with higher growth and benefit all'.[33]

In particular, 'reallocation of public spending towards infrastructure and education... raise[s] income in the long run, whereas increasing social welfare spending can reduce inequality'.[34] This broad conclusion was very similar to Kyle McNabb's conclusions in an exhaustive review (2018), whereby higher taxes can 'provide governments with the potential to invest in, for example, infrastructural improvements, education or R&D, all of which can increase the economy's productive capacity'.[35]

A striking conclusion from recent research is that what is taxed is very important. Broadly speaking, tax affects an economy in four basic ways: it alters (1) the supply of labour, (2) the readiness to invest in physical and intellectual capital, (3) the rise in productivity or innovation, and (4) best practice.[36] There is a broad consensus that the structure of taxation *does* affect the rate of growth, and that income taxes create more distortions and slower GDP growth than consumption taxes (although the effects, concluded Kyle McNabb, 'are often quite small').[37] What appears to make the most difference for promoting long-term growth, according to one of the most widely cited pieces of research, is a cut in personal income taxes and social security contributions for *low-income households*.[38]

The UK's extraordinary history of scientific endeavour helped create this modern world, transforming knowledge and prosperity in the process. Past glories do not pay the bills, but they can help inspire a culture of innovation to build the bigger knowledge-based economy with a bigger supply of better paid jobs, which is the bedrock of any strategy to reverse wealth inequality. But building creative states backed by a sensible storehouse of tax revenue is merely the first step. If we want to build a democracy of wealth, we have to make sure that innovation is not simply something that happens in parts of the nation that are already relatively wealthy. We have to nurture knowledge-intensive jobs in every sector – and in every region. And to do that requires Whitehall not to hoard power, in some attempt to order innovation from on high, but rather lets it go.

England's regional inequalities are infamous. According to the *Financial Times* in 2019, the UK is cursed by regional inequality that is 'one of worst in developed world'.[39] Almost half of its knowledge-intensive jobs are in just two regions – London and the South-East – and naturally this has an impact on where wealth has been created. In fact, the *growth* shown in wealth in London and the South-East over a recently documented ten-year period – at £2.8 trillion – is more than the rest of the country put together.[40]

Such inequalities persist because England's regions have never been given the freedom to design the institutions that suit them best. Institutions are important. Since the turn of the twenty-first century, a new appreciation has grown of the critical role of institutions in fostering healthy economic development.[41] The key, as economist Paul Romer once explained it, is that 'the most important job for economic policy is to create an institutional environment that supports technological change'.[42] Daron Acemoglu and James A. Robinson, in their fine book *Why Nations Fail* (2013), explained how a nation's institutions make or break national success.[43] Forces in every society, they argue, shape economic institutions, which shape economic incentives: the incentives to learn, to save, or to invest, to innovate and to advance new technologies. 'As institutions influence behaviour and incentives in real life,' they argue, so 'they forge the success or failure of nations'.[44] Institutions shape our behaviour and structure our relationships.[45]

Across the countries of the capitalist west we have evolved two basic flavours of these institutions: a 'liberal' market model in the United States, UK, Australia, Canada, New Zealand and Ireland, where coordination is pretty loose; and coordinated market economies, as in Germany, Japan, Switzerland, The Netherlands, Belgium, Sweden, Norway, Denmark, Finland

and Austria, where firms rely much more heavily on non-market relationships to coordinate their behaviour with other actors – especially in organizing factors of production like labour and finance.[46]

The challenge for England is that its institutions, like its tax and spend system, are still *very* centralized. Yet its regional economies are the size of small countries. They differ in their specialisms and comparative advantages, as well as in their challenges. But local leaders remain trapped in national systems, which entail huge effort in bidding into central programmes and then finding ways to join in, after the event. England has barely any flexibility for creating institutions at the regional or sub-regional level for developing economic growth. While some regions might need or want the flexibility to take a 'liberal market' approach, others, like manufacturing areas, would benefit from a 'coordinated market economy' approach. If we want to transform our rate of growth, build new resilience and autonomy in key supply chains, decarbonize our economy, and crucially, reduce regional inequalities, we need a decisive shift in the country's power and money towards our regions, cities, towns and villages.

When, in 2021, I entered the race to become Mayor of the West Midlands – though I did not win – I set out to understand how new freedoms were needed for our regions to build the institutions we needed to mobilize money, people and ideas.

First, to help us mobilize money – capital and investment – we proposed a regional bank to recycle local savings and help pension funds drive finance into green homes and the green and digital economies. This is not an original idea. The German *Sparkassen* ('savings banks') have helped mobilize finance for regional industry for a long time. Regional banks today could help supply the green and digital economies with funds to start up and, crucially, to 'scale-up'. In addition, we explored the creation of regional 'Yozma' funds, which in Israel, have brought together venture capital, investment banks and government funding (of \$1.50 for every \$1 raised by the private sector). By 2010, Yozma funds were managing £2.4 billion and supporting hundreds of new Israeli companies.[47] If a small country like Israel can do this, then so can an English region.

Second, we realized that we needed a plan for skills. This problem, too, is not new. For well over a century, the UK has had a problem with its technical education system. Devolving more control of education and skills would help. Attempting to *centrally* plan across the myriad relevant issues – skills, education, crime, worklessness, transport, physical regeneration, health, housing, environmental sustainability, social regeneration, spatial planning, and economic development – is so complex as to be a fool's errand. Yet that is exactly what the British government tries to do today. We proposed a break with this. I wanted a new (regional) Commissioner for Education to connect together schools, colleges, universities and apprenticeship agencies to transform technical education. I wanted to make sure we were training people for good jobs in the Green Industrial Revolution and the burgeoning digital sector, with better systems to educate people from cradle to grave, from ABC to PhD.

Part and parcel of these proposed changes would be a radical change to the way Job Centres (now branded JobCentre Plus) work, devolving back-to-work services to local areas, for the first time bringing together one team with the right incentives to make a difference. But the cornerstone of the new system we suggested was the Technical University Trust, to build on the good practice emerging in the further- and higher-education systems, where institutions are coming together to sponsor schools and align curricula.[48] These Technical University Trusts would – drawing on our already rich educational infrastructure – connect elite universities, working with the UK's top companies, to create a new 'gold standard' of advanced vocational education.

Third and finally, we proposed pushing new ideas into the bloodstream of industry with University Enterprise Zones and a regional system of German-style Fraunhofer Institutes, focused on applied research. As Professor Richard Jones has pointed out, demand for R&D among SMEs in the UK is generally very low, and so SMEs make up a tiny fraction of UK R&D spending.[49] We suggested ways to change this with a range of ideas, from tax credits and 'innovation vouchers' for SMEs to spend with local universities, to better funding for 'translational' research funding – and more. The aim would be to promote partnerships between small businesses and the research, knowledge and expertise available in universities. Alongside this, I wanted to see a federation of universities and research centres in every region with the same clarity and simplicity of the mission of those 76 Fraunhofer institutes and research units, which is 'to provide the R&D department to Germany's *Mittelstand*', its mid-sized firms. This needs supporting with a funding model that strongly incentivizes researchers to go and hunt out research contracts from SMEs, knowing that, in effect, there is a 2:1 funding match from the public sector.

I may have lost my election as West Midlands Mayor – but I am convinced these ideas are right. And mobilizing the money for this agenda would be an awful lot easier if we ended the ludicrous centralization that bedevils England today. Using Parliamentary Questions in 2022, I exposed 149 different educational spending programmes, totalling £65 billion, that were run from Whitehall, which is a disastrous approach for building innovation.[50] This money dwarfs the approximately £700 million in funding that was devolved at the time to England's seven metro-mayors.

To compound this problem, the UK has one of the most centralized fiscal regimes in the world. '[A]lthough all modern UK governments have talked about greater devolution within England,' noted Professor Iain McLean in 2019, 'none has done anything fiscally material.'[51] Now, I am not much in favour of tax freedoms that simply allow local areas to cut revenue taxes, because it risks impairing a *level* of redistribution from richer to poorer regions that already exists.[52] But the fiscal flows today are a reflection of significant regional economic inequalities, as well as large differences in infrastructure investment and skill levels around the nation. As such, allowing local areas to raise more and, crucially, raise funds for capital projects is absolutely vital.

Any freedoms to raise debt at the local level will have to sit within some sort of national control regime, as ultimately the UK Treasury is the guarantor of last resort. But today's fiscal freedoms are extremely limited; only 15 per cent of the English population live under a serious subnational government. The risks in today's level of fiscal federalism, such as it is, are very manageable, and new freedoms could be safely managed with brakes in the system, such as balanced-budget rules, which bite on the local authority – as is common in the United States and many other OECD countries.

The final piece of the creative-state jigsaw is a set of complementary reforms at the centre of government. The UK Parliament needs regional select committees to bring together scrutiny of the executive around place. We need full-time regional ministers to be full-time warriors-in-Whitehall for every region, battling to get things done. They would coordinate policy on physical regeneration, business support, skills strategy, housing – and generally advocate for their regions. A Council of Regional Ministers and Mayors would provide a proper forum for local government to have its say, creating a proper junction between Whitehall and the town hall. *Personally,* I would go a step further and reorganize the House of Lords with a more formalized Senate and representatives elected – on proportionate basis – from regional constituencies, but I have been in Parliament too long now to have much faith that this will ever be delivered.

John F. Kennedy never lived to see men walk on the moon. But that moment was lauded by his foe, President Richard Nixon, as 'the greatest week in the history of the world since the creation'.

Watching from Downing Street, Harold Wilson spoke for millions when he declared the national feeling of 'tremendous admiration. Admiration first for the way in which this great and historic achievement was conceived and planned'.

It was a mission that became a hieroglyph of hope; a banner boasting of optimism, self-confidence and advance. Above all, it showed what creative states could do. We should roll them forward, not roll them back. It would work wonders for boosting the earnings of every worker.

Yet a new strategy for growth is not enough. To improve earnings and reduce inequality, we will need to rewrite the rules of our key marketplace institutions, to stop them so ruthlessly driving down wages in the short, medium and long term. To put the common good back into the marketplace, we will need a plan for civic capitalism.

9

Paying the People

Civic capitalism, earnings and deferred wages

One wintry November day, I went off to hunt for the oldest charter in English capitalism. Past the magnificent gothic mass of King's College chapel in Cambridge, up a higgledy-piggledy staircase and down a lino-covered corridor covered with threadbare rugs, I found it in the library.

The Bricett Manor charter dates back nearly nine centuries, to 1152. Written on parchment about the size of a paperback, it is adorned with the magnificent Great Seal of King Stephen, a great wax coin, brown and black with age, and bearing a stylized image of the king crowned on his throne, with sword and orb, and crested with a little square cross and an eagle. Above, set out in eleven lines of text penned in the 'Caroline minuscule' script of Domesday Book, with its odd mixture of Latin and Old English, are the rules: the right to hold a weekly market and fairs on 5 and 6 July, to mark the festivals of St Leonard and St Lawrence.

Bricett Manor's charter is not only an exquisite piece from the puzzle that makes up our long economic history; it is a simple reminder of an economic truth: that the 'free market' in this country has never been a free-for-all. Markets have always had rules.

Dr Richard Blakemore, based at Reading University, is one of the UK's experts in early English capitalism. 'The word "market",' he told me, when I rang him, 'literally means a regulated space in which to conduct business... without regulations you don't have markets, you just have people meeting each other.' All markets – like towns – were granted by royal charter, because the role of the sovereign was to mediate on behalf of their subjects, and that meant creating an environment in which they could conduct trade, safe in the knowledge they would not be cheated. And so, markets evolved. 'The idea that you can somehow develop a totally anarchic market system,' Richard concluded, 'is, to my mind, a complete misunderstanding of the history of markets.' As it happens, this was precisely the point that Franklin Roosevelt liked to hammer home in the 1930s: 'we must lay hold of the fact,' he once thundered, 'that economic laws are not made by nature. They are made by human beings.'[1] Or, as Pope Benedict XVI put it eighty years later, 'a free market... is shaped by the *cultural configurations* which define it and give it direction'.[2] (My italics.)

All markets have rules. We write rules not simply for the marketplace but also for the commercial company, and these were rules intended for the common good – because the creation of both the modern exchange and the modern enterprise were meant to benefit all.

On the eve of the First Industrial Revolution, England boasted perhaps just twenty companies, and at that time the creation of anything new had to be approved by Parliament, and the partners were liable for the company's errors.[3] However, at the height of the Crimean War, in 1855, new laws swept away the past to permit the creation of a new concept: the *limited liability company*. Away went the requirement for Parliament to license new firms along with old stipulations that all partners were individually liable for the entire debts of the firm. For the first time, an investor's financial liability for a company's debt was limited to a fixed sum, generally the value of a person's investment in a company or partnership. If a company with limited liability was sued, the claimants sued the company, not its owners or investors. When the bill came to Parliament in the summer of 1855, it was fiercely attacked as a recipe for fraud, but Prime Minister Viscount Palmerston carried the day. The reform, he declared, would allow Britain's army of small savers to combine their small pots together to create the great firms of the future 'for *the advantage of the community at large*'. (My italics.) 'It is a question of free trade against monopoly,' he declared, before his rousing peroration: 'There is nothing,' he told the Commons, 'that would tend more to the *general advantage of the public*.'[4] (My italics.)

What would Palmerston think if he could see Britain today? Despite his best intentions, he would survey a scene where *both* our enterprises and our exchanges are run on rules which reward a lucky few far more than others, through power structures and incentives that hold down the wages of millions of workers and short-change the return on those 'deferred wages' which we know better as pensions.

Palmerston was known for his analytical mind, so perhaps he would appreciate a few numbers. And as noted above, we need look no further than what has happened to the 'labour share' of our national income since the Second World War to illustrate the point. The 'labour share' combines the wages paid to employees, the value of social contributions paid to employees, such as pension contributions, and an estimated portion of self-employment income.[5] Since 1955, the Office of National Statistics has published figures showing how much national income has flowed to labour and how much was accounted for by the profits of companies and the self-employed.[6]

What the records show is that in early decades (1955–75), labour's share of national income held steady at around 70 per cent. But then it began to fall and fall, until 1996, when it bottomed out at 55 per cent. A recovery commenced in the first years of Tony Blair's government, and labour income rose, back to around 60 per cent of total national income. But it has stubbornly stuck there ever since, at a level that is far lower than those earlier, post-war years.

That line on a graph represents a gigantic loss of earnings for working people – and indeed it masks the full challenge for working people, because a good chunk of labour income now goes to those at the top. For years, the public has been treated to the most egregious stories of stratospheric pay enjoyed by corporate chieftains like Sébastien De Montessus, head of mining firm Endeavour, who took home £17 million in 2021, or construction boss Albert Manifold, who pocketed £12 million. But both pale into insignificance compared to Denise Coates, of the gambling empire Bet365, who took home a pay-packet of £214 million in 2022.[7]

If we take a step back and look at what happened in 2022, the challenge becomes quite clear. Over the course of the year, pay for the 'median' worker rose by 6 per cent, to £33,000. But pay for the average FTSE 100 CEO increased by *12 per cent*, to £4.15 million.[8] Meanwhile, the income flowing to capital surged even further. The value of regular dividends paid out of profits to investors who owned shares in UK-listed companies – what we might call the returns to capital – soared by 17 per cent, to £85 billion.[9] And in turn, that was dwarfed by the rising value of UK share buybacks – the means by which companies return company cash-hoards to shareholders, usually on excellent terms. These almost tripled between 2021 and 2022, to £57 billion.[10] At the time of writing, 2023 looked set to prove even more extreme: according to the High Pay Centre, in that year FTSE 100 chief executives had earned more than the average wage in Britain by 2 p.m. on Thursday 5 January, after just thirty hours' work; and median pay for a CEO reached '103 times the median full time worker's pay of £33,000', representing a 39-per-cent increase in CEO pay levels as of January 2022.[11]

Yet, to add insult to injury, it is not just workers' wages today that are being shortchanged. It is their deferred wages – their pensions – which are not as high as they should be, because the investment management industry is not serving the common good either. Indeed, one recent analysis found that UK savers were paying on average *five* times too much for their pension compared with low-cost pensions that exist now.[12] This has a gigantic impact on the pension pots that workers might retire with, and hence on the income they can enjoy in their golden years.[13]

It is very hard to see how all this tallies with the 'Palmerston test' of a *'general advantage of the public'*. Indeed, a little thought experiment helps illustrate the scale of the loss to most working people. If the wage share of national income in 2021 returned to the heights enjoyed in the 1950s and 1960s, workers would have gained an extraordinary £191 billion in extra wages each year. Roughly speaking, that is worth more than £7,000 per worker – or a pay rise over median earnings of more than 20 per cent.

If we are to rebuild a democracy of wealth in Britain, we first have to raise earnings. That is very hard to do without a faster growing economy. But as this analysis shows, even if our economy grows faster, we need a second step: a plan to rewrite the rules that currently channel such a large share of national income either to shareholders or into the pay packets of those at the very top.

To get a sense of the change the public thinks is needed, I worked with the Policy Institute at King's College, London (KCL), to build a catalogue of ideas for reform – and we then tested them out in polling. We asked people to rank the new employment rules they would support to tackle inequality. Perhaps because the media have covered the scandal of top pay so extensively, most people picked, as their top choice, the fixing of the top pay rate for CEOs at twenty times the pay of the lowest paid employee in the firm. This was especially popular with baby boomers; in fact, almost a third (30 per cent) of the older generation picked this as their No. 1 idea. Nor was there much difference in levels of support for this policy between Labour and Conservative voters.

Not far behind was support for raising the national minimum wage, which was especially popular among Gen Z, a third of whom picked this choice. But while three in ten (29 per cent) thought raising the minimum wage from the existing level of £9.50 would be the best policy for reducing inequality in the next five years, almost a fifth (18 per cent) thought fixing the pay of CEOs would work best. The public not only supported these ideas but felt they were perfectly credible as policies to be put into effect.[14]

These changes could all make an important difference to raising workers' earnings in the short term. But for the long term, we have to move beyond ideas that just patch up the worst damage of the day towards those that actually shift the *system* towards a *civic capitalism* that genuinely rewards the common good and so restores the moral foundations on which our market institutions were built.[15]

And in order to understand how we might set about this task, we must first inspect the broken system of bamboozled savers, blind stewards and selfish captains that bedevils the marketplace today.

Our story starts with the saver. When Palmerston persuaded Parliament to create modern-day companies, he inspired support by invoking the humble saver with 'small capitals', which the prime minister wanted to 'set free' so 'that they may be turned to profitable employment'. In theory, these workers saving up for a pension or a rainy day should have a lot of power. All told, the UK now boasts an estimated £6.5 trillion of UK pension wealth, along with an estimated £1.9 trillion in financial wealth.[16] By investing in well-run companies that paid workers well, the saver-worker could be a powerful force for good. And the evidence is that, given the choice, that is exactly what they would like.

In its research, the Centre for Progressive Policy think-tank found that though ethical concerns were a long way behind a desire for returns (the top priority for 82 per cent of pension savers) and concern about fees charged, nevertheless 31 per cent prioritized investing in companies in line with their own social or moral values.[17] My research with the KCL Policy Institute shows that attitudes may be changing fast. In fact, we found that *three-quarters* (72 per cent) of voters *do* think that fund managers have a responsibility for only investing in ethically behaving companies, compared to just one in ten (11 per cent) who *do not* believe fund managers have a responsibility to behave ethically.

Now, views are split as to whether ethical priorities should be pursued regardless of profitability. But over a third (36 per cent) felt that pension-fund managers should ensure that they are investing in ethnical companies even if it reduces returns a little, with the same percentage believing they should invest ethically but only if that does not reduce returns. Still, exactly half (50 per cent) said they would switch pension provider if they learned that their fund manager was not properly ensuring they were investing in ethically behaving companies. Just 20 per cent said they would leave their money where it is. But the problem today is that it is almost impossible for savers to understand which companies are behaving badly and which are behaving well.

In order to understand this better, I worked with the Centre for Progressive Policy (CPP) to sponsor a piece of work studying what an inclusive firm promoting 'good work' might look like.[18] It was very difficult to pin down answers. For a start, despite several studies, there is no agreed single definition of 'good work'.[19] Not to be defeated, the CPP heroically assembled a 'Good Employer Index' that combined data from fourteen different indicators to virtue-rank the twenty-five largest UK employers, which together employ 2.3 million workers using criteria like pay and benefits, terms of employment, training and progression, working conditions, voice and representation, diversity and recruitment, and promoting an inclusive economy.[20]

Finding the data needed was very, very difficult. In fact, it was hard enough even to establish the twenty-five biggest employers. Company law requires that some data, such as the pay of a company's highest paid director, is published. But this information is generally not usefully collated. Nor is there much information published on other indicators of 'good work', with the exception of gender pay reporting. The government reports on certain violations (non-payment of the minimum wage; employment tribunals; health and safety breaches), but poor data presentation and complex corporate structuring often make it hard to form an overall picture of companies. Some organizations do help supply useful information, like employee reviews of their employers, but comprehensive information on the terms of employment, and therefore on job security, is notably absent.

This absence of data is a large problem. Empowering workers to invest their savings in ways that stop firms holding down wages, dodging taxes, poisoning the planet and generally contributing to exorbitant levels of inequality would be a huge step towards reversing inequality and helping increase the labour share of national income. Yet until we find a way to help the 'bamboozled saver', we are not going to make much progress, especially as the problem is compounded by the challenge of 'blind stewards'.

By and large, few of us actively manage our own savings or pensions. We pay someone to do it for us. And these investment managers are now giants. Globally, in 2022 the world's asset managers invested, on our behalf, an extraordinary £74 trillion.[21] In the UK, the members of the Investment Association own nearly a third of the entire listed equity market.

But these investment managers are *not* working especially hard to manage the individual businesses in which they invest. In fact, they are more concerned about which firms go into a *portfolio* rather than any one firm's particular performance.

Once upon a time, in Venice's Rialto Square or on the quays of Amsterdam, investors could look their ship's captain in the eye and make a cool-headed assessment of whom to trust and whom to spurn. Investors learned the hard way that it was risky to put all one's eggs in the same basket. One sunk ship could a man's ruin make. So, cautious investors diversify. But today, investors diversify *so much* that they have lost any meaningful connection with the management of any individual firm. In this sense, they become almost blind stewards in the management of the people's capital. Indeed, we have actually made a science of it. It is called 'modern portfolio theory' (MPT), and it dates back to Harry Markowitz's seminal paper 'Portfolio Selection' (1952), which earned the economist a Nobel Prize.

Markowitz explored risk, return, variance and 'covariance' (that is, the directional relationship between the returns on two assets). He concluded that the best way to maximize returns for a given level of risk was to study the variance and correlation in the behaviour of share prices across a *family* of different shares. 'In essence,' argued Markowitz, 'a portfolio of multiple risky securities is less risky than a singular risky security, since some will zig while others zag... Zigzags will partially cancel out, reducing the overall risk.'[22]

Thereafter, the practice of investment management became obsessed with how best to construct a portfolio of shares in which the risks of any particular share price falling were offset by the likelihood of another share price rising. In turn, this revolution in thinking gave birth to the 'Capital Asset Pricing Model', taught to all investment bankers and business school students, which helps investors assemble a portfolio of multiple assets designed to maximize returns for a given level of risk.

The downside of this approach, however, is obvious: it stunts detailed shareholder engagement in the management of any particular company. The science of assembling shares whose prices supposedly rise and fall in a harmonious relationship to one another is considered more important. Indeed, it is now estimated that 90 per cent of the variation of return enjoyed by an investor is explained by the return from a particular risk profile – and *not* by the actual stock selection undertaken by the asset manager.[23]

When *all* investors hold portfolios, 'ownership' of a firm becomes very, very dispersed, and shareholders become very, very passive. They become poor guardians against risky behaviour. When investors can diversify their risks by holding a broad portfolio of assets – and buy and sell shares so fast – they become less sensitive to risky firm behaviour and less likely to rein in risk-taking by wayward managers.

This trend has vastly accelerated since the Financial Crisis of 2008. The result is, as Philip Fisher puts it, that while 'no investment principle is more widely acclaimed than diversification', we now have 'the disadvantage of having eggs in so many baskets... it is impossible to keep watching all the baskets after the eggs get put into them'.[24] When everyone only has a little at stake, there is not much incentive to intervene in the running of a firm. But this is now the norm in the UK, where less than 20 per cent of firms have a controlling shareholder – almost the lowest ratio in the world – and where long-term investors like pension funds and life insurance companies now own just 6 per cent of UK listed shares.[25]

This problem of blind stewards contributes to a heightened risk of a third problem, which we might call the 'selfish captain': the corporate chief executive who (if the FTSE 100 is anything to go by) might only be in post for, say, five years,[26] and who is free to behave in ways that maximize their own gains but hold down workers' wages and short-change the investment that might help those wages rise in the medium term. The problem is now so acute that even the world's largest investment managers are complaining about it. '[M]ore and more corporate leaders have... [adopted] actions that can deliver immediate returns to shareholders, such as buybacks or dividend increases,' says Larry Fink, the chief executive of BlackRock, the largest investment firm in the world, 'while underinvesting in innovation, skilled workforces or essential capital expenditures necessary to sustain long-term growth.'[27]

The relationship between the company investor and its manager has long been fraught with risk. Known as the 'principal-agent' problem, it was described by Adam Smith: 'The directors of such [joint-stock] companies,' he wrote, 'being the managers rather of other people's money than of their own, it cannot well be expected, that they should watch over it with the same anxious vigilance with which the partners in a private co-partnery frequently watch over their own.'

But to guard against this risk, investors began paying the CEOs of their companies in shares rather than simply in cash. Surprise, surprise, company leaders began to make sure that more of the company's profits went to shareholders rather than to workers or into investment. The science of this was crystallised in ground-breaking work by Michael Jensen and William Meckling, which showed how to align the interests of shareholders and managers by paying the managers in the same coin in which investors reaped their harvest – either dividends or via a happily upward-spiralling stock price.

Total alignment of a chief executive's rewards with the performance of the company would require the chief executive actually to own the firm, which is not possible. Indeed, UK FTSE 100 CEOs own, on average, just 0.1 per cent of the stock in the firms they manage. So, boards issue a mix of a base salary plus performance-related pay calculated either annually or according to a Long Term Incentive Plan (LTIPs). Today, performance-based pay dominates this mix; it makes up around three-quarters of the maximum remuneration for CEOs of companies on the FTSE All-Share index.[28]

These strategies have proved remarkably effective at ensuring that dividends now flow to shareholders – some of whom will be pension savers – at the expense of both the pay of workers and medium-term investment. In fact, the effect is so powerful that even though profits tend to rise and fall, as Andy Haldane, former chief economist at the Bank of England noted, 'after 1980... we see a one-way street. Dividend payout ratios almost never fall.'[29] The short-term quest for smoothing shareholder returns dominates payout behaviour, almost irrespective of profitability. And so, we are left with a tragedy beautifully described by the late Lynn Stout of the Cornell Law School, in relation to the United States: 'This dogma drives directors and executives to run public firms with a relentless focus on raising stock price,' she writes, and so:

> In the quest to 'unlock shareholder value' they sell key assets, fire loyal employees, and ruthlessly squeeze the workforce that remains; cut back on product support, customer assistance, and research and development; delay replacing outworn, outmoded, and unsafe equipment; shower CEOs with stock options and expensive pay packages to 'incentivize' them; drain cash reserves to pay large dividends and repurchase company shares, leveraging firms until they teeter on the brink of insolvency; and lobby regulators and Congress to change the law so they can chase short-term profits speculating in high-risk financial derivatives.[30]

How, then, would we build a better, civic capitalism from this system? Five steps are key.

As a first step, we have to change the way the boardroom works. This is not some radical left-wing Marxism. It is actually an agenda shared by many leaders of Anglo-American capitalism. Almost a decade ago, Dominic Barton, the former head of management gurus McKinsey & Co., declared that 'boards aren't working'.[31]

This concern reflects a sense that companies *do* have obligations to society beyond simply the shareholders who pay in equity. A March 2020 *Fortune* magazine poll found that 41 per cent of Fortune 500 CEOs agreed that solving social problems *should* be 'part of [their] core business strategy'. CEOs and others are coining new terms such as 'compassionate capitalism' and 'inclusive capitalism'. The American Business Roundtable, which brings together some of the most prominent US corporate captains, declared that this new perspective was driven by a shift in public sentiment – for as many Americans (64 per cent) say that a company's 'primary purpose' should include 'making the world better place' as say it should include 'making money for shareholder' – as well as by pressure from employees, especially younger workers.[32]

Change should therefore begin with a change to company law to crystallise an obligation on company directors to declare the *purpose* of their business – and enshrine a fiduciary duty to maintain that purpose in the company's proceedings. Initiatives such as the UK charity Blueprint for Better Business already try to help firms focus harder on purpose and inculcate these values from the boardroom down. Some firms, like Unilever and Danone, can boast some success. So-called 'B Corps' are another model, which do away with the business of distributing profits and reinvest in the purpose they set out to pursue. But today's rules of the game in the UK are a constraint on this sort of approach, as Will Hutton recently explained to me: 'Unlike any other advanced industrialized country,' said Will, the UK's company code 'insists that the over-riding priority of a company is the fiduciary obligation to pursue profits rather than the firm's wider health and purpose.'[33]

This deficiency dates back to the Company Law Review Steering Group in 1998, when the doctrine of shareholder primacy was not just retained but made *legally explicit* in Section

172 of the UK Companies Act (2006), which says: 'A director of a company must act in a way he considers, in good faith, would be most likely to promote the success of the company for the benefit of its members (i.e. shareholders) as a whole...' Directors must merely 'have regard to' wider stakeholders. Like customers. Or workers. Or creditors. The Review had asked whether companies should have responsibilities broader than maximizing gains for shareholders, but its members concluded that directors' duties should not be spread wider because that risked giving directors too much to think about; it risked turning 'company directors from business decision makers into moral, political or economic arbiters'.

This response, argues Will Hutton, was the wrong one. Today's laws make it harder in Britain to create a group of anchor shareholders who get behind a company's mission and stand behind it through thick and thin. As a result, Will explained, we have 'a Wild West of fractionalized, dispersed, uncommitted owners in which the opportunity to demonstrate sustained inventiveness over time in a healthy organization by binding all the stakeholders into a common cause is made impossibly hard'. He concluded that 'Profit should be a means to an end – ensuring the survivability and sustainability of an enterprise – but it cannot *be* the end. The end is a business's purpose which should be its north star.'

As a second step, in order to buttress this reform, we need people in the boardroom who are genuinely motivated by the long term, and who genuinely have skin in the game. As we have seen, today's investors are highly diversified and do not tend to hold onto shares for very long – unlike other stakeholders in the company, like employees, customers and clients, for whom diversification of company-specific risks is hard. Most workers cannot easily invest in a portfolio of jobs or products or supply lines, and lacking a seat on the board, most creditors, suppliers, debt providers – and workers – are powerless to help steer a company on a better long-term course. If we are to create the freedom for managers to think long-term, we need to give greater weight to those who cannot diversify their risk away: to creditors, and to workers past and present.

For the third step, we need to ensure that there *is* a big, deep UK capital market of worker-savers prepared to invest in these firms. And there is now a way to do this by asking the new National Employment Savings Trust (NEST) to draw up new, defined benchmarks and standards for environmental and social goals for companies to meet, and so help to foster a country of good work.

This is not as novel as it might sound. The investment industry knows there is a problem. In recent years there has been a flurry of 'stewardship codes', such as the 2020 UK Stewardship Code, which requires signatories to 'systematically integrate stewardship and investment, including material, environmental, social and governance issues, and climate change, to fulfil their responsibilities'. It sounds sensible. But frankly, it is close to meaningless, because of the way asset managers shy away from using their voting rights on certain 'difficult', 'excessively onerous' or 'burdensome' issues.[34]

Yet there is change underway when it comes to climate change. A huge amount of work has created benchmarks that companies must meet to declare themselves 'Paris compliant', referring to the goals of the COP21 Paris Agreement (2015), and there is also work on reforms to financial reporting, so that investors can see how firms are really behaving. This, in turn, creates pressure on investment managers to create solid portfolios of firms that are doing their bit to hit the Paris goals.[35] If we can create investment codes that are good for the environment, then surely we can write investment codes that are good for equality? It is harder in some respects – there is no simple headline goal, such as avoiding a 2C temperature rise. But we *can* create lists of behaviours that we want firms to avoid and behaviours that we would like to see; and crucially, organizations like NEST can both specify and then make investments according to these criteria, setting new norms in the investment marketplace for firms committed to 'inclusive growth'.

Indeed, failing to harness NEST in this way would be to miss one of the biggest opportunities for change in the investment industry in decades. Since February 2018, all UK employers have been required to set up a pension scheme and *automatically* enrol their staff. As a result, the number of workers in occupational pension schemes had risen, by 2022 estimates, to more than 19.4 million people.[36] This has meant a grand total of 73 per cent of UK employees saving for the first time.[37] NEST is the default investor for those funds, which will now multiply very quickly. According to its chief executive, Helen Dean, 'More than 80 per cent of UK workers are participating in a second pillar pension through work – the highest rate we have ever had, and far higher than in the golden age of defined benefit pensions.'[38]

This new army of pension savers, saving 8 per cent of their salary (after matching contributions from government and employer), will produce a flood-tide of new investment capital. Over the course of our savings career, we adjust how much we invest in equities, bonds and cash, but the average over our lifetime of pension saving for equities comes to around £34,000. If we multiply that by 12 million savers, we can see more than £415 billion of new money heading into equity investment in the years to come.[39] Channelling this much to firms that offer to 'do the right thing' could form quite a bargaining chip. We should start using that leverage.

In order to get to the bottom of this, I invited Helen Dean and a host of experts to meet together one very hot afternoon in the House of Commons. Helen is almost unique in Whitehall, in that she worked for years on the policy of auto-enrolment into company pensions before getting to run the organization that implements it. And she has already found that the power of NEST's influence is substantial.

'We've gone from zero to over 11 million members now and growing,' she told us. That is one in three workers in the UK, who have already built up savings of £24 billion. This size and scale gives NEST the power to use its influence. 'We're able to leverage our buying power,' Helen went on. 'We can do extremely good deals on behalf of our members, in the admin space, to drive down costs.' But crucially, Helen can appoint investment managers who are skilled in investing in companies with good values.

'At first it was pretty hard to do,' Helen explained.

We were tiny, and we were investing in funds, and we had very little leverage... but as we've grown bigger, we've been able to do more. And we don't do responsible investment because it's the right thing to do. It may well be the right thing to do. But that's not why we do it. We do it because we have a strongly held belief that integrating ESG (environmental, social, and governance) into our investment strategy will actually enable us to generate the best long-term risk-adjusted financial returns.

The bottom line is that companies that have decent values are best placed to thrive: 'we think that well run companies with good environmental practices [and] social practices are more likely to be sustainable and more likely to be profitable'. Companies that treat staff well have less staff turnover and are more likely to be productive. 'We're interested in diversity,' Helen explained, 'because we think companies are better companies that are diverse, particularly at senior levels.'

NEST has already begun coordinating with others that share their interest – and that is helping make sure that companies set good Net Zero targets, pay the living wage and have boards that are as diverse as the customers they serve. If we are careful, this approach could help us fix the shortfalls of the old science of portfolio management. In fact, it takes us beyond modern portfolio theory to a *systems theory* that works on three levels: the security, the portfolio *and* the system-level effects. 'The biggest theoretical failing of Modern Portfolio Theory,' write James Hawley and Jon Lukomnik, 'is the assumption that the non-diversifiable risk of your investments – the effects of market crises, global warming, political risk and other systemic issues – affect your and my investments, but is unaffected by those same investments.'[40] Encouraging everyone to invest in ways that are good for equality lowers the systemic risks – that is, the overall risk that cannot be diversified away – across the marketplace, because, as we now know from the groundbreaking work of both the IMF and the OECD, excess income inequality *drags* on growth and makes growth less sustainable over time. Conversely, lifting the income share of the poorest *accelerates* growth.[41]

Our fourth step is to make absolutely sure that we maximize the market power of investment funds devoted to this sort of virtuous behaviour by rolling up our crazy industry of 4,500 tiny defined benefit schemes, and 27,000 miniscule defined contribution pension funds, into a group of five or six pension fund giants known as 'super-funds', with sums of £300–400 billion under their management – just as the Australians and Canadians do. This would solve a problem that has been getting worse for twenty years. A series of bad regulations have meant that British pensions have disinvested from UK shares on a staggering scale. Back in 2001, funds invested 50 per cent of their portfolio in such shares. Now it is down to 4 per cent. The money has been switched to government bonds, and the London Stock Exchange, once a global giant, is now only just about in the top ten. This shift starves British firms of risk finance, and of course it limits the influence of pension savers on business behaviour.

But there is a model solution.[42] The Pension Protection Fund, created in 2004, mops up pension funds and their liabilities from firms that have gone bust. Today, it is huge. It manages £40 billion (around 100 times the size of an average UK pension fund), and like the biggest pension funds in places like Canada and Australia, it enjoys vastly superior returns, of around 9 per cent – much better than the the 6-per-cent average return of UK pension schemes.

A couple of steps are needed to deliver this. On the one hand, a short, sharp incentive is needed to encourage pension fund trustees to merge their little funds into the new super-funds. The best way to do this is to jeopardize their tax breaks (worth around £10 billion a year) if they do not at least actively consider merging into a super-fund. In order to help, we then need to clarify fiduciary duties to ensure that pension-fund trustees can enjoy a clear definition of what constitutes 'inclusive growth' firms, with the confidence that their fiduciary duties permit them – as stewards of company pension schemes – to invest in ways that stretch beyond demanding simplistic financial returns. Today, trustees often defend appointment of the same old investment managers by hiding behind risk-averse legal advice. Worse, they are required to insist on triennial valuations, which encourage a very short-term performance focus. We should change this. Our challenge is that our investors today do not think long-term, because they do not invest long-term.

Together with consolidation of the £360-billion local government pension schemes and a new investment fund for public sector pensions, we could see a new family of super shareholders genuinely able to drive long-term investment in both companies but also national infrastructure.

Harnessing the power of NEST and new super-funds to lead new benchmarks on 'investing for good work' could help us radically expand the number of firms delivering good work. But there is one final, fifth, step that is needed to ensure that we do not simply maximize wages in the short term but rather improve the value of 'deferred wages', pensions. And that will require some common-sense reform of the investment industry, which frankly needs to rediscover its purpose.

Over the past seventy years, the finance industry has grown enormously, but today its purpose is neither very clear, nor much debated, despite the clarity of what savers seek.[43] Once upon a time, investment management could argue that its principal purpose was the efficient allocation of capital. But surely it is more important now to manage risk for individual savers, and ensure they have a good, predictable income to retire with? In my polling with the KCL Policy Institute, we found that voters are generally dissatisfied with the support that the UK government provides for people trying to improve their finances, and 60 per cent think the government does too little to help everyone save enough for a pension. Around 39 per cent of pension savers are looking forward to a predictable income in retirement, around 19 per cent are looking for a lump sum when they retire, while 43 per cent are seeking a mixture of both.

Yet the investment management industry effectively holds down the value of this deferred income because the industry is so inefficient and expensive. One rigorous study by Professor Thomas Philippon reviewed the amount of money deposited in the care of the finance industry, over 130 years to 2015, and the sums then invested.[44] Philippon discovered *no* improvement whatsoever in the industry's productivity; the industry that finances the Internet is no more productive than the one that financed the railways. This is an astonishingly poor performance, which means that investment charges, 'the price of stewardship', remain high for many pension savers – and high annual rates exert a gigantic impact on the eventual return pensioners are likely to enjoy.

If we are to create a finance industry that better fulfils its purpose, we have to begin a new debate about what a *purposeful* industry would look like. Without 'purpose' it is impossible to write the right rules. We know that we will not agree on everything. But unless we find the overlapping consensus and regulate to deliver these outcomes, we will consign a critical section of our economy to ever greater costs, lose the progress we need to build a more inclusive economy, and profoundly damage our ability to mobilize investment towards creating the jobs of the future. We might then back this up with a sort of Hippocratic oath for everyone who works in the finance industry, to encourage better behaviour among asset managers and create a kind of 'nutrition label', specifying a manager's performance, along with the beginning balance, the final balance, the net return and a list of every cost and fee so that savers are far clearer about how much investment managers are charging for their services.

Over the centuries, the rules of the strange arena we call the 'marketplace' have been carefully and deliberately written, as choices were made about what sovereign governments would, and would not, permit or license or tax. But change was always justified in terms of the common good. Today, that common good has got lost. We have defeated the good intentions of reforms like those overseen by Viscount Palmerston. It is time that we rediscovered them. If we get it right, workers will enjoy earnings that are higher, in firms that are more productive. And that is the raw material for wealth-building.

But to maximize the gains for ordinary people, we need a force multiplier. We have now seen that building a genuine wealth-owning democracy involves changes to raise earnings, with a proper strategy for growth and a reformed civic capitalism. In order to make sure that everyone is able to turn those earnings into wealth, we need something additional: a system of universal basic capital.

10

Supporting the People

A social security fit for the twenty-first century

It is said that Sir William Beveridge wept when asked to pen his famous wartime report that became the blueprint for the welfare state. He hankered to be in charge of manpower on the Home Front, organizing to defeat the Nazis. But Britain's Minister of Labour, Ernest Bevin, who had asked Beveridge to help run the ministry, was told in no uncertain terms that the distinguished knight was impossible to work with.[1] So, in 1941, the good Sir William was tasked instead with leading an enquiry into the future of social security. He did not take long to seize the moment.

Timing is everything in politics – and Sir William's was perfect. In November 1942, the Allies defeated Rommel at El Alamein, counter-attacked at Stalingrad and triumphed over the Japanese navy at Guadalcanal. It was not the beginning of the end. But it was, as Churchill put it, the end of the beginning. Interest in the future that the country was fighting for hit a new high, and that swept the Beveridge Report – or, more properly, the report on *Social Insurance and Allied Services* – off the shelves when it was published that month. It became the most popular government publication until Lord Denning's Report into the Profumo scandal in 1963 – when it comes to government inquiries, it seems sex outsells social security.

Beveridge was a Liberal, but his blueprint helped define a new centre-ground in politics. The Labour Party placed his work at the very foundation of its 1945 General Election manifesto, and coupled with a plan for full employment, it helped propel the party to power. Less than one year later, at 3.48 p.m. on 6 February 1946, the Minister of National Insurance, Jim Griffiths, got to his feet to move that the National Insurance Bill be read for a second time, replete with its first clause: 'Every person who on or after the appointed day being over school-leaving age and under pensionable age... shall become insured under this act.' And so, after just four years of work, the Beveridge Report began its journey onto the statute books.

Social security is the way we honour our deepest instincts to cooperate, look after one another, and share the windfalls that, morally, should be shared. True, in the old debate about human nature, there are plenty of cheerleaders for Thomas Hobbes and his proverb *homo homini lupus* ('Man is wolf to man'), but, as Frans de Waal has explained, that is 'a questionable statement about our own species based on false assumptions about another species'. In fact, 'cooperation is our species' first and foremost inclination'.[2]

Humans are social animals, and over the long run of our evolution, that instinct for mutual aid has proved the best security. 'Security is the first and foremost reason for social life,' de Waal goes on, because 'every human life cycle includes stages at which we either depend on others... or others depend on us.'[3] These instincts are so powerful that neurobiologists like Donald Pfaff believe that our brains have actually evolved mechanisms to automatically shut down fear-inducing thought when altruistic behaviour is appropriate. This helps explain why, in an emergency, people can be found running *towards* danger, seeking to save others.[4] But not only are we programmed to ensure the survival of the destitute, we are also hard-wired to share good luck when it comes our way. When any one of us makes a little breakthrough, or even a large one, whether it is killing a mammoth or discovering electricity, part of our programming tells us that the fruits we have won should be shared, not hoarded. The reason, as historian Ian Morris writes, is that we have been foragers for 90 per cent of our history and 'refusing to share the good things that come your way is a forager deadly sin'.[5]

Over time, the basic instincts of aiding and sharing became the foundation for the most successful societies, as Charles Darwin suspected, and as the revolution in sociobiology and evolutionary psychology of the last thirty years has confirmed. Darwin was struck by the paradox of how selfless behaviour could 'arise by natural selection, which is seemingly its antithesis'.[6] The paradox is resolved (as Darwin surmised) by understanding – as Professor Martin Nowak explains – that 'the *whole* colony is the unit of selection'.[7] David Sloan Wilson has summarized the principle pithily: 'Selfishness beats altruism within groups. Altruistic groups beat selfish groups. Everything else is commentary'.[8] Over time, the most cooperative prevail, and so, over the long arc of our evolution, 'pro-social' instincts are diffused throughout the human population, the length and breadth of the planet.

Beveridge knew what he was doing when he rooted his famous report in these instincts. He was clear that 'organized altruism' was not only desirable in rebuilding a war-battered nation; it was essential. '[C]oncrete expression is thus given,' said the Report, 'to the *solidarity* and unity of the nation, which in war has been the bulwark against aggression and in peace will be its guarantee of success in the fight against individual want and mischance.'[9]

Under the duress of war, the Beveridge Report was almost exclusively focused on one element of the mutual aid equation: the prevention of destitution. And so, he sought to provide social insurance for those moments in life when earnings were interrupted, or when earnings could not cover the extra costs of family – when, for example, children arrived or sickness struck. But Beveridge's plan for 'social insurance' was merely one part of what he called a 'comprehensive policy of social progress' and which, all in all, was a far more ambitious post-war plan for wealth-building, including municipal housing, free education and universal pensions to guard against poverty in retirement. Or, to put it another way, it was a plan for housing capital, human capital and pension capital.

In order to build a wealth-owning democracy today, we need to rediscover the grand ambitions on which social security was constructed but adapt them to our new world. As it happened, a twist of political fate threw me into a role that confronted these very challenges.

When I was young and ambitious, I had my own back-of-the-envelope sketch of how I would have loved my career to unfold. I think it is fair to say that leaving certain notes at the Treasury was not on it. And nor was becoming Labour's social security spokesman, a post I succeeded to in a reshuffle, after the great Alan Johnson suddenly resigned as Labour's shadow chancellor in 2011. Westminster was stunned at Alan's departure, and in the commotion I got a call from Ed Miliband, asking me to step up and become Shadow Secretary of State for Work and Pensions on top of the job I already had, chairing Labour's policy review.

It was a nightmare. There was a heavy load of very tricky laws to respond to, as the Conservatives took aim at slashing the social security budget. In the years of austerity after the Great Financial Crash, the Tories, seeking *huge* savings, cleverly reprised Ronald Reagan's tactics of attacking the 'undeserving poor'. The tide of public opinion was on the Conservatives' side, and as Labour's Opposition spokesman, I am afraid I made the mistake of following the polling too religiously, half thinking of 'out-toughing' the Tories. 'Labour is the party of hard workers not free-riders,' I exclaimed, in a speech on the Conference floor. 'The clue is in the name. We are the Labour Party. The party that said that idleness is an evil.' But 'welfare reform' had become the sharpest edge of austerity. All politicians must be party managers, and I managed to offend deeply many in my party. After two hard years, I was sacked along with the remaining Blairites in the Shadow Cabinet, and Jeremy Corbyn went on to ride the Left's surge-tide of anger about rising levels of inequality and welfare cuts, and so become Labour's leader.

While in the social security role, and navigating hundreds of hours of legislation, I had tried to read everything I could about the history, economics and policy of welfare. As we sailed further into the twenty-first century, it was already crystal clear to me that our social security system was no longer much of a social pact, nor much of a guarantee of security. I concluded in my initial advice to Ed that our first task was to stop talking about 'welfare reform', which had become such a mantra in the New Labour years, and start talking instead about refounding social security. 'We reframe the debate about the welfare state,' I wrote in one memo, 'around the new risks that families face in the 21st century.' As it happens, this remains the right strategy, but there were two basic problems.

First, social security no longer supplied the solutions to fixing the problems of modern Britain. Beveridge famously named the five giants blocking the path to Britain's post-war reconstruction as Want, Disease, Idleness, Ignorance and Squalor. But when I looked at my constituency of Hodge Hill – the most income-deprived constituency in Britain – I saw different evils. Yes, Want was, and is, still with us, but its co-conspirators now were Exploitation, Disability, Inability and Poor Places. They represent twists of life and circumstances that are outside the individual's control, and combined, they create an insurmountable wall, blocking the path out of poverty.

The second problem was that a large slice of society no longer thought it got anything out of the system. They thought the system was broken and that it offered – as the then TUC leader Brendan Barber memorably put it – a 'nothing for something' problem: people paid in, but got nothing back.[10]

If we are to renew social security for new times, we need to remember that it is not only one of the most important ways in which we protect the poorest; it is also how *we share the harvest of the nation's progress more fairly*. This requires one philosophical shift from the days of Beveridge. He was squarely focused on cauterizing the wounds of fate, and he wanted to minimize the disruption to earnings. Today, we need a different philosophy to *maximize the potential* of earnings as the world of work changes all around us.

Much of the debate about social security today is, accordingly, about fixing the problem of income shortage, and among the most fashionable proposals for reform is the idea of a Universal Basic Income (UBI). It is an old idea with new traction – an idea that was once associated with Milton Friedman's concept of a 'negative income tax' but is now in vogue on the Left. Pioneered for over thirty years in the UK by the Citizen's Income Trust, UBI is a hot topic internationally as people look at the state of the world now for millions of workers – and then glance at the world to come, with artificial intelligence and automation growing in power and threatening to erase millions of jobs. UBI has a great philosophical and ethical appeal in a country like the UK, which believes in the right to basic subsistence. As Guy Standing points out, the Charter of the Forest – sealed in 1217, two years after Magna Carta – is one of the two foundational documents of the British constitution and asserts the truth that 'everybody had a *right of subsistence*, realisable in and through the commons'.[11]

Many different models of UBI have been proposed. In essence, all involve a basic payment being made, providing enough to make a difference but by no means total security. The payment would be in money rather than in anything paternalistic like vouchers or food stamps. It should be regular and predictable, and it should be paid automatically, as of right; it should go to an individual rather than a household, unconditionally, which means to every legal resident; and it should be non-withdrawable.

How much might the UBI be worth? Figures vary, but these are what the Royal Society of Arts has proposed: a Basic Income of £3,692 for all qualifying citizens between twenty-five and sixty-five, with a pension of £7,420 for those over sixty-five.[12] At current levels, that's a little over 10 per cent of the median wage, and around 80 per cent of the state pension. But children, too, would receive payments (replacing child benefit): the first born in every family would enjoy a Basic Income of £4,290 before the age of four, with £3,387 for their siblings, falling to £2,925 for those aged five to twenty-four.

My polling shows that the ideal of a Universal Basic Income is popular, especially among Labour voters.[13] We found that a fifth of voters (20 per cent) ranked this as the measure they supported most and the one considered (out of the options offered) to work best for reducing inequality within the next five years. I am not surprised. Recent data shows that 'around 1 in 20 (5 per cent) of adults reported that in the past two weeks they had run out of food and had been unable to afford more'.[14] I hear the heartbreaking stories behind the statistics in my constituency every week.[15]

A challenge, though, is that a fairly high proportion (48 per cent) in polling do not regard Universal Basic Income as a credible solution.[16] Personally – and I am open to being proved wrong – I too suspect that the political and administrative barriers to UBI are insuperable. I cannot see how the idea slays those 'five giants' of the *modern* age. A UBI might address Want, but no-one is proposing that it could provide total security. It would also be very, very expensive. An income paid to all UK citizens (including children) at the levels of recent Jobseekers' Allowance payments would come to around 13 per cent of UK GDP, or more than 30 per cent of recent government budgets.

A more modest and realistic scheme, modelled by Howard Reed of Landman Economics, proposed £60 per week for each adult over twenty-five.[17] But even this would cost £140 billion. Most proposals for paying for UBI draw attention to a long list of tax breaks that need binning. But this skirts the challenge I learned the hard way as a chief secretary to the Treasury. In any change to social security, one has to ask: 'Who are the losers?' In the Royal Society of Arts scheme, the losers are individuals earning more than £75,000 *and* those 'locked for prolonged periods of time on very low hours'.

A better approach may be that suggested by the Trussell Trust and the Joseph Rowntree Foundation, which proposes an Essentials Guarantee: a level of income, based on the recommendation of the independent process, that would ensure benefit levels were set at the minimum required to afford rent, food, utilities and vital household goods.[18] Analysis showed this would require £120 a week for a single adult and £200 for a couple. But even this is expensive, costing around £22 billion a year. Yet the polling I undertook with the KCL Policy Institute confirms that there is support for this sort of approach. When we asked voters how to use the social security system to reduce inequality, we found that 'ensuring benefits for those with ill-health are high enough to prevent poverty is the most popular measure'; a fifth (22 per cent) ranked this as the measure they supported most from the list of solutions, and 60 per cent considered this a credible approach.

Improving the basic safety net is a vital way for us to roll back poverty. But if we want to create a wealth-owning democracy we cannot simply worry about income; we also need a social security system that helps everyone build *assets*.

James Meade understood that it is impossible to build a democracy of wealth if a large slice of society is without savings. Not only did Meade emphasise the importance of building human capital, stressing 'the great importance of investment in education in raising earning power', he went on to note that 'arrangements which encourage *the accumulation of property* by those with little property are certainly as important as those which discourage further accumulation or encourage dispersal of their fortunes by large property owners'. [19] (My italics.) Today, this requires nothing less than a system of Universal Basic Capital (UBC).

In the early 1990s, Michael Sherraden – the father of 'asset-based welfare' – began to make just this argument. He rightly believed that a system which fostered assets (or wealth) had a multiplicity of virtues, because while 'income only maintains consumption... assets change the way people think and interact in the world... In other words, while incomes feed peoples' stomachs, assets change their heads.'[20] As he went on to argue, 'without some emphasis on assets people will not be given the maximum opportunity to realise their potential and escape poverty'.

Sherraden reconceptualized welfare as an investment, because access to assets multiplies the life-chances open to everyone. Helping individuals and families to build assets cultivates a sense of independence, not dependence; it provides a store of future consumption, improves peoples' resilience to twists of fate, creates an orientation towards the future, stimulates the development of other assets, provides some space for entrepreneurialism, boosts social and political buy-in and, above all, enhances the well-being of children.

Much of this theory has been confirmed by subsequent research. The most comprehensive study in the UK found that 'early asset holding does have positive effects on later wages, employment prospects, excellent general health and in reducing malaise'.[21] Equally, the *lack* of assets has been found to have all sorts of ill effects. According to one recent US study, net wealth poverty 'is associated with detrimental effects for child development'.[22] And in the UK, the Joseph Rowntree Foundation found that 'Those with minimal savings reliably reported far more distress than substantial savers, with twice as many admitting to taking less care at work, and three times as many reporting feeling worthless.'[23]

As it happens, UBC would also help us fix that 'nothing for something' *political* problem that imperils the foundations of the welfare state, because it could also help people see that social security *is* a system that benefits us all. Today, this is unclear because, as Richard Titmuss observed in the 1950s, whereas the poor rely on 'social welfare', the well-off enjoy 'fiscal welfare' – that is, help for the well-off to build assets through gigantic tax subsidies. And the scale of those subsidies is vast. In 2020–21, higher-rate taxpayers in the UK (about 13 per cent of workers) enjoyed tax subsidies on their pension savings worth £21.3 billion a year.[24] The best paid fifth of the population enjoy around £1.7 billion in tax subsidies on their savings.[25] The capital gains tax exemption for windfalls arising from the sale of family homes costs the public coffers £30-odd billion annually.[26] Those who take a degree course at university enjoy a collective write-off of student debt that is currently worth around £10 billion a year.[27] Together, these subsidies are worth roughly £62 billion, and they are enjoyed by a very small slice of society. This sum is not far off the bill for Universal Credit and other legacy benefits (that is, income subsidies for those out of work or low paid), which totalled £72 billion in 2022–23.[28] Yet by definition, if you have no income, these tax subsidies are denied you. By contrast, creating an integrated system of Universal Basic Capital would help everyone see that they are, indeed, in the same boat – a boat we build together.

Inspired by the work of Michael Sherraden and others, the idea of asset-based welfare caught on in the UK at the turn of the twenty-first century. The 2001 Labour manifesto made the grand promise 'to add a fourth pillar to the welfare state':

assets, along with specific commitments to a universal child trust fund, and a vaguer promise to strengthen support to help poorer groups save.

The Child Trust Fund (from September 2002) went on to award all new British babies a £250–£500 bond, while the Savings Gateway incentivized saving among low-income families with a government match of £1 for every £1 saved, up to a limit of £375.[29] Nor was the concept the exclusive territory of the Labour Party. David Willetts, for example, also developed ideas for a lifetime savings account. Yet somehow the ideas died away for want of political support – because the benefits were too narrowly shared.

We should learn from this with a new approach to UBC. Not least because, as we saw in the Meade Equation, ensuring that everyone has access to a pot of capital is a key component of ensuring that we diffuse wealth better. Today, the level of savings among the less well off is appallingly low. As the Joseph Rowntree Foundation's Tom Clark recently noted, 'the poorest tenth own vanishingly little – with a wealth share of just one-fiftieth of 1 per cent'.[30] The Money and Pensions Service suggests that just over a quarter of UK adults have less than £100 put away, and nearly half of households in the bottom tenth of total wealth owe more than what they have in ready cash.

The savings challenge is especially harsh for young people who now face an almost impossible savings life cycle. As we have seen, those born around the turn of the twenty-first century earn less than the generations that came before. But their bills are higher, too. When young people graduate – and while many will never pay off *all* their student loans – they are required to repay 9 per cent on everything they earn over £27,295.[31] Then they pay more for a pension: the low interest rates that have generally prevailed, plus greater longevity, means saving more to have the certainty of retiring comfortably, so that is around another 5 per cent of income. Then comes the rent, and rents are now close to their highest level for decades as a share of tenants' incomes, while rent subsidies from government, social housing and rent controls have shrunk by a combined value of around £45 billion.[32] At the time of writing, this means that rents are now, on average, £795 a month, but £1,450 in London.

From what is left, young people are expected to save for a deposit on a home – but of course, because prices are so high and lending rules are so tough, this is a much bigger sum than in the past. Some, of course, will benefit from their parents, either alive or when they die.

One new study has discovered that individuals from the luckiest families (with well-educated homeowner parents) 'are *three* times more likely to report housing wealth by age 35', and furthermore their average level of housing wealth 'is roughly ten times higher on average compared to individuals from the most disadvantaged background'.[33]

But many of today's renters will struggle to get on the housing ladder and for many young people, home ownership is becoming an impossible dream. In 1988, a house for a first-time buyer cost, on average, £36,000; now it costs almost ten times more, around £358,000.[34] John Burn-Murdoch, who has been following this issue for the *Financial Times*, estimates that 'Forty years ago it took the average couple three years to save for a deposit to buy a home in the UK. Today it takes nine, rising to 15 in London.'[35] Ironically enough, the recent spike in interest rates *might* make things easier. Interest rates on savings are higher and house price falls might be steep. Experts think that an 8 per cent fall in house prices could knock a couple of years off the average time it takes to save for a deposit, from 15 years to 13 years – but only if young people can continue to save at the same rate as before.[36] And there's the catch, because saving more is highly unlikely. In 2022, a rising cost of living and rising rents meant that almost half of adults (44 per cent) said they were not expecting to be able to save any money in the year ahead.[37]

Despite the challenges that savers face, the way the government offers to help is with a maze, not a model. Those £62 billion of tax subsidies described above are aimed at higher-rate taxpayers saving for a pension, squirrelling money away in an ISA (Individual Savings Account) or enjoying capital gains on the sale of property. (And the student loan system provides an effective subsidy to graduates, as we shall see.) When people *do* save in government-backed schemes, there is little flexibility to – for example – move savings from one purpose to another, while the employer contribution to the whole system is relatively small: employers, for instance, do not pay National Insurance contributions on their pension contributions, in a loophole that costs the Treasury some £14 billion a year in lower revenues.[38] Because the incentives are so skewed towards those who already have assets, today's system is not helping solve Britain's savings crisis. In fact, for four out of five years since 1980, the UK has had the lowest savings rate of any major economy.[39]

When Michael Sherraden first proposed his ideas on asset-based welfare, he suggested the simple truth that 'To create wealth in poor households, begin with assets.' He proposed Individual Development Accounts, which combined support for education, housing, self-employment and retirement.[40]

I would suggest something similar: a system for accumulating human capital and pension capital, together with short-term savings (e.g. for deposit on a home). The backbone of a new system would be to enrol *every* UK citizen in a universal National Savings Account, when they started paying National Insurance. To prepare young people for this, we should overhaul financial literacy training in schools. This one-stop-shop account would connect to two further accounts, one of which already exists – auto-enrolment pension accounts – and one of which, as we will see, is now on the cards to support lifelong learning.

Within this framework, we should – as resources allow – progressively universalize the coverage of pension savings accounts and increase the amount saved, and expand the support for first-time buyers and the value of subsidies for learners – and so democratize the way we help everyone build wealth over the course of their lives.

Let us start with the pension account. Thanks to an extraordinary cross-party consensus, as we have seen, since 2012 the UK has been able to build a pension system whereby some 13 million pension savers now have an auto-enrolment pension account. The government chips in by way of tax relief, while the employer chips in with cash.[41] The scheme has contributed to a tenfold increase in the membership of defined contribution (DC) occupational schemes.[42]

However, right now a huge number of people are *still* left out of the scheme, because of several factors: it does not cover the self-employed or young people between the ages of sixteen and eighteen who might be working.[43] Nor is the current savings rate of 8 per cent enough to safeguard against poverty in retirement. The result is that millions still do not have adequate pension coverage, and this will simply result in a new generation of pensioners living in poverty.[44] It is, effectively, a tax on the lowest paid when so many people earn too little to qualify for an auto-enrolment account, and thereby lose out on both government and employer contributions. What is more, the total contribution in auto-enrolment schemes (8 per cent of earnings) is not enough to deliver the sort of income that most people would want in retirement: to deliver that, the savings rate needs to go up to something more like 12 per cent.

Today, UK pension savers save around £115 billion a year,[45] but despite auto-enrolment, very few people think that the government does enough to support pension savers. In my polling with the KCL Policy Institute, we found that 60 per cent of respondents thought the government did too little to help everyone save enough for a pension.[46] Crucially, we need to radically expand eligibility to the low paid and increase its generosity.

Expanding eligibility and increasing government contributions to the scheme will be expensive – but the Institute for Fiscal Studies (IFS) has shown that we *can* raise billions of pounds to help finance these changes by restoring some good old-fashioned fairness to the system.[47] It proposes, first, capping income tax relief on pension contributions at the basic rate of tax (or a little higher, at 30 per cent), and second, asking employers to pay National Insurance on their pension contributions (worth around £12.5 billion, albeit reduced by a subsidy to employers).[48] Today, pension savers can withdraw a quarter of their pension pot as a tax-free lump sum, meaning that the wealthiest of them can extract as much as the limit of £250,000. So third, the IFS proposes reducing that cap to £100,000 – along with other changes, such as charging income tax on any inherited pensions. Where there's a will, there's a way.

Following pensions, the second leg of Universal Basic Capital is a support to help everyone boost their knowledge capital over the course of a working life. As it happens, at the time of writing the UK government is planning some common-sense reforms.

In 2020 it was estimated that those who studied up to degree level could look forward to net earnings, over the course of their lifetimes, of £100,000 more than those who did not go to university.[49] Yet, despite this rather large advantage, the training subsidies enjoyed by graduates have dwarfed those of everyone else. Currently, the average student debt on graduation is around £47,000, and yes, very high levels of interest then rack up, but the average graduate only repays around £45,000 before the loan is written off after thirty years – costing the government an estimated £87,187 per student.[50]

This inequality in subsidy, between university study and vocational study, is very large. But nor has the system been flexible enough to allow a return to study later in life – something that is going to be essential. The speed of technological change and automation now will mean that we have to reinvent our systems for retraining and reskilling. According to World Economic Forum forecasts, '65 per cent of children entering primary school today will ultimately end up working in completely new job types that don't yet exist.' I have heard these fears when canvassing. ('How am I going to survive,' asked one resident at the last election, 'how am I am going to support my family when I'm on the scrap-heap?') Those doorstep impressions are confirmed by polling I undertook with Opinium: we found that 54 per cent of C2DE voters thought automation would make it harder to earn a decent wage, and 46 per cent of ABC1s agreed.

The implications are especially serious for the least trained. 'Opportunities for lifelong learning,' writes Katherine Mullock at the OECD, 'are particularly important for low-skilled workers, who are less likely to receive training from their employers, but who may most need to upskill or retrain to remain employable in the context of technological change.'

Fortunately, having consulted in 2022, the UK government announced important changes, scheduled to begin in 2025, and similar to the Australian FEE-HELP loans.[51] In the UK, all learners (between the ages of eighteen and sixty) will have a 'Lifelong Loan Entitlement' of £37,000 to cover four years' worth of education for qualifications at levels 4 to 6, in either colleges or universities.[52] Study can be part time or full time. Learners will have a personal account they can access throughout their life, displaying their 'balance'; in addition, eligible learners will be entitled to maintenance loans for living costs, and there will be targeted grants for those in need. The system is open to postgraduate students, part-timers and mature students who did not qualify for previous help on the basis of studying a low-intensity course, or retraining, having already earned a degree. Such a scheme could go a long way towards rebalancing the state subsidy between those taking the traditional three-year degree and those who choose a different path. These changes might make a big difference, so long as ministers genuinely allow learners to study for a wide range of technical qualifications and improve support for level 3 studies (A-levels or NVQ level 3).

One change more would help. If we want to truly improve people's freedom to save and invest in improving themselves over the course of their lives, we should make it easy for people to be able to top up the entitlements provided by the government. And that could be accomplished by building the third leg of our system of Universal Basic Capital: a new type of savings account.

Today, the way the government supports short-term savings, or getting a foot on the housing ladder, is an unholy mess, but it is not a total void. Those in the know can open a Lifetime Individual Savings Account (LISA). If you are wise enough to do this, the government will give you a 25 per cent bonus on everything you save. If you put in the current maximum of £4,000 per year, therefore, you will be rewarded with another £1,000 for free. But there are restrictions on how you can use the cash, so you cannot do useful things like repay student debt, or endow a pension, or invest in education or training that will allow you to upskill and earn more. For those on benefits, there is 'Help to Save'.[53] This scheme allows you to save up to £50 per month and offers a bonus of up to £1,200 over four years. And finally, there is the good old ISA, the Individual Savings Account introduced by John Major, which lets anyone save £20,000 a year tax-free.[54]

Altogether, it is a patchwork of disconnected schemes, which also happen to channel vast sums to those who already own vast sums. The Resolution Foundation concluded that: 'Taking the existing schemes together, current policies are either poorly targeted... or are too small in scale to achieve a significant broadening in the distribution of household savings.' The take-up of Help to Save is so poor that only 10 per cent of those eligible have opened an account.[55] And although the scheme is targeted at those most in need, the government invests just £43 million a year in it. Support for LISAs is more generous – but again, it is very badly targeted. In 2022–23, LISAs cost the government around £671 million, but more than £300 million of it went to the richest individuals. Yet even this kickback for the better-off is dwarfed by the tax subsidy for ISA savers, which costs around £4 billion, of which £2.2 billion a year to those with ISA savings above £100,000).[56]

Personally, I think we need a fairer, universal system. And happily, there is now a model in the type of savings accounts that recently finished a four-year road test run by the National Endowment and Savings Trust (NEST).[57] The pilot involved automatically opening a 'sidecar' savings account attached to auto-enrolment pensions. Individuals working for a participating employer chose how much they wanted to save each payday and set a savings target. And henceforth, that amount was deducted from their salary and placed into an instant access savings 'jar' sitting alongside their workplace pension pot. Once the savings target was reached, the surplus was dispatched into the pension pot on top of their normal pension contributions. Four years of research have now confirmed that, on average, 99 per cent of accounts were active after eighteen months, and during this time, savers had built up an average savings balance of £384. Employees said the system gave them greater peace of mind and confidence with money. Given that one in four UK adults currently have savings of less than £100, this is an extraordinary step forward.

So, we should universalize this type of sidecar savings account, and merge it into the subsidies currently available through both LISAs and Help to Save, to create one system of Universal Savings Accounts.

If we can transform Britain into a nation of savers, we create a new foundation for the way we support a particularly important group in the battle against inequality: those struggling to save enough to buy a home to call their own.

As we have seen, home ownership among young adults has fallen off a cliff. Back in the late 1980s, more than half of young people were homeowners, yet by 2016 that proportion had shrunk to a quarter, with black young people less than half as likely to own a home as white young people.[58] Worse, on current trends, there is not much hope that things will improve; some have forecast that more than a third of Millennials will still be renting in retirement.[59] Yet three-quarters of renters would prefer to own their home.[60]

The problem is basically five-fold. While young people earn less than the generations that preceded them, houses have continued to become more expensive. But after the 2008 Financial Crash, banks demanded bigger deposits; in fact, the average deposit, which used to be 5 per cent of house values in 1989, had risen to 15 per cent by 2019, as banks restricted the multiple of earnings they were prepared (or were allowed) to offer. As a result, just 8 per cent of young non-homeowners aged twenty-five to thirty-four have saved enough for a 10-per-cent deposit on the average first-time-buyer home in their region; and half (48 per cent) have less than £1,000 in the bank. It is no wonder that two-thirds of young people say the lack of a deposit is the chief problem in buying their own home. To make things more difficult for them, rents have ballooned so fast that it is now harder than ever for young people to squirrel away the savings needed.

Result? The Resolution Foundation has estimated that just 4 *per cent* of young non-homeowning family units have *both* the required earnings *and* savings to access home ownership. Falling house prices might change this picture – but not by much: the Resolution Foundation suggests that an 8-per-cent fall in house prices might only enable an extra 30,000 (or just

0.7 per cent more) potential young buyers to enter the house market.[61] And though, ultimately, the UK must build more homes, transforming supply has only a modest impact on house prices over a generation.[62]

Because almost all first-time buyers rely on mortgage finance to buy a home, some serious changes to the mortgage market would be fundamental to reshaping the landscape for young people. These include expanding the availability of 95 per cent mortgages, and (once lower interest rates return) raising the earnings multiple allowed for lenders to make mortgage offers, in order to increase supply of very long-term fixed-rate mortgages.[63] Some bold measures on tax might be required, too.[64]

The Conservative government's 'Help to Buy' equity loans (available 2021–23) made *some* difference. However, many have argued that the scheme also fed into higher prices for new-build homes.

Right now, the way we support first-time buyers is very poor. And the public feels it. In the polling I did with the KCL Policy Institute, we found that over half of voters (55 per cent) did not think the government provided adequate support for those saving for their first deposit, while seven in ten (71 per cent) think the UK government can do more to help savers build their savings faster. [65] And even if we do see an expansion of longer-term 95-per-cent mortgage deals, that still leaves the challenge of saving that deposit of 5 per cent.

This is where a Universal Savings Account could really help. Analysis by the Tony Blair Institute for the years 2014–16 and 2016–18 showed an average shortfall of £10,000 on the deposit for an average first-time-buyer property.[66] Our polling found that the most popular ways to support savers and first-time buyers were by providing matching contributions to savings (33 per cent supported this idea) and providing a tax relief on saving contributions (backed by 30 per cent).[67] So, within new Universal Savings Accounts, the government should *increase* the amount by which it matches every pound saved by the under forties, and radically increase the maximum match-funding available, up to a capped subsidy, for every young person, worth £10,000. This step, in combination with others – notably 95-per-cent fixed-rate mortgages – would knock years off the time it takes for an average earner to build a deposit without the help of the Bank of Mum and Dad.

Naturally, the government would not be able to introduce these measures overnight. Proving a £10,000 match to savings for young people would cost around £7.4 billion a year. But there are three ways in which we could free the resources needed.

First, we should allow employers the chance to contribute to these accounts tax-free. Second, we should redistribute the tax subsidies enjoyed by the very richest through the ISA system and redirect them towards improving the generosity of matched funding for young savers. And third, we could meld some ideas from the IPPR and the Resolution Foundation's Inter-Generational Commission.[68]

The Commission proposed a one-off payment of £10,000 for everyone at the age of twenty-five, to provide a start in life. But our polling found voters were very divided on the idea: 35 per cent supported it, but 38 per cent opposed it.[69] Yet there is a better way, as the polling also suggested: if the dividend was paid to young people as a *tax incentive*, support levels were transformed: 41 per cent were in favour, and just 22 per cent opposed.[70] The misallocation of tax incentives that exists right now has delivered huge rewards to the very rich and exacerbated wealth inequality. As the *Mirrlees Review* put it in 2010–11, '[t]he current system of savings taxation in the UK is beset by complexity and unequal treatment' – and that remains the case.[71]

Building Universal Basic Capital – of pensions, savings and knowledge (or skills) – will not be easy. It does not come cheap, nor does it come overnight. But it is part of the fundamental infrastructure we need to build if we are to create a wealth-owning democracy.

There is, though, another piece of the puzzle that would ensure not only access to capital, but also access to the sort of returns that are today enjoyed only by the super-rich. Indeed, this could even be the source for that vital £10,000 in tax incentives or matched savings for every twenty-five-year-old, paid into their Universal Savings Account.

It goes by the name of a sovereign wealth fund.

11

Investing for the People

Nurturing the wealth of the nation

Across the park from Buckingham Palace is the stately pile of Lancaster House, beneath which is one of Britain's strangest stores. Commissioned in 1825 by the 'grand old' Duke of York, Frederick Augustus, the house was once the hub of fashionable London. In would sweep *le beau monde* of the day, through the red and gold reception halls so redolent of Versailles, to chit-chat in the magnificent long gallery – where Churchill would give Queen Elizabeth II her coronation reception – or to enjoy the dripping luxury of the Gold Room, the Eagle Room, the Green Room, or the State Drawing Room where the occasional treaty is still signed. Thanks to William Lever, Lancaster House was gifted to the nation. I have enjoyed the odd state lunch there myself with visiting leaders. And, for toasts on any special occasion, ministers need only order up from the deep cellars that are home to a special treasure: the government's wine. I can tell you, their contents are excellent.

A century ago, the grand panjandrums of the Government Hospitality Fund concluded that the nation could simply no longer cope without an advisory committee for the 'Purchase of Wine'. So, the wine stocks of Whitehall were gathered in from Downing Street, Carlton Gardens and beyond, and during the Second World War, the fruits of a raid on the cellars of the German Embassy added to the racks. Today, overseen by a former diplomat and four Masters of Wine, the committee buys young wine (half of it English) to mature and to lubricate government receptions. At the time of writing, the store was home to 32,921 bottles of wines and spirits. None of it is Fairtrade ('none was of a sufficient quality'), but the stores now include a rather good 1878 Grand Cognac from the Fins Bois *terroir* worth at least £1,000 and labelled 'Drink very sparingly'; fifty 'A1' bottles of red, including a 1955 Château Latour 1er Cru Classé worth £1,700; sixty bottles of gin; and five bottles of whisky. All in all, the government's cellar has been conservatively valued at £3.2 million.[1]

Back in 2009, after the government blew £6,000 on wine for the G20, I once tried to make the Foreign & Commonwealth Office sell the collection and briefed my ambitions to *The Times*. But my hair-shirted efforts were defeated. With predictable *sang froid*, the Wine Committee 'regretted the manner in which the matter had been raised and the lack of consultation', before agreeing it 'would continue its work'.[2]

Of course, the nation owns stranger things than wine. The Crown Estate, which technically belongs to the monarch of the day, nevertheless surrenders its revenues to the Treasury in return for the payments from the Civil List. It boasts a portfolio that dates back to the Norman Conquest. Now worth £15.6 billion, its assets include everything from retail parks in Southampton to a large chunk of London's West End, to the nation's river-beds and seabeds out to a 12-mile limit, along with half of the nation's foreshore. If you want to harvest seaweed, you need the Crown Estate's permission.[3]

Yet even this loot is dwarfed by the contents of the vaults in the Bank of England. Rebuilt by Sir Herbert Baker in 1839, the ten-storey Bank, built from Portland stone, limestone and bronze, nestles on its island site in the City of London's Threadneedle Street. It is arranged around an exquisite courtyard, where only the governor can stroll to admire the exquisite little mulberry trees. The Bank's interiors are a neoclassical hotchpotch – 'a pasticcio, a patch-work of symbolical odds-and-ends' in the words of one governor – that includes spotlessly clean parlours that could double as sets from *Downton Abbey*. But deep beneath the drawing rooms is a labyrinthine layout, reminiscent less of an English country house and rather more a nuclear bunker. The endless identical corridors are full of the rumbling hum of nearby Underground trains, which serenade 400,000 gold bars, worth around £120 billon, locked in conditions so secure that the vaults have been breached just once – accidentally, by a nineteenth-century sewer worker.[4] Most of the ingots there no longer belong to the UK, but rather to other central banks; the Treasury does retain, however, on behalf of the nation, 24,000 bars worth around £15 billion.

Even the Bank of England's hoard represents a mere fraction of the UK government's assets. In fact, all in all, the assets of the UK public sector today total an extraordinary £2.14 trillion. This includes everything from the rail and road network (£460 billion) through to shares in 515 companies the government bought during Covid-19 lockdowns – including a chunk of Bolton Wanderers Football Club, a 'holistic' whisky distillery called 'The Lakes', and a firm that throws international sex parties called 'Killing Kittens'.[5]

But nor is this the sum total of the national worth. For years, Credit Suisse has issued a databook that looks at the household wealth of countries around the world.[6] And in its most recent edition at the time of writing (covering the two years 2020–21), the United Kingdom retained its No. 5 spot, with total wealth amounting to an incredible £13.1 trillion. To put that in context, that is one-fifth the size of China's wealth, a country with over a billion people.

News of this Aladdin's cave of riches would, I suspect, astound many UK citizens for the simple reason that the gulfs between the haves, the have-nots and the have-yachts are now so great. Indeed, Oxfam's boffins calculated in January 2023 that the richest 1 per cent of Britons now hold more wealth than the poorest 70 per cent.[7] This is not simply a problem for the here and now. It is a problem for the future, because of the force that James Meade knew all too well: the 'to-him-that-hath-shall-be-given' principle, or the old truth that 'money begets money'.

The state of equality in any society, argued Meade, depends on the balance between equalizing and 'disequalizing' forces. If the rates of return enjoyed by small savers are somehow vastly greater than the returns enjoyed by the very rich, then society will slowly move towards a more equal state. But the opposite is true, as Thomas Piketty proved in 2014. 'It is perfectly possible,' he wrote in *Capital*, 'that wealthier people obtain *higher average returns* than less wealthy people...[and therefore] It is easy to see that such a mechanism can automatically lead to a radical divergence in the distribution of capital'. (My italics.) A powerful 'disequalizing' force today is the reality that the rich carry on getting richer than the rest of us because of this problem of 'differential returns': big money makes more money than small money. So, if we want to build a democracy of wealth, we must not only improve earnings for all and spread capital to all. We must also provide *everyone* with access to the sort of superior returns that are currently only possible if you are lucky enough to own a giant amount of assets.

We can learn a lot about why the very rich enjoy such high returns by looking at their investments. Not that this is easy. Professor Brooke Harrington, who literally wrote the book on the wealth-management habits of the super-rich, told me that it is hard to generalize about their portfolios because 'the defining feature of financial services to these clients is customization: you and I get "off the rack" clothes while the ultra-rich get bespoke clothes, cut and tailored specially for them. Same with their investment plan.'[8]

One attempt to make some generalizations was made by Altrata, a firm that researches and publishes each year its 'Wealth-X' report. It reckons that the wealth managers of the world's 400,000 ultra-high net-worth individuals (those individuals worth a cool £24 million) allocate somewhere between 4 and 13 per cent of the assets they steward into 'real estate and luxury assets' like yachts, classic cars, jewellery and art. Another third of wealth goes into liquid assets like cash, and the balance is split evenly between public and private holdings.[9] Among ultra-high net-worth men, an extraordinary 73 per cent boast cars worth more than £160,000, while 80 per cent own either outright or a share in a yacht worth £4 million plus, and 81 per cent have a plane or access to one.[10]

The property firm Knight Frank has a slightly different take. It surveys hundreds of 'private bankers, wealth advisors, intermediaries and family offices' every year for its *Wealth Report*. Their research for 2021 (published 2022) found that, on average, those people who fitted their definition of high net-worth individuals (worth $1 million or more) parked around 27 per cent of their fortunes in property.[11] The reason is simple, as William Matthews, head of Knight Frank's commercial property team explains: the value of property is somewhere between a bond and cash, so it 'enjoys the upside of rising rents and values in times of economic expansion, but also security of income during times of volatility'.[12]

The very wealthiest can afford lovely things like mansions in Monaco, where £27 million will be needed to buy quarters that are among the world's most expensive.[13] But many of the super-rich own things that are rather more speculative: 11 per cent have invested in non-fungible tokens, and 18 per cent own some sort of crypto-currency.[14] But by and large, most of the wealthiest spread the balance of their investments across shares, bonds, real estate and a bit of venture capital, alongside plenty of chi-chi collectibles, which, in order of returns in 2021, included fine wine, watches, art, coins, rare whisky, handbags, cars, jewellery, coloured diamonds and furniture.[15]

As dazzling as this sounds, what is truly remarkable is that these investment strategies have broken the link between risk and reward. Risk is quite low. But returns are sky high. Sometimes, these are flattered for some by tax avoidance. But, as Brooke Harrington explains, other factors are at work. 'Some special investments are only available... to the ultra-rich,' Brooke goes on, 'with high rates of return *and lower risk of losses* than are available to regular people like us. That's really important, because that defies the laws of finance, where *risk* is supposed to be rewarded with returns, and low risk means low returns.'[16] (My italics). These are the sorts of investment opportunities that are simply not available to the poor. In fact, most of the poorest keep their savings in current or savings accounts which, while interest rates were low for so long, have paid a return of next to nothing.

This *gulf* in returns enjoyed by the rich and poor was recently mapped by economists from the IMF and elsewhere, who got their hands on some rare data from Norway – almost the only country actually to publish tax returns.[17] The results are astounding. Looking at twelve years' worth of data, the team confirmed that some individuals earn a markedly different average return on their net worth, and they confirmed that these differences were *not* explained by some taking risky bets that came off while others – like the unfaithful servant in the parable of the talents – buried their gold in the garden, but found instead that returns *were* 'positively correlated with wealth'. The scale of the differences was incredible. In fact, the richest 10 per cent enjoyed returns *18 per cent* higher than the poorest tenth. And these differences persisted over time, and down the generations: you were more likely to enjoy higher returns on your assets if your parents enjoyed higher returns too.

There is no one simple explanation. Risk tolerance is a factor.

The wealthy can withstand risk and were found to 'allocate (persistently) a larger share of their wealth to risky assets... [which] are compensated with a return premium'. By contrast, those at the bottom of the pile are generally paying a lot more for their debt. A second factor is persistent differences in wealth and a positive effect of the *scale* of wealth on returns, as Thomas Piketty suggested. However, a third broad explanation is that the wealthiest enjoy a level of financial sophistication, and the ability to process and use financial information, as well as access to investment opportunities, which are denied to the poor. As the authors summarized it, 'we interpret our evidence as implying... persistent heterogeneity in returns reflects also differences in ability to generate returns and superior information about investment opportunities'.

The agreeable returns enjoyed by the wealthiest affect the make-up of the income that flows into the bank accounts of the very richest. As we have already seen, what unites the wealthy is that they draw a significant chunk of their income from investment, not wages. I found this for myself when I asked the House of Commons library to take a look at tax data. The results showed that people earning more than £1 million draw, on average, a fifth (19 per cent) of their income from capital, while those earning £20,000 to £30,000 typically draw just 4 per cent from whatever capital they have.[18] The picture is best clarified by asking: where does investment income in the UK go? And the answer is unsurprising: it goes to the rich. In fact, investment income is far more unequally distributed than any other form of income: an extraordinary 57 per cent of total investment income goes to the richest 10 per cent of households.[19]

There is one obvious way in which we can fix this inequality of access to the best returns on investment. We can create one giant fund, owned by all citizens, in which all citizens have a share, and from which all citizens enjoy a dividend. This is not some radical flight of fancy. It is called a sovereign (or social) wealth fund (SWF). It has been around for almost a century, and it is now one of the most important features of the global investment landscape.

The basic concept of a sovereign wealth fund is simple. As Matt Bruenig explains in his paper 'Social Wealth Fund For America', 'the government owns a large pool of income-generating assets and then uses the return on those assets for social welfare purposes.'[20] Once upon a time, the concept was proposed as the ultimate phase of socialism, whereby the workers could finally own the means of production. But modern advocates of the idea now range from inequality guru Tony Atkinson to former Greek Finance Minister Yanis Varoufakis, from Democratic presidential contender Hillary Clinton to Conservative MPs.

Some experiments in social wealth funds have, indeed, been fairly radical. After a long debate, the Swedish social democratic leader Olof Palme created the country's 'wage earner funds' in 1984, based on a plan developed by two Swedish trade unionists, Rudolph Meidner and Gosta Rehn. The government imposed a small excess-profits tax on companies and used the cash to buy shares in Swedish companies, eventually amassing 7 per cent of Swedish company stock by 1991. But that idea did not survive a change of government, and a new centre-right government quickly privatized the funds.

But the idea did not die. Indeed, in neighbouring Norway a family of sovereign wealth funds was founded in 1990, and four years later the state began squirrelling away the proceeds from the country's oil boom to safeguard that wealth for the benefit of future generations, given that oil-related income would inevitably decline. Nowadays, the fund is worth an incredible £1 trillion – around £185,000 for every Norwegian. Figures for 2022 showed that the fund invests in 9,300 companies globally and owns 1.3 per cent of all listed stocks in the world.[21]

But nor is the SWF idea a mere lodestone of Scandi-socialism.

Republican Alaska has a similar model. Often lauded as 'the most popular program in the history of the US', it dates back to 1976, when Alaska's maverick governor founded the fund with royalties from the oil industry. By 2018, it was worth 113 per cent of Alaska's GDP. Among outcomes paid for by its dividends are lower poverty, increased attainment by disadvantaged young people and, it is said, a rise in employment of up to 17 per cent. Australia, too, has followed the pattern: its Future Fund was created to help pay for future civil-service pensions, while a second fund, the DisabilityCare Australia Fund, supports Australians with significant and permanent disability.

These are just a few examples from a constellation of more than seventy such funds in countries as diverse – politically, geographically and culturally – as Singapore, New Zealand, France, Ireland and most countries in the Arabian Gulf, as well as nine US states.[22] And at least forty of these funds have been created since 2005.

Estimating the combined value of SWFs worldwide is a murky business, but without doubt they are worth a fortune. At the time of writing, the world's largest funds have been estimated at £5.7 trillion.[23] That is a bigger asset base than the £3.3 trillion invested in private equity and the £2.7 trillion invested in hedge funds.

But what defines a sovereign/social wealth fund? Most have a few things in common. They are owned by a sovereign government, but crucially, they invest in assets that generate excellent returns, far outstripping the sort of returns the humble saver might enjoy. As such, they *can* help conquer today's inequality of access to the best returns, because they are – like the super-rich – able to build diverse and substantial portfolios of assets far beyond the reach of the poorest households, especially when interest rates are low. In a 2022 study, State Street Global Advisors found that the average five-year return for a sovereign wealth fund based in Europe was an extraordinary 8.3 per cent.[24] And between 2018 and 2020, the assets of sovereign wealth funds grew at an annual clip of 11.3 per cent, the explanation being that 'the acceleration in AUM [assets under management] growth is largely a function of market gains.' Needless to say, these sorts of returns have been radically bigger than the tiny percentage returns enjoyed by low-income savers in desultory bank and savings accounts.

There is now, slowly but surely, a growing consensus on the need for a UK sovereign wealth fund. From the right of the aisle is the Conservative MP John Penrose, who began to argue some years ago that 'There is one more piece of the puzzle that would reinforce an important aspect of social solidarity... a UK sovereign wealth fund to pay into these accounts dividends from our common wealth.' The centre-left think-thank, the Institute for Public Policy Research (IPPR) has also advanced the idea, while the *Financial Times*'s Martin Wolf has also weighed into the debate, declaring that 'Public Wealth Funds are an idea whose time has come'. Public opinion appears to agree.[25]

The returns seen with sovereign wealth funds are, in themselves, compelling. But I think there is a more instinctive reason why this idea is commanding support now in the UK, from both Left and Right. It resonates with a deep, perhaps too-long buried, ethical memory that the 'commons' is vital to our survival. After all, common land is ancient land. In medieval times, it covered most of the country's less productive acreage, spread across the mountains, moorlands, heathlands and marsh.[26] It was a place of strange and ancient rights – to graze animals, to fish, to take sods of turf for fuel, to turn out pigs in the autumn to eat the beech mast and acorns, to collect wood, and to dig for minerals. These are rights that date back to at least the Norman Conquest and, as we have seen, were crystallized in the 1217 Charter of the Forest's prerogative that 'everybody had *a right of subsistence*, realisable in and through the commons'.[27]

These 'commons' – which even today, cover nearly 3 million acres – were to become the very foundation of England's wealth-owning democracy, for they were the land on which grazed the nation's sheep flocks, which, by the middle of the thirteenth century, meant up to 18 million animals. Their wool, declared the barons, was 'the sovereign merchandise and jewel of this England' making up half the nation's wealth.[28] A sovereign wealth fund taps into this history and cultural memory, for it is a common wealth fund.

Now, we must not pretend that these funds are perfect. There are plenty of risks to worry about. Some funds, because they invest abroad, can lead to capital improvements at home getting ignored. Some funds have made poor investment choices. Others have objectives that could be achieved with some good old-fashioned fiscal rules around keeping budgets in balance. Some do not provide the sort of transparency that, these days, would be essential to ensuring popular support. Many funds are bedevilled by issues around governance, transparency and resilience. And investment strategies would inevitably become a matter of debate in public.

But we cannot let the perfect become the enemy of the good. What we need to do is focus on the two key questions: Where does the money come from? Where does the money go?

Let us start with what the fund could be used for – where the money could go. Around the world, the precise purposes of SWFs vary. Everything depends on the specific needs of the country concerned.

Some nations need to stabilize the volatility that is inevitable with exporting natural resources. Some funds – like Chile's ESSF – are 'rainy day funds' or stabilization funds, on which governments can draw to cover the odd financial crisis in exchange rates or a government budget. Recently, the governments of Qatar, Russia, Singapore and Norway each drew down directly from their SWFs to stabilize public finances when deficits soared. Others made investments to support Covid-stricken economies. In the UAE, the Mubadala Investment Company provided rent relief in the residential, office and hospitality sectors. In Singapore, funds stepped in to recapitalize local firms. The Russian Direct Investment Fund was a key investor in the country's national vaccine programme.

Other funds are designed to invest for the long term, to diversify from, say, a dependency on oil. These 'savings funds' focus on building up national assets – converting assets and revenues in the present into renewable assets and revenues for the future. They tend to have long investment horizons and have often been set up using the proceeds from exploiting natural resources. Others are just looking for higher returns for their foreign exchange reserves, but some are trying to carve out a new position in the world, by, for example, hosting the World Cup. These 'strategic funds' focus on supporting the domestic economy. They may, for instance, concentrate on development (start-up and growth) of strategically important firms and industries, or on seeing mature businesses through periods of change, or on building critical national infrastructure, as in the case of Ireland's ISIF.

Finally, some countries want to boost savings and opportunities for future generations. Singapore's GIC is deliberately designed to transfer wealth from one generation to the next. Recognizing that the Fourth Industrial Revolution will mean that adults will have to start retraining, and retraining again, Singapore decided to begin routing the proceeds of its sovereign wealth funds into individual skills accounts. It uses dividends to credit skills training by way of individual learning accounts, in this way helping to safeguard workers against the wipe-out of jobs by automation and artificial intelligence.

Here in the UK, the basic choice to wrestle with is this: we could either pay out, each year, a little money to everyone; or we could pay out a larger sum to a smaller number of people who need it.

John Penrose, with whom I worked in Parliament, set out

his case in a series of pamphlets and Parliamentary debates. He advanced the view that such a fund would help mobilize investment in critical new national infrastructure, as well as raise funds to help pay down the national debt and offset the gigantic size of future public-pension liabilities.[29] It would, he argued, 'affirm British social justice by ensuring we are not saddling our children and grandchildren with the bills for our lifestyle today, through future debt repayments'.[30]

The centre-left has approached it from a different angle. IPPR research has proposed a Citizen's Wealth Fund, which, it argues, could quickly build to £186 billion by 2029–30, yielding a 4 per cent real return, which would be enough to pay all UK-born 25-year-olds a one-off capital dividend worth £10,000.

The 'dividends for all' model is, in one way, a twist on the concept of Universal Basic Income. Rebadged as a 'Common Wealth dividend', it could be a sum paid to every citizen, into their Universal Basic Capital account. This is an intriguing idea, which, as it happens, reminds us of the history celebrated in the parlours of the Bank of England. There, on the walls, is an 1859 painting of *Dividend Day at the Bank of England*. Painted by George Elgar Hicks, it is a jolly Victorian crowd scene, set in the handsome stone-arched Soane-designed banking hall. The 'quarter-day' was when dividends on bank stock and government securities, or 'Consols', were paid out to personal applicants. With their unvarying interest of 3 per cent per annum, they were the only investment permitted to the trustees of widows, orphans and veterans. Hicks depicts a unique cross-section of Victorian life, a democracy of savers from every social class, drawing their return on the money that had been invested in the engine of Britain's imperial economy.

The IPPR idea carries several big benefits. First and foremost, it is likely to have a lot more impact than an annual payment to everyone from a similar size of fund. In fact, a 4 per cent payout to all adults from that sized pot would only amount to £129 – unlikely to make much of a difference to many individuals. But a one-off payment of £10,000 to twenty-five-year-olds would be a huge contribution to getting started in life. For some, £10,000 might not sound much, but it is a lot more than the net financial worth of 40 per cent of British households. And £10,000 would cover between a third to a quarter of the deposit on a home in eight of Britain's regions.[31] If the dividend were paid into the sort of universal lifetime savings account I have proposed, it would attract tax benefits and provide a down payment to which savers would then add, in a tax-incentivized way, and this could knock more years off the timescale for amassing the savings needed to fund a deposit on a home (bringing down the age at which someone may have enough to buy a house to the early thirties).

There are other potential benefits, too. Such a bonus might well encourage good habits that last a lifetime. Many studies have shown an 'asset effect' on life chances. In fact, the IPPR noted that 'Having some wealth aged 22 is associated with positive impacts when reaching age 33, including participation in work, higher wages, good health, absence of depression and greater political agency.' But it is worth facing up to the political challenges involved. In our KCL Policy Institute polling, we asked the public where the dividends should go. Adding to pension savings was the top choice, with two-fifths (38 per cent) choosing this option, while cutting taxes came second (at 34 per cent). Helping young people to buy a home was ranked as the fifth choice, with just 20 per cent supporting it. So, there would be a task of persuasion ahead.

There is, though, an even bigger challenge: where would the money come from to supply the fund? And here, there is even less consensus.

Around the world, SWFs tend to be set up by countries that generate persistent fiscal or trade surpluses, neither of which the UK enjoys. Some of these funds – like Norway's NBIM – invest abroad, while others, like India's NIIF, invest only at home. But most, like Abu Dhabi's Mubadala, do both. Generally speaking, the funds are used to store windfalls of national wealth to ensure that the money is not all spent at once and that there is a semblance of a wealth transfer to the next generation. The money that goes in tends to come from a wide variety of surpluses – like a balance of payments surplus, or a surplus on a government budget, on foreign currency operations, or through privatizations – and, of course, natural resource exports. The research group Global SWF has reported that:

> 51 per cent of the capital managed by SWFs comes from the revenues derived from the sale of commodities, including oil, gas, copper, phosphate, and diamonds. The other almost half comes from foreign exchange reserves, budget surpluses, issuance of securities, and proceeds from Governments' land sales or other privatizations.[32]

Having spent many months after the Great Financial Crash as Chief Secretary to the Treasury trying to sell things the country did not need, I can tell you it is not easy to find large chunks of cash. And today, the state of the public finances is much worse than it was in 2010. This has been laid bare in an under-studied document, which was one of my innovations in government: the Whole of Government Accounts, which lays out the assets and the liabilities of the entire public sector.

As we saw at the beginning of the chapter, the total value of the nation's public assets is a huge £2.14 trillion. But what I did not tell you is that the nation's liabilities are £5 trillion, dwarfing those assets. The biggest obligations are the public-sector pensions bill, out to the year 2067, which totals £2.2 trillion, or 40 per cent of the liabilities. Gilts – the money that the government has borrowed from people to run the country – total £1.2 trillion. Bank deposits held in the Bank of England and repayable on demand amount to a further £560 billion.

The Treasury's dirty secret is that the net worth of Britain's public sector has been in steep decline since the late 2010s. In fact, it deteriorated by 50 per cent between the Brexit vote and

Covid-19. In 2015, public-sector net wealth stood at a *negative* figure of £1.9 trillion; by 2020, it was a negative figure of £2.8 trillion.[33] If only the UK had saved the money from North Sea oil. Between 1980/81 and 1989/90, oil raised an incredible £166 billion in taxes.[34] Instead of saving that cash, like the canny Norwegians, we cut non-oil taxes. If the UK had been more Norwegian about things, and invested oil revenues in a sovereign wealth fund, it would be worth more than £500 billion today.[35]

However, we are where we are. So we need to be imaginative, and, as Matt Bruenig explains in his excellent short study, there are basically five ways of raising the money for a social wealth fund: we can solicit voluntary contributions; we can ring-fence existing state assets; we can borrow at low interest rates and invest the money in higher yielding investments; we can re-deploy foreign currency reserves or some part of the monetary base; and we can impose judicious levies.[36]

The first source, voluntary contributions, is basically a form of philanthropy. It might be a possibility – after all, the very rich do bequeath assets to the nation – but it feels like a case of hoping for the best, while having to plan for the worst. Then there is potentially ring-fencing some state assets. Now that *is* a good idea. As it happens, the UK still has significant chunks of shares in British banks, which, when sold, could add up to £29 billion. The IPPR recommended using asset sales, including the government stake in Royal Bank of Scotland and the wind-down of the UK Assets Resolution programme. To this, we could also add the Crown Estate and fold in what are called 'dormant assets' – the cash in UK bank and building society accounts that have lain untouched for fifteen years. (These accounts have been valued at £3.7 billion, of which just £2 billion is ever expected to be reunited with their owners.)

In a report published by University College London, Martin Wolf argued that by taking equity in firms with good long-run potential, the funds 'will help create businesses and so an economy that would otherwise never come into being. The public would share in the risks, but also take a share in the rewards'.[37] Future sales of the future radio spectrum for mobile services could add another £10 billion.

An even bigger asset is the state's knowledge capital. Since South Korea's Intellectual Discovery fund first opened in July 2010, sovereign patent funds (SPFs) have begun to show how smart use of intellectual property can be a money-spinner. The UK government's 'knowledge assets' – intellectual property, tech, data and other intangibles – have been valued at around £150 billion. We should fold our public-sector-owned intangibles together and work harder to maximize the yield.

Third in Bruenig's possible money sources is the possibility of borrowing to provide some of the capital base for the fund. Even after the debacle of the short-lived Conservative government of Liz Truss, and her even shorter-lived first chancellor, Kwasi Kwarteng, interest rates on government ten-year bonds were only 3.312 per cent – whereas average returns for sovereign wealth funds, as mentioned, have been north of 8 per cent. So, with these sorts of differentials, it would still be profitable to borrow to invest.

Fourth, there are the foreign currency reserves, which are, in my experience, the most under-discussed assets in British politics. Using foreign exchange reserves has cross-party support. John Penrose, for example, proposed that a UK SWF could be capitalized by using foreign reserves – mimicking the approach taken by Singapore, which is another country without a significant natural-resource base. As it happens, the UK's foreign currency reserves are in remarkably good shape, after a ten-year programme to build up the pot to around £155 billion,[38] where today it sits in the nation's Exchange Equalisation Account. As luck would have it, in 2021 it had a little windfall, as the UK was gifted £19 billion in IMF 'special drawing rights', as part of a global issue of £443 billion worth of new paper, effectively valued against a basket of international currencies. Now, in theory, we should be sharing a chunk of this back with the IMF, to lend on to poorer nations. But we could always move half of the cash equivalent – say, £10 billion – into a social wealth fund.

If we put these four pools of potential sources of investment capital together, we could probably see our way fairly easily to somewhere between £50 billion and £70 billion. That still leaves something of a gap of around £100 billion in order to create a fund of £180–£190 billion, which is probably the minimum investment needed to generate the sort of dividends that would make a difference to the lives of young people. And that implies that a degree of tax revenue – or levies – will be needed to plug the gap. The IPPR has, for example, proposed so-called 'scrip taxes' on the sale of new company shares (up to 3 per cent on listed companies), which require companies either to issue equity to government or pay a tax of an equivalent value. However, this is a similar idea to the founding funds in Sweden that caused such controversy, and which I doubt would command much political support in the UK, because the shares of existing shareholders (who include pension savers) would be diluted.

That therefore leaves us with one further option, which is Matt Bruenig's final source of funds: taxes on capital income and even on wealth itself, rather than just on earned income – and the restoration of some kind of fairness to the UK's crazy tax system...

12

Sharing Among the People

From carpet-bagging to a moral tax code

The great hall of the Royal Institution was crowded for the evening for a display of what looked like magic. On stage, Michael Faraday was about to demonstrate a 'mysterious force'. Born in poverty and apprenticed to a bookbinder aged just thirteen, Faraday had managed to secure work as a young man assisting the great scientist Sir Humphry Davy. Like the sorcerer's apprentice, he was allowed to play with the equipment after clearing away his master's work, and over the course of 1831, Faraday stumbled across the elemental force we now call electromagnetism. Soon, his fame as an accomplished speaker was such that his Christmas lectures, delivered from his now famous bench, were attended by Queen Victoria herself.

But one man, so the story goes, was underwhelmed, as friends of Faraday once described. When Faraday explained the importance of his electrical discoveriess to the lion of British Liberal politics, Sir William Gladstone, the great knight's only comment was: 'But, after all, what use is it?' Quick as lightning, Faraday replied: 'Why, Sir, there is every probability that you will soon be able to tax it!'[1]

In that moment Faraday revealed an evolutionary instinct: that we are hardwired to share. Indeed, sharing is the key to the cooperative instinct that has made us the most successful species on earth, supremely able to act in concert with kin and stranger alike, to combine force, control violence and divide labour. Combining force is especially useful if you like meat and need to kill the larger animals out on the savannah, but hunting in packs is a rarity in nature, and it only works if the hunters share the prey.[2] Equally, our exceptional ability to divide labour allows us to create a hearth to rear our long-dependent children while others go out to forage, but this too rests on our talent to share.[3] So, as humans multiplied and societies grew complex, the invocation to generosity became a defining part of the faiths and fables that Daniel Harari calls the 'imagined orders' – the cultures and religions that enabled millions of strangers to live together in peace.[4] Helping bind together these societies are organised religion, and the mythical storylines that we recognize so well today, variations on battles against a demonized, selfish and egocentric monster. From Humbaba, in the first recorded tales of the hero Gilgamesh, to the Biblical Goliath, from the Greek Medusa and Minotaur to the Norse Grendel, and on to the modern Dracula and Darth Vadar; '[t]he monster,' as Christopher Booker astutely observed, 'is heartless; totally unable to feel for others... Its only real concern is to look after its own interests, at the expense of everyone else in the world.'[5] Until, that is, it is slain by the selfless hero.

Today, these basic instincts to share, and to shame the selfish, are what underpin the ruler's right to tax. And that is the power that is the quintessence of the states – 'the strongest, the most pervading of all the powers of government'.[6]

Admittedly, no-one relishes paying tax. But most of us know, as the famous former Supreme Court Justice Oliver Wendell Holmes put it: 'Taxes are what we pay for a civilized society.' But truly civilized societies are fair societies with tax codes that reflect our moral codes, where the rich support the poor, where windfalls are fairly shared, and where we help each other to flourish. Sadly, today the tax system in the UK is riddled with unfairness. It poorly shares windfalls of gifts and grace, and so we fail to mobilize the resources needed to help everyone live the life they could. Without progressive taxation, as James Meade argued all those years ago, the rich will carry on getting richer and inequality will simply grow. To fix today's inequality of wealth, we have already seen how we must raise the rate of growth and earnings, create a Universal Basic Capital and back it with a sovereign wealth fund. The final piece of the puzzle is to return fairness to the tax system.

As it happens, my polling with the KCL Policy Institute revealed that the British public has an excellent sense of where to start. Overall, we found that that UK adults see tax reform as the No. 1 way to fix inequality in Britain – more important than improvements to social security, health, education, housing, employment or equalities policy. And the two priorities the public preferred most were, first, reducing tax avoidance and the use of tax havens – by far the most popular choice, supported by a third (32 per cent) – and second, introducing a new annual wealth tax on individual net wealth of over £10 million (16 per cent).

It seems that if we want to raise the resources we need to build new institutions like sovereign wealth funds, to pay out dividends to the young, or to build more social housing, we need to mobilize the money by overhauling the way we tax (or do not tax) carpet-bagging and capital.[7]

The original carpet-baggers were American Northerners who swept into the South to exploit the economic chaos after the American Civil War – to make a fast buck and leave without paying their dues. But the history of Britain's Exchequer reveals that we too have been cursed by the same sort of behaviour for at least seven centuries. Back in 1340, Edward III threw his Baron of the Exchequer, William de la Pole, into the Tower of London after widespread fraud wrecked his plan for wool taxes. Almost seven hundred years later, as I sat down to write this chapter, tax controversy engulfed another exchequer chief, Nadhim Zahawi.

In July 2022, the day after Zahawi took the helm of the Treasury, the *Independent* newspaper reported that the National Crime Agency was looking into his finances. A flurry of threatening letters from his lawyers failed to stem the flow of further revelations. Days later, it emerged that HMRC was probing the chancellor's tax affairs, only to provoke a protest from Mr Zahawi, who asserted that 'I've always declared my taxes, and paid my taxes in the UK.' In January 2023, however, the *Sun on Sunday* revealed that Mr Zahawi, then Conservative Party chairman, had agreed to stump up a *seven-figure* sum to settle a dispute with HMRC, including a substantial fine for *not* paying the full sums owed.[8] When the prime minister finally confirmed that none of the income in question had been declared as it should have been, Mr Zahawi was sacked.

To understand carpet-bagging better, I spoke to the journalist and former tax adviser Dan Neidle, who first helped reveal the Zahawi affair, which was described to Dan by an HMRC tax inspector as the result of 'man-in-the-pub-level tax advice'. At least in this case, as Dan explained, 'the law worked the way it should. HMRC did the job they should have done'. But the case underlines a basic truth: like Gollum guarding his stolen magic ring, many of the very rich go to great lengths to hide their treasure. In fact, the economists Abhijit Bannerjee and Esther Duflo recently noted that 'Even in famously honest Scandinavia, [where]... only 3 per cent of personal taxes are avoided... the very rich are much more serious offenders.'[9] In fact, one study showed that the richest 0.01 per cent of people in Norway, Sweden and Denmark evaded 25–30 per cent of the personal taxes they owed.[10]

Carpet-bagging costs Britain a fortune. There is an enormous 'tax gap'. The difference between tax that is collected and that which is 'theoretically due if all individuals and companies complied with both the letter of the law and HMRC's interpretation of the intention of Parliament in setting law' cost the UK an incredible £36 billion in 2021–22, the highest level for seven years.[11]

For several years now, Robert Watts, editor of the *Sunday Times* Rich List, has also published a Tax List. It is not perfect, he admits, but it gives a good feel. And what it shows is that the big employers – especially the large high-street retailers – seem to pay a lot of Employer's National Insurance, corporation tax, stamp duty and VAT. But at the same time, Robert told me, 'there still are many, many people who are featured prominently in the *Sunday Times* Rich List, who do not *ever* appear in the *Sunday Times* Tax List.'

Tax avoidance has been around since tax began, but the modern form of the cancer dates back to the years after the First World War, when the shifting of income offshore was first described in Parliament as 'legal avoidance' in contrast to 'evasion by omission'. In later years, those keen to avoid tax became masters of moving headquarters to a low-tax country and loading cost on subsidiaries in high-tax nations, to keep the overall global tax liability of businesses low. In addition, the very rich learned to swaddle their assets in a mystery, inside a privilege, inside another low-tax country. So, assets were moved to 'trusts' that were hard for tax inspectors to peer into. These were often owned by companies in privileged offshore 'secrecy jurisdictions', half of which were in the Anglo-zone of British Overseas Territories and Crown dependencies, like Jersey or the British Virgin Islands. In turn, these companies were owned by organizations headquartered in very low-tax jurisdictions, like Luxembourg.

The sheer scale of wealth held in these offshore networks today is staggeringly unclear, but also, very likely, staggering in size.[12] Alex Cobham is chief executive of the Tax Justice Network and a pioneering campaigner for tax reform. His Network estimates that an incredible £17 to £26 trillion in financial assets are sitting offshore in tax havens, avoiding almost £350 billion in tax every year.[13] When we sat down to chat, he made a critical point. The secrecy that surrounds these numbers is a violation of the deal we struck with business more than a century ago, when the status of 'limited liability' was created. 'We allow limited liability for companies,' Alex explains, '[so] you don't have to put your children's house or whatever at risk to set up a business. We give you limited liability. But the deal is you give us transparency, you publish annual accounts, you tell us who's behind the company so that anyone doing business with you can have confidence.' After all, it is in the public interest for us to know that there is not a secret monopoly at work, or that the company is not actually bankrupt, and that the company is not owned by someone able to make or adjudicate the rules, such as the regulator or politicians. The bottom line, Alex explains, is that 'no market works better when we don't know who's behind the people acting in the market'. Yet that is exactly what has happened, as the rich seek to obscure what they own.

In the wake of the Great Financial Crisis, the G20 was whipped into action to begin fighting international tax fraud with rather more rigour. At the time of writing, we are yet to see whether new reforms led by President Biden, to ensure a global minimum corporation tax of 15 per cent, will bear fruit. But currently, we sabotage the best of our intentions when we sign international trade deals that forget about tax. A few years ago I sat on the International Trade Select Committee. One afternoon, in the Houses of Parliament, I asked one of the UK's most senior trade officials about the way we put tax into the mix of negotiating new trade treaties. I was stunned by the answer: 'I think I am right in saying that including tax commitments in free trade agreements would be quite novel. It certainly is not something that was considered in [the] TransAtlantic Trade and Investment Partnership.'

So how do we end the injustice? Well, Step One is perhaps the simplest – and it almost sounds banal: hire more tax inspectors. It is a good investment. Tax collecting costs His Majesty's Revenue and Customs less than a penny for every £1 it collects. That is a pretty efficient way to raise revenue, yet even though tax fraud costs the Treasury an estimated £20 billion – *nine times* more than the £2.2 billion lost to benefit fraud, HMRC employs 3.5 times fewer officials than the Department for Work and Pensions on compliance checks. Between 2009 and 2019, there have been 85,745 criminal prosecutions for benefits crimes, compared to just 3,665 prosecutions for tax crime.[14]

Step Two requires new rules to combat tax avoidance. Historically, UK tax law was targeted at specific problems; there was never a 'general anti-avoidance rule' to bar egregious behaviour designed to subvert the spirit of the law. Instead, ministers played 'whack-a-mole', hammering problems as they came to light. There has been some progress. There was a slew of changes to tighten up the system following the advent of 'mass marketed tax avoidance', sold by banks like Barclays and adopted by so many famous figures. This included the introduction, in 2013, of a 'general anti-abuse rule', which allows HMRC to 'call in' schemes if 'one of the main purposes' is to secure some sort of 'tax advantage'.[15] Dan Neidle told me that with these new provisions now in place, 'tax avoidance today is really, really hard. With a few exceptions it tends to be done by total chancers and fraudsters selling schemes to greedy people who don't know any better'. But there is still the basic weakness that the relevant criminal offence – 'cheating the public revenue' – is extremely difficult to prove in avoidance cases where, however outlandish the evidence, the 'accused' can claim that they were honestly following professional advice. And then, the professional advisers can claim that they were giving an honest opinion.

All this shines a light on the role of the dominant accounting firms. 'You have to look at the role of the big four and a couple of law firms, who are really doing the key lobbying on corporate tax,' Alex Cobham told me. 'We can think of, you know, Amazon and Google and these guys [who pay very little], but they're not really doing [the lobbying] for themselves. It's their sets of professional enablers who take the key lobbying role.'[16]

Step Three is to build better radar: specifically, global registers, so that we actually know who owns what, or at least who is the beneficial owner of which assets, together with the automatic exchange of information between banks of all tax havens and foreign tax authorities, backed by proper sanctions for bad actors. Here, we *are* slowly making progress. After the outrage of Russia's invasion of Ukraine in 2022, the UK government was shamed into rapidly passing an Economic Crime Bill. It was hopelessly inadequate at first, and the rage that was provoked sparked my favourite WhatsApp group – the Russian Sanctions Group – in which twenty cross-party MPs, myself included, quickly developed amendments to toughen up the bill. The government accepted almost every idea. And yet, as I write, the key idea of a register of beneficial ownership of property looks set to be defeated by hundreds of people disguising their ownership of UK real estate by means of registering it in blind trusts, located in – yes –tax havens.

Finally, as Step Four, we need actually to give Parliament some proper oversight of the system. Given that the English fought a civil war about Parliament's role in granting tax, it is frankly bizarre that Parliament is kept so far away from the way our tax system operates. There is more Parliamentary oversight of the Intelligence Services than there is of the tax authorities. Given what is at stake, that has to change.

Like the trials of Sisyphus, the war on carpet-baggers will be long, boring and never complete. It remains vital. But even victory will not be enough to reverse the inequality of wealth we have allowed to grow. And so, with taxation, we need a second front. As Dan Neidle put it to me: even if outright tax avoidance is now hard, the key issue is that 'there are still lots of ways for the rich to not pay tax... ways the Parliament has either enabled or permitted. It's a policy failure.' So, if we want to raise the money to reverse the inequality of wealth, to build new social homes, or raise an additional £30 billion a year to help create our new sovereign wealth fund, we will need to restore fairness to the tax system and reform tax, either on capital gains, capital income or capital, or all three.

Historically, the UK compromise on tax was to tax the income of the living and the wealth of the dead. But unlike the days of William the Conqueror and his son, we do not even have a comprehensive picture of the wealth of the nation.

It is not a simple task to see the Domesday Book today, guarded as it is, deep in a temperature-controlled vault in the UK's National Archives. But the book is a testament to the bureaucratic precocity of Norman England. In desperate need to pay his mercenaries, William urgently required a survey of his new dominions to see what taxes he could levy. And so, at Christmastime 1085, he ordered that surveyors be sent out to all quarters of their counties to gather evidence and carefully record the value of things as they were in the days of old King Edward 'the Confessor' – who ruled England until 1066 ushered in Harold's brief tenure – along with the values in 1066 and 1085.

It was a huge undertaking. William died before the job was finished, but the result was actually two books, known later as 'Little Domesday' and 'Great Domesday', catalogued as part of the Exchequer Treasury of Receipt and recording – on parchment made from sheep, goat, roe deer and calf – the £73,000 that constituted the nation's eleventh-century wealth, from that of the king down to every cottager.[17] The books revolutionized writing, just as they transformed the art of record-keeping: there was nothing so ambitious until the Victorian census. And it would be impossible to write today. Because we no longer know where the wealth of the nation is squirrelled away, especially by those in possession of a healthy fortune.

But we do know that wealth has multiplied, and so the debate about tax reform has grown louder. UK net household wealth has tripled since the turn of the century from £4.3 trillion in 2000 to £12.2 trillion in 2021,[18] but tax revenues on wealth, as a proportion of GDP, have remained broadly unchanged. In 2022–23, UK government revenues were £1,017 billion, and income tax, National Insurance contributions and VAT receipts made up three-fifths of all revenues – around a quarter of GDP.[19] But taxes on 'capital' are just 1.8 per cent of GDP, with council tax on property adding just 1.5 per cent of GDP: tiny fractions.

This muddled design means that the wealthiest pay taxes at roughly the same rate, if not a lower rate, than the poorest. As you can imagine, this is a contentious argument. But if someone draws income from wealth, like investments or a second home, they pay lower tax rates than someone earning the equivalent amount from wages, and some, like those with the controversial 'non-dom' status, are allowed to live in the UK but not pay British taxes on their overseas investments. When the Resolution Foundation looked at this, it found average tax rates from 1977 to 2017 to be 'remarkably flat across the income distribution, with rates of between 27 and 36 per cent for all income groups in 2017'.[20] The reason was a combination of 'progressive direct taxation (income tax, National Insurance and council tax) and regressive indirect taxation'. How can this be so?

Well, at the time of writing, the top rate of tax, when all is said and done, is 47 per cent.[21] But income from 'capital' is taxed at much lower rates: income from dividends is only 39.35 per cent, at the highest ('additional') rate, while tax on capital gains can be as low as 10 per cent. These perks benefit the richest most, because, as mentioned, an incredible 57 per cent of investment income in the UK goes to the richest 10 per cent of people. Indeed, if you are lucky enough to be earning more than £1 million, then you're likely to take almost one-fifth – 19 per cent – of your income from capital.[22] And that is five times more than for those earning £20,000 to £30,000.

Dr Arun Advani and his colleague Andy Summers have taken a look at the taxes paid by the UK's richest individuals.[23] They found that the average person with more than £2 million in taxable income paid only 40 per cent, and one in ten people earning more than £1 million paid tax at a lower overall rate than someone earning just £15,000. In fact, the average person earning more than £10 million had an effective tax rate of just 21 per cent – which is around the rate paid by Prime Minister Rishi Sunak on his £2 million of income.[24] That rate is less than the rate that would be paid by someone on median earnings of £30,000.

To improve on these iniquities, we need better taxes for the wealthy. James Meade himself recognized the point. 'The case for an annual tax on capital wealth is... a strong one,' he wrote, and the least worst tax to halt rising inequality, while protecting incentives to invest, was, in his view, a tax 'upon the value of the total property owned by the taxpayer'.[25] But care is needed to get this right. Traditional economic analysis would tell us that taxing wealth has problems. If wealth is 'productive capital' (think machines, houses, etc.), then taxing its returns is inefficient, because it can reduce growth by discouraging investment in productive capital. A second problem is that the rich may simply pass on the cost of increased capital taxes to the poor by cutting wages.[26] Moreover, much of the increase in wealth in recent years has been due to low interest rates pumping up the value of housing and pensions, which now account for almost £4 in every £5 of UK household wealth. Many holders of this wealth could only wallow in it if they were to liquidate the assets and consume the capital. But if they cannot liquidate their assets, it is very hard for them to pay an annual levy – especially if the tax goes up automatically, simply because asset prices rise every time interest rates fall.

Despite these challenges, it will prove impossible to reverse today's sky-high levels of income inequality without some measure of tax on capital gains, capital income or on big pots of giant fortunes worth over £10 million, which have of course been inflated by almost £1 trillion of quantitative easing. As Alex Cobham puts it, 'ultimately, you can taper income inequalities through taxing incomes and profits. But if the stock of inequality isn't being changed, then we are locking in generational inequalities that aren't going to change'.

The UK government last considered a wealth tax in the mid-1970s, when a government review concluded that a wealth tax was 'not sufficiently justified... apart possibly from a tax on occupation of high net value property'. There are now just three OECD members (Norway, Spain and Switzerland) that have such a tax in place, compared to twelve in 1990.[27] But none of the G7 economies has raised more than 1 per cent of national income in revenue from estate, inheritance and gift taxes in any one year over the last forty. Nevertheless, most economists believe that wealth taxes could help reduce global inequality if we could solve a slew of problems.[28] A better philosophy than taxing 'wealth' may, in fact, be to 'tax the wealthy' – and the most obvious place to begin is to tax the capital value of assets when they are transferred.

Dr Arun Advani has been one of the two driving academic forces behind the first UK Wealth Tax Commission to look at this question, properly, in fifty years. In a set of remarkable papers, he and his intellectual partners have transformed the debate about how to restore fairness to the tax system. And of course, the first problem is the challenge William the Conqueror wrestled with all those years ago: the lack of a good register of who owns what. As Arun explained, 'HMRC could ask questions about these things,' but it does not, and 'that hinders policymaking'. So, even if a minister were asked for options to develop a wealth tax, it would be pretty hard for officials to answer. So, 'we don't have good data because we choose not to collect', and this means, as Arun continued, 'the closest thing people have to look at the super rich is things like the *Sunday Times* Rich List'. And there, the sudden appearance of Rishi Sunak and Akshata Murthy, with a hitherto unknown wealth in excess of £700 million, illustrates the data problem. 'There are countless other Rishi Sunaks out there who aren't in the list,' Arun went on. 'Anecdotally, we know from advisers, there's a lot they can name.' The fact that we do not know about wealth levels means that in politics we cannot think or debate clearly about what a wealth tax might bring.

After debating his ideas for the last two years, Arun is now very clear about three priorities. First, we have to think beyond the idea that we can only raise tax from the current big three of income tax, National Insurance and VAT. Second, if we want to raise more money, we have to start equalizing tax on investment income. But third, if we want to reverse wealth inequality, Arun is clear that we *will* need some form of one-off wealth tax on the 20,000 largest fortunes, worth over £10 million.

Let us start with the easiest changes, beginning with 'non-doms'. Being non-domiciled, as Akshata Murthy was before she changed her tax status, means living in the UK but claiming that your permanent home is somewhere abroad.[29] UK residents must pay full UK tax (and inheritance tax) on *all* income and gains, wherever in the world they have made it. Non-doms do not. In 2017–18, for example, this lucky group of 26,000 individuals made about £1 billion in UK investment income and capital gains, and £19.9 billion abroad. It confirms something that Robert Watts noticed when he was putting together the *Sunday Times* Tax List. 'We are a haven in this country to the super-rich,' he told me:

> ... and many politicians over the years have told us it's very good for us to have these people here because they create jobs – but actually often that's just not the case. They may be paying up a chunk of stamp duty on that house they bought

in Belgravia. But not in terms of actually creating businesses here that create jobs and pay a lot of tax.

Ending the non-dom tax break would yield £3.2 billion.[30] And some polling suggests that more than half of the public would support making this change.[31]

Second, if we want to start equalizing tax on investment income, we could insist that National Insurance is paid on such income, just as it is on wages.[32] National Insurance raises a huge amount of money: £143 billion in 2020–21, to which NI on investment income could bring in an additional £8.6 billion. (National Insurance is also politically acceptable: it happens to be rated second among the 'fairest' taxes, after taxes on cigarettes and alcohol.)

Third, we could equalize the rate of capital gains tax with income tax which would return us to the days of 1988, when Margaret Thatcher's chancellor, the decidedly unsocialist Nigel Lawson, did exactly this. It would raise £15.6 billion. There are many reasons why this is fair, among them the fact that much of the wealth accumulation of the last twenty-five years has simply been driven by lower interest rates, and there is very little basis in economic theory for allowing windfall gains like that to go largely untaxed. In particular, the Bank of England's £895 billion injection of quantitative easing knocked, at best guess, 0.8 per cent off interest rates, which helped inflate asset prices and dramatically increased absolute levels of wealth inequality. The idea enjoys big support in polling.[33]

These changes alone – run for just three years – would be almost enough to raise the money needed to complete the build of a £186 billion sovereign wealth fund (assuming we start with around £85 billion in state assets, and deliver the average 8 per cent return). But if we are feeling braver, we might add reform of inheritance tax to the list, not least because once someone amasses an estate worth more than £10 million, the rate of tax collected effectively collapses – because the richest have found ways to give away the money. There was a minor hullabaloo when it emerged that King Charles III was to pay nothing on his inheritance from his mother, but the truth is that, had the king paid tax, he would have been the exception, which is one big reason why inheritance tax is widely seen as unfair.

The best reform might require us to cease levying the tax on the estate and rather to levy it as a gift tax, paid by the person who receives the money – as happens in most OECD countries.[34] And perhaps the level could be based on how much recipients get in their lifetimes. This is much fairer, because it means that those who have inherited more in the past pay tax at a higher rate on additional receipts.

Perhaps most controversial of all are the taxes on property, largely a combination of council tax and stamp duty on buying new homes. Today, this is about 3.4 per cent of GDP,[35] but it is widely unfair, because council tax does not have regular revaluations, unlike business rates, and it is based on a series of bands rather than a precise valuation. As a result, the average home in Blackpool pays around £2,000 a year, compared to a home in Westminster which pays on average £829.[36] This means, as campaigner Andrew Dixon from Fairer Shares told me, that the owner of a Hartlepool property worth say, £150,000, is paying over 1 per cent of the value of the house in tax, whereas the owner of a Westminster property worth £8 million is paying just 0.02 per cent. Altogether, the UK housing stock is currently valued at nearly £4 trillion, so the Fairer Share campaign estimates that an annual tax rate of, say, 0.48 per cent would raise enough funds to cover the £36.7 billion currently raised by both council tax and stamp duty.[37]

However, like Alex Cobham, Arun Advani makes the case that if we care about *reversing* the wealth concentration at the very top – say those worth £10 million or more – we have to look beyond capital gains tax, inheritance tax and the like. 'They're all good things to do,' concludes Arun, 'but that's not going to reduce wealth concentration at the very top. So, if you see that as a problem, your only option is an actual wealth tax.'

Until the UK Wealth Tax Commission was established in 2020 and produced its report, the most comprehensive recent proposals for such a change were tabled in the United States, by the Democratic senators Elizabeth Warren and Bernie Sanders.[38] They proved popular: one poll found Warren's ideas were supported by 54 per cent of the public and opposed by just 19 per cent. But to design a wealth tax, we have to answer some basic questions about who pays, on what, when, how much – and how.

So, should we charge only adults, or should we consider children as well? Should taxes be levied on individuals, or should an assessment be made of couples? Any new wealth tax will need to deal with issues like residency, domicile, citizenship, the very location of assets and the stubborn business of who is telling the truth. What about trusts? Should non-residents pay tax on their assets parked in the UK? Should non-doms be exempted? Most countries limit tax on non-residence to real estate and business enterprise, but should the scope be wider than this?

Then there is the 'what'. If it were to be truly comprehensive, a wealth tax would cover all forms of personal wealth. But should a pension pot be taxed? What about somebody's main home minus the mortgage? How do we value things? Around the world, many wealth taxes are based on open-market value but allow fixed discounts, compared to a past transaction, or use some kind of banded approach, and this tends to lead to complexities and distortions. Market value can be affected by the legal form in which the estate is owned. If we are trying to levy wealth taxes on these every year, the problems become particularly acute. How, for example, do we value paintings in a booming arts market? What about unquoted company shares? Or land that is likely to get planning permission? What should be the deductible liabilities? And so on.

The third design question is *when* to levy the tax. Inheritance tax applies to the value of somebody's wealth when they die and the wealth is transferred to heirs. Stamp duty taxes apply when a property is transferred (bought), and stamp duty bites on the sale of shares. As we have seen, the UK also taxes returns of wealth, so that income tax is paid on dividends from shares, rent from property and investment income like savings interest. Capital gains tax, on the other hand, bites on the gains realized when an asset is sold.

Then there is 'how much' and 'how'. If we have a regular tax on wealth, instead of, say, a windfall tax, we would need to consider who can actually pay it.[39] There will be many people who own assets but do not have the income to pay tax on them.

There is, therefore, a long list of design issues. And this is before we tackle the lobbying for all kinds of exemptions that reflect political priorities – like investing in farmland or small businesses, or pension assets, or artwork – or crucially, the rights or wrongs of taxing something retrospectively. Finally, despite the theoretical possibility of acquiring more data on wealth holdings and their values, we must acknowledge that wealth is notoriously hard to track down.

Despite all these daunting challenges, the Wealth Tax Commission cut through many of the issues. It proposed that tax be levied on an individual on a one-off basis, each year, for five years, and the basis for taxing included *all* property. Assets would be valued based on their open-market value. However, householders would have the right to challenge the valuation. For those without cash to hand, payments could be deferred by those who are 'asset-rich-cash-poor', and some measures would be needed to reduce unnecessary hardship.

Arun's big conclusion was that there is virtue in setting a high threshold for those who are levied. Why? Because this gives tax authorities a small number of people to survey, who can therefore be surveyed in a great deal of detail and precision. As Arun explained to me, 'They already have accountants and whoever else, so their stuff is fairly well managed already.' And the fruits could be extraordinary. A 1-per-cent tax on everyone with assets of more than £10 million could bring in between £10–£11 billion a year.[40] And what is even more intriguing is the level of political support for the idea. In a poll conducted in late 2022, Professor Ben Ansell found that a wealth tax 'was significantly more popular than other ways of raising revenue across all taxpayer groups'. Well over half (56.3 per cent) of people agreed with the statement that we should have a net wealth tax on the wealthiest, and the idea was three times more popular than raising the top rates of income tax.

Reforming wealth taxes, or taxes on the wealthy, will be hard. For Conservatives, tax in general, and low tax in particular, has become almost sacred, a defining part of the creed. However, down the ages – from the Plantagenets to the Victorians – tax strategy has proved critical to national strategy. There is no 'grand strategy' for any country without a strategy for collecting and sharing the harvest. And if we want to build a wealth-owning democracy in the twenty-first century, we cannot avoid the argument on tax – but we should not underestimate the political battle. In his research, Ben Ansell identified several lines of objection he heard from the public:

'Wealth can follow circumstance. A modest house in the right neighbourhood can become quite valuable.'

'Taxing wealth of OAPs in expensive properties would be punitive. Income may wax and wane with some high incomes.'

'People have worked for their possessions but will not miss a percentage from source as much.'

'People who inherit wealth shouldn't be punished, neither should people who work hard and start their own successful business.'

'People work hard and risk their capital in stocks; they shouldn't be punished for success.'

Assuaging these concerns will not be easy. And so, the first step may need to be an exercise in information gathering: effectively setting a 0-per-cent tax on assets above £10 million, in order to allow the HMRC to build a comprehensive picture, a modern Domesday Book, of who has which assets, and from which sources. With a few facts at hand, the political argument may be an awful lot easier to win.

Ultimately, the argument for fair tax has got to be presented as a strategy for rebuilding a country where there is just reward for hard work. Fair tax must be the means by which we can build societies where everyone can get on in life, no matter where they are born. The morality of most would say that your success in life should reflect what you merit, not simply what you inherit. But today your wealth owes far less to your dreams and abilities; it is more about your genes: what the market of the day happens to pay for the gifts you happen to be born with and, more important, the gifts you happen to enjoy from your parents – be that education, estates, endowments or an entrée to useful networks. The British public know this.

In my polling with the KCL Policy Institute, we found that the public is more likely to think that wealth comes from factors outside one's own control, rather than from personal hard work. More than four in five (85 per cent) felt that factors linked to *social background* were now the most important explanations of why some people have wealth and others do not; 73 per cent of our survey said that coming from a wealthy family was the most important explanation for wealth, followed by 41 per cent who cited 'having useful networks'. By contrast, *just over a third*

(35 per cent) thought success was all down to hard work, and only a tenth (11 per cent) saw wealth as coming down to positive factors such as being organized.

A country that no longer believes in hard work as the way to get on is a country in jeopardy. That is why we must repair and rebuild the ladders that help people climb up in life. And that is not free. The money has to come from somewhere. And it *can* come from restoring fairness to the tax system.

Ultimately, the key to the argument must be an appeal to the 'fairness' triggers that have evolved over millennia of history. We have to insist that the tax code reflects our country's moral code. So, when voters ask whether their taxes will go up, the answers are 'only if you are dodging your dues', or 'only if you pay yourself in capital gains, because your tax rate is lower than your cleaner's', or 'only if you are pumping greenhouse gas pollution into the air and accelerating the climate crisis'. As it happens, the majority of the public agree with these ideas.

As Brooke Harrington told me, in a world where norms change faster than laws, it may be perfectly possible to harness our basic psychology to build support for paying taxes, much as the campaign group of high net-worth Americans called the 'Patriotic Millionaires' have shown. Their line, 'patriots pay their taxes', is frankly one of the best lines I have seen in politics anywhere. Brooke argues that we cannot beat tax avoidance by simply changing laws. 'I don't think you can fight them on that terrain,' she told me.

> Any new law you might throw at them will be unsuccessful because they have more money than you do. They have more time than you do. They can do this all day. And you can't. So does that mean you can't win? No. You just have to fight on a different terrain.

We have to appeal to their thirst for respect and dignity – and their fear of shame in being exposed as avoiding their dues. In

Brooke's view, 'If millions of people all over the world can be persuaded to do dumb and self-destructive things like planking, eating Tide [detergent] pods, dumping buckets of ice water on their heads, they can also be persuaded that paying your taxes is cool.'

Nothing in the battle to solve inequality is easy. As I have tried to show in these last few chapters, there is no one silver bullet, but there is a combination of ideas that could, together, make a difference. These ideas are not impossible with the requisite political will, economic sense and public support. Together, they are far, far better than war or revolution, which historically is the only way serious inequality has been reversed. If we do nothing, the chasm between those with the greatest wealth and those with the least, between the riches of assets and the poverty of wages, looks set to grow. It is time to reverse that trend.

In the spirit of Kennedy, we must choose to tackle inequality not because it is easy, but because it is hard, and 'because that goal will serve to organize and measure the best of our energies and skills'.

Conclusion

Freedom and the Moral Economy

After a long and painful illness, Adam Smith breathed his last on 17 July 1790, at Panmure House, his home in the heart of Edinburgh's Canongate district. In the years that followed, politics and economics were transformed by an epic battle between an old tradition and a new discipline.

On the one hand, there were the old ideals of the moral economy – a just wage, just prices and justice in exchange. On the other, there was the new 'science' of the market economy, extolled by William Pitt the Younger and his so-called 'Friends', whose 'divinities' were said to be the 'the ledger and the cashbox'.[1] At war with revolutionary France abroad, it was Pitt who prevailed at home, as his alliance swept away 'the old Tudor paternalism' in the name of utilitarian 'progress'. This represented – in the words of the Fabian Sidney Webb, a century later – the 'destructive criticism of all the venerable relics of the past', creating a new world in which the '"devil-take-the-hindmost" became the accepted social creed of what was still perceived to be a Christian nation'.[2] Old protections of wages were abolished. The Corn Laws set prices to favour the rich. The laws that guaranteed a 'right to live' and which subsidized low wages were wound down and then abolished. 'Never perhaps in all modern history,' wrote the anthropologist Karl Polanyi, 'has a more ruthless act of social reform been perpetrated.'[3]

Yet the ideals of the moral economy never died. Artists, politicians, Christians, Chartists, trade unionists, the pioneers of the Cooperative movements, and even industrialists and entrepreneurs like Robert Owen, George Cadbury and John Spedan Lewis, kept the flame alive. Few were as influential as John Ruskin. His violent reaction to the utilitarians and 'political economists' was a paean to the virtues of the moral economy, which he dated to 'the first commercial words' written in 1090 in the church of San Giacomo di Rialto in Venice, the first great commercial emporium of Europe: 'Around this temple, let the Merchant's Law be just, his weights true and his contracts guileless.'[4] Ruskin's best-selling book of essays, *Unto This Last*, was said to be the single most influential volume among the first Labour MPs. The work took its title from the parable of the vineyard workers in the Gospel of St Matthew (20: 1–16), and it put centre-stage a simple notion of justice: 'the economic relationship between employer and employee' it argued 'is not one of profit and advantage, but of justice', rooted in a recognition that all people have equal needs and reciprocal responsibilities.[5]

This was the tradition not of market supremacy, but of the supremacy of society – a tradition that dates back to the first marketplaces of Babylon, to the dialogues of the Greeks, to the laws of the Romans and to the canons of the Christian Fathers. It was well understood by Adam Smith, who wrote in *The Wealth of Nations* that 'Every man, *as long as he does not violate the laws of justice,* is left perfectly free to pursue his own interest his own way.' And it was a tradition renewed for the twentieth century by Roosevelt's New Dealers and Clement Attlee's Labour landslide in 1945.

*

For the last fifty years that radical tradition of moral economy has been hard to see through the smoke, as it was torched across the West. But the market supremacism that took its place has delivered, with its privilege, technopolies and bubbles, an inequality that is rising so fast that it threatens the politics of cooperation today. Which is why it is time, once more, for the radical tradition to enjoy a renaissance. This *is* possible, given the changes that lie ahead. At stake is the nature of freedom in the twenty-first century.

Freedom is never fixed. Progress shifts its frontiers. And over the decades to come, we *could* have liberties, options, choices and control that we can only dream of today for the simple reason that the possibilities of life are about to be transformed.

Change is now so fast that the fantasies of science fiction have become reality before our eyes. Ideas that featured in *Blade Runner, Star Trek* or *Star Wars* – like bionic limbs, mobile phones, artificial intelligence, 3D printing, tablets, space stations and driverless cars – are already with us. The pace of change will only get faster as 9 million scientists – 90 per cent of all the scientists who have ever lived – sweat to invent the future.

The baby born today might grow up in an age where billions of people are more enlightened than frightened about what tomorrow might bring. That child might still be around well after the year 2100, thanks to a transformation of health care, where a dozen game-changing biotech and pharmaceutical breakthroughs could, together, add a decade to the human life, as genome sequencing, gene-based medicine, AI, quantum computing and cellular medicine all combine. The nearly real-time speeds of 5G will let haptic interfaces transmit the physical sense of touch, transforming telehealth, telesurgery and emergency A&E services.

These changes will help the world's population expand by one-sixth – another 1 billion people – by 2050. And despite the catastrophic setbacks of Covid-19, the global middle class will likely swell by another 2 billion people before 2030, creating an ever bigger global market. Almost everyone will be online. Within our lifetimes, we will see global gigabit connectivity joining together everyone and everything, everywhere, at ultra-low cost. As early as 2030, the entire planet might well be connected to the Internet, drawing in another 3 billion individuals, and driving tens of trillions of pounds into the global economy.

Within a generation, these consumers will spend more on content than any other product category. Two billion people already have the tools to create and distribute original content. And everyday goods and services (finance, insurance, education and entertainment) are being digitized and becoming fully demonetized, available to the new middle class on mobile devices.

Meanwhile, quantum computing will soon outgrow its infancy, and a first generation of commercial devices will help us solve real-world problems, like simulating complex chemical reactions and slashing the cost of research and development. Quantum chemistry will let us design new materials faster.

Soon, carbon footprints may be viewed as being as socially unacceptable as drink-driving. With a few exceptions, the whole world knows it must go green, creating gigantic opportunities for those who make the technologies that cut carbon. In transport and logistics, the rise of electric vehicles, autonomous vehicles and drones will not only cut carbon, they will collapse the costs of geography.

Taken together, these changes will drive a doubling of the world's annual economic output by 2060, adding nearly £100 trillion.[6] But to whom will this new wealth flow? Will it go to those who already have so much? Or will we seize the moment to change course, to turn back from the road to dystopia and set a different course towards building a renewed wealth-owning democracy?

Let us be clear about the risks. If we fail to reconstruct that wealth-owning democracy, we risk a catastrophe in the 'heartland of democratic capitalism'.[7] We risk a world of private power sentinelled by plutocracy, where the wealthiest snap their fingers at their servants in the marketplace and their puppets in the corridors of power.[8] We risk the rise of 'private government', where freedom is lost to a new corporate domination, where we have little choice but to comply if we want to stay in any kind of work, trapped in an obedient hierarchy, a servile dependency, always at the mercy of others.

Because wealth seeks power, our politics will 'drift to oligarchy', a land described by Martin Wolf as one of 'connections capitalism', in which 'the political system is exploited for the personal gain of the powerful and their relatives, favorites, and supporters'.[9] In this world, where the strong have licence to exploit the weak, the trust that is required for market exchange breaks down.[10]

It would be naive to think that this kind of inequality will not affect politics. It will. Not only will it risk new levels of corruption, it will ossify and embitter societies, where, quite simply, it will become ever harder for ordinary people to get on in life. A surge-tide of super-inequality may spark a chain reaction of graft that leads to rage; and rage leads to schism. As notions of the common good evaporate, some states may even break apart for the simple reason that they will have weakened the cords that bind a nation. Populists will be empowered, because, ostensibly, they rage against elites. But populists in power tend to weaken states and sow division, and so they simply strengthen the hand of separatists, who grow stronger.

The worst-case scenario is very bad. In a more fractured world, smaller states, giant corporations, megacities and non-state actors (like terrorists and organized crime groups) all compete for power. It will become harder to govern the 'global commons' – the poles, the seas, our airspace, outer space and cyberspace on which all advanced nations now depend. Responses to natural disasters will be uncoordinated, with private companies stepping in to provide assistance in exchange for rights to resources. Technological change, advanced by private corporations, will be governed only weakly, allowing all kinds of abuse and misuse. Unregulated worlds of information will become battle-spaces, while the boom in digital transactions will be mined mercilessly by intellectual property thieves.

While states struggle to manage the shift to a more digital economy, corporations, as well as cities, will end up designing new models of help without waiting for national governments to act. Organized crime will grow unchecked. Wildfire conflicts will proliferate, and so defence and security spending will stay high. Hard power will be needed to survive and project influence, while 'grey wars' will spread. Crucially, it will become ever harder to broker the global consensus we need to tackle climate change.

This may all sound like Doomsday. But these are not my theoretical fears. They are part of the scenario-planning for the British military.

Happily, there is another, better way. With the right choices now, the future could offer us a rich mix of freedoms: freedom from the arbitrary, unaccountable will of others;[11] and the positive freedom that comes from a life blessed with a rich menu of options. The promise of this world is 'the freedom to be you', to live your life the way you choose. But that world requires us to build – as generations of progressive thinkers have understood – both security for all and power for each.

It was an old Whig lord high chancellor, Robert Henley, who once said: 'Necessitous men are not free men.' That was something Roosevelt understood. In his State of the Union address of January 1944, he declared that 'true individual freedom cannot exist without economic security', for '[p]eople who are hungry and out of a job are the stuff of which dictatorships are made'.[12]

Security frees us from the prison of fear, anxiety and worry. But power gives us agency, options and control over our lives. Freedom cannot mean, merely, a nice view of the Promised Land if we actually lack the ability to get there. In the real world, we need power to pursue our dreams.

We enshrine freedom, security and power with rights, which we sustain by law, but we underwrite them with *wealth*. Which is why, if we want to build a new democracy of freedom, we have to rebuild a wealth-owning democracy. When we diffuse wealth, we diffuse power. We guard against the ability of others to dominate us at work or at home, so that no-one can lord it over us. We encourage traditions of prudence and engagement in public life, themselves the best guarantor of a lively democracy and the best defence against a life lived at the mercy of others.[13] We maximize the agency, self-sufficiency and control each of us has over the life we choose to live.

Today, too many of our fellow citizens are trapped between a rock and a hard place. They have lost their freedom from fear to today's insecurities, and they are now in peril of losing their freedom to rise and to enjoy the new possibilities of tomorrow.

We can change this if we decide to alter course and *fairly* share the future. But the time to decide is now.

Acknowledgements

This story begins a decade and a half ago in HM Treasury and No. 10 Downing Street. There, I was fortunate enough to be able to develop this analysis with Professor Nick Pearce, Gavin Kelly and Torsten Bell, and my special advisers Tony Danker and David Mills, along with the brilliant Treasury Productivity Team ('Prod') led by Simon Gallagher. Both Alistair Darling and Gordon Brown were generous enough to let me get stuck into the research.

Many of the ideas here are the fruits of hundreds of hours of debate and conversation in Parliament, and I am enormously indebted to His Grace the Archbishop of Canterbury, Justin Welby, who first suggested to me the creation of a cross-party Parliamentary group to identify the overlapping consensus on fostering a more-inclusive growth. Over the years, I have learned a lot from my fellow Parliamentarians in the work we have done together – in particular, among the Labour family, my colleagues in the Tribune Group of MPs and its indefatigable chair, Clive Efford MP; and from 'across the aisle', George Freeman MP, John Penrose MP, Lord David Willetts and Lord Ian Wrigglesworth. Over the last decade we have been honoured to host, at the House of Commons, some individuals and organizations who have helped develop this thinking, not least Will Hutton, Marianna Mazzucato, Michael Jacobs and the IPPR Commission on Economic Justice, along with representatives of the CBI and TUC, and the polling research team at Opinium, led by Chris Curtis, Priya Minhas and Jack Tadman, who transformed our understanding of political possibilities. Ángel Gurría, Gabriela Ramos and Anthony Gooch were fantastic leaders at the OECD; they worked closely with us on developing this agenda, along with my partners at the IMF and the World Bank.

The team at the Centre for Progressive Policy, led by Charlotte Aldritt together with Ben Franklin, have been the intellectual powerhouse for much of this work. We have been blessed, too, with incredible interlocutors from our universities, especially Colin Hay, Tom Hunt and their colleagues at the University of Sheffield Political Economy Research Institute (SPERI), to whom I owe the phrase 'civic capitalism'. And over the last year we have been able to really deepen our work with Professor Bobby Duffy and his colleagues at the Policy Institute, Kings College London, and Will Snell at the Fairness Foundation. My former colleagues at Nuffield College (University of Oxford), professors Jane Green and Ben Ansell, transformed my understanding of the roles of insecurity and wealth inequality in the rise of populism, and Jane in particular was a brilliant mentor during my time as a Gwilym Gibbon Research Fellow, as I tried to understand the importance of plausibility in driving voting behaviour. I was lucky enough to be able to work with a hugely talented Viviana Baraybar Hidalgo in developing this.

Lots of people were kind enough to offer time and interviews on the key areas of research, including Robert Watts, editor of the *Sunday Times* Rich List, who was a brilliant guide to the evolution of serious wealth in Britain, along with the ONS Wealth and Assets team, especially Hilary Mainwaring, who talked me through the ways we measure wealth in Britain, and Molly Broome at the Resolution Foundation. Rolls Royce and Pendennis were generous enough to offer me time understanding the amazing things they make.

I have worked with many people to understand the rise of rent-seeking around the world, including Senator Bernie

Sanders and James Crabtree. Professor Brooke Harrington was an incredible guide to the psychology of the super-rich, and I am especially grateful to Oliver Bullough, Paul Caruana Galizia and Catherine Belton for the work they have helped inspire, tackling the economic crime that emanates from Russia in particular, and the insights they offered for this book. Dame Margaret Hodge, with whom I worked closely on the most recent economic crime bill, has been a constant source of wisdom and example, together with many of my colleagues on the Parliamentary Foreign Affairs Committee.

Professors Kate Pickett and Richard Wilkinson (University of York) helped me understand the risks of inequality, while professors Steven Durlauf (University of Chicago) and Miles Corak were generous and insightful in explaining the dynamics of the Gatsby Curve. Professor Joe Stiglitz first alerted me to the critical role of institutional rule sets in understanding how our markets really work, and both Professor Barry R. Weingast and Andy Haldane helped develop my thinking about institutions and their reform. Amanda Bevan and Oliver Finnegan, at the UK's National Archives, were kind enough to indulge my fascination with the foundational documents of English capitalism, along with the archivists at King's College, Cambridge. Dr Richard Blakemore was generous enough to spend time with me unpacking that history.

Dr Arun Advani, Dan Neidle and Alex Cobham all helped me understand far better the inequities of our tax system and the options for its reform. Helen Dean, Chief Executive at NEST, along with Norma Cohen were enormously important in helping me crystallize ideas for Universal Basic Capital, though I owe a debt to Professor Paul Gregg for first starting me down that line of thinking.

Much of the anger and energy behind this book comes from the streets of my Birmingham constituency of Hodge Hill, where I have been blessed to be able to work with a passionate team there and in the House of Commons – Gill Beddows, Sarish

Jabeen, Jamie Tennant, Kate Evans, Lisa Homan and Olivia Coyle – along with an incredible group of community activists working in our food banks and striving to end homelessness: they are too many to name. Birmingham is immeasurably stronger for the radical compassion they wake up with every day. But the book is dedicated to the people who taught me most: the residents of East Birmingham, where five generations of my family have lived and worked. They share an uncommon decency, common sense, passion and optimism that things can, and should, be better. Over twenty years, they have always been the people I listen to hardest about what needs to change, and how it needs to change.

There are three more debts I owe: to my agent, Georgina Capel, who first suggested the idea of a book on this agenda; to my publisher Anthony Cheetham and the amazing team at Head of Zeus; and to Mark Hawkins-Dady, my editor, who with patience, kindness and rigour helped shape, clarify and polish what I was trying to say.

Finally, none of these ideas would have seen the light of day if it were not for the encouragement and forbearance of my wife Sarah and our three incredible children, Alex, John and Kyla, who inspired, listened, argued, read and helped with the odd translation as the book took shape. I hope this book helps re-shape a better world for their amazing generation.

Notes

Introduction

1   For this and other excerpts from the speech, *see* Franklin D. Roosevelt, 'State of the Union Message to Congress' (11 January 1944): https://www.fdrlibrary.org/address-text.

2   Ibid., 'Address accepting the presidential nomination at the Democratic National Convention in Chicago' (2 July 1932): https://www.presidency.ucsb.edu/documents/address-accepting-the-presidential-nomination-the-democratic-national-convention-chicago-1.

3   Barack Obama, 'Remarks by the president on economic mobility', White House press release (4 December 2013): https://obamawhitehouse.archives.gov/the-press-office/2013/12/04/remarks-president-economic-mobility.

4   The explosion in the literature of the 'New Inequality' has been especially influenced by the likes of Thomas Piketty, Tony Atkinson, Mike Savage, Lane Kenworthy, Joseph Stiglitz, Robert Reich, and Adair Turner, through to Thomas Phillipon (*The Great Reversal*), Elizabeth Anderson (*Private Government*), Martin Wolf (*The Crisis of Democratic Capitalism*) and Sohrab Ahmari (*Tyranny, Inc.*).

5   The phrase 'end of history', alluding to the ostensible 'unipolar' dominance of the United States and of Western liberal democracy at the start of the 1990s, is associated most with Francis Fukuyama, *The End of History and the Last Man* (1992).

6   The name was a very Treasury homage to E.P. Thompson's classic study, *The Making of the English Working Class*.

7   *See* Alec Ross, 'Understand Your Industries of the Future', in Liam Byrne (ed.), *The Future of the Work for the People We Serve* (2019).

8   Hans Jakob Christoffel von Grimmelshausen, *The Adventures of Simplicius Simplicissimus* (originally in German, 1668–9).

9   *See* 'Property and ownership', in *Stanford Encyclopedia of Philosophy* (2004; revised 2020): https://plato.stanford.edu/entries/property/.

10 Aristotle, *Politics*, 1263a.

11 *See* Jean-Jacques Rousseau, *The Social Contract*, Book II, Chapter XI (1762).

12 In his pamphlet *Agrarian Justice* (1797), Tom Paine noted that for £15 apiece, a young couple could buy a cow and a few acres and so 'instead of becoming burdens upon society... [they] would be put in the way of becoming useful and profitable citizens'.

13 *See* Noel Skelton, 'Constructive Conservatism', *Spectator* (19 May 1923), p. 5: http://archive.spectator.co.uk/article/19th-may-1923/5/constructive-conservatism-ivdemocracy-stabilized.

14 Labour's great revisionists all argued for a society in which private property was distributed much more equally between individuals. *See* Ben Jackson, 'The Conceptual History of Social Justice', *Political Studies Review*, 3/3 (September 2005), p. 243; and J. E. Meade, *Efficiency, Equality and the Ownership of Property* (1964), p. 41.

15 John Rawls, *Justice as Fairness: A Restatement*, edited by Erin I. Kelly (2001; revision of his *A Theory of Justice*, 1971), p. 136. Rawls put the idea of a property-owning democracy centre-stage in his theory of justice. He argued that the basic institutions of property democracy should use progressive taxation plus markets 'to disperse the ownership of wealth in capital, and thus to prevent a small part of society from controlling the economy and indirectly political life itself'. A property-owning democracy, argued Rawls, avoided this hazard 'not by the redistribution of income to those with less... but rather by ensuring the widespread ownership of production of assets in human capital'. Ibid., p. xiv. John Rawls is happily enjoying a renaissance: *see* Daniel Chandler's wonderful *Free and Equal: What Would a Fair Society Look Like?* (2023).

16 As Henry Kissinger once put it, 'Democracies evolve in a conflict of factions. They achieve greatness by their reconciliation.'

17 An insight that we all owe to Jonathan Lynn and Antony Jay's *The Complete 'Yes Prime Minister': The Diaries of the Right Hon. James Hacker* (1989).

Chapter 1: The Absurdity of Affluence

1 '*Ahpo*': https://www.lurssen.com/en/new-build/yachts/ahpo/.

2 'Amazon Billionaire Jeff Bezos Rode a Dick Into Space and the Jokes Make Themselves at This Point', BuzzFeed (20 July 2021): https://www.buzzfeednews.com/article/adeonibada/amazon-jeff-bezos-space-blue-origin-dick-rocket.

3 'Britain's most expensive houses', *Evening Standard* (15 December 2021): https://www.standard.co.uk/homesandproperty/luxury/britains-most-expensive-houses-channel-4-b971960.html.

4 '£110m mega mansion for sale on Rihanna and Robbie Williams' former street in north London', *Evening Standard* (2 November 2022): https://www.standard.co.uk/homesandproperty/luxury/st-john-s-wood-avenue-road-ps110m-megamansion-rihanna-robbie-williams-b1035754.html.

5 '£30 million to live on UK's most expensive street – Tite Street', Halifax press release (22 December 2021): https://www.lloydsbankinggroup.com/assets/pdfs/media/press-releases/2021-press-releases/halifax/halifax-most-expensive-streets-2021.pdf.

6 'Rolls-Royce car sales hit 119-year record as US drives demand', *Financial Times* (9 January 2023): https://www.ft.com/content/7d4ca641-728e-4b87-ab7c-06d1e6558410.

7 '"Glittering smokescreen" of auction highs masks a nervous market', *Financial Times* (14 December 2022): https://www.ft.com/content/5cc5e24b-1e1f-496b-92ff-8751ec237c60.

8 'Private jet sales likely to reach highest ever level this year, report says', *Guardian* (1 May 2023): https://www.theguardian.com/world/2023/may/01/private-jet-sales-likely-to-reach-highest-ever-level-this-year-report-says.

9 'US Billionaire Wealth Surpasses $1.1 Trillion Gain Since Mid-March', Institute for Policy Studies (25 January 2021): https://ips-dc.org/u-s-billionaire-wealth-surpasses-1-1-trillion-gain-since-mid-march/.

10 'The billionaire boom: how the super-rich soaked up Covid cash', *Financial Times* (13 May 2021): https://www.ft.com/content/747a76dd-f018-4d0d-a9f3-4069bf2f5a93.

11 '2010–2020: A Decade of Billionaires', *Forbes* online: https://www.forbes.com/consent/ketch/?toURL=https://www.forbes.com/decade-of-billionaires/.

12 James Crabtree, *The Billionaire Raj: A Journey Through India's New Gilded Age* (2018).

13 'Cost of Taj Mahal', housing.com (4 April 2023): https://housing.com/news/shah-jahan-may-have-spent-nearly-rs-70-billion-to-build-the-taj-mahal/.

14 'Chinese rich kids go on the rampage', *Irish Times* (2 April 2016): https://www.irishtimes.com/life-and-style/people/chinese-rich-kids-go-on-the-rampage-1.2595099.

15 'The burden of wealth', *China Daily* (updated 29 April 2015): http://www.chinadaily.com.cn/culture/2015-04/29/content_20571936_2.htm.

16 Paul Caruana Galizia, 'How the Lebedevs partied their way to power', *Tortoise* (28 June 2022): https://www.tortoisemedia.com/2022/06/28/londongrad-paul-caruana-galizia/.

17 'Meet the Crazy Rich Russians who grew up in London', *Tatler* (22 July 2020): https://www.tatler.com/article/wealthy-russians-in-london.

18 'The *Sunday Times* Rich List 2023 revealed', *Sunday Times* (19 May 2023): https://www.thetimes.co.uk/article/sunday-times-rich-list-2023-revealed-b3kxb5kx3/.

19 In 2023, the combined wealth of billionaires on the *Sunday Times* Rich List was £684 billion. Ibid. In 2022, the wealth of UK billionaires was reported to have risen more than £55 billion: '*Sunday Times* Rich List 2022: Sunaks join wealthy elite as UK billionaires swell to record level', *Sky News* (19 August 2022): https://news.sky.com/story/sunday-times-rich-

list-2022-uk-has-a-record-number-of-billionaires-12617181.

20 *See* Molly Broome, Ian Mulheirn and Simon Pittaway, 'Peaked interest: What higher interest rates mean for the size and distribution of UK household wealth', Resolution Foundation report (July 2023): https://www.resolutionfoundation.org/publications/peaked-interest/.

21 'House of Commons Library Research on the shift in UK wealth to national earnings ratio', All Party Parliamentary Group on Inclusive Growth (22 May 2023): https://www.inclusivegrowth.co.uk/house-of-commons-library-research-on-the-shift-in-uk-wealth-to-national-earnings-ratio/.

22 Jack Leslie, 'The missing billions', Resolution Foundation (3 January 2021): https://www.resolutionfoundation.org/publications/the-missing-billions/.

23 For the £2.5 trillion figure, *see* Broome *et al.*, op. cit.

24 A point well made by Daphne Merkin, 'The Rich in Fiction', *New Yorker* (12 September 2015).

25 There are numerous examples, such as the remakes of *Dallas* and *Dynasty*, *Downton Abbey, Gosford Park, Brideshead Revisited, The Kardashians, Real Housewives, Below Decks, Paris in Love, Big Rich Texas, Triangle of Sadness*, Bong Joon-ho's film *Parasite,* HBO's *White Lotus* or the recent hit *Succession.*

26 A phrase I owe to Professor Brooke Harrington, personal interview.

27 Fiona Sturges, 'The *Succession* effect: how TV dramas got angrier about the rich', *Financial Times* (21 November 2022): https://www.ft.com/content/b3a10aeb-184d-46b8-9d64-9f5ea8a0d659.

28 Ibid.

29 'New figures suggest top 1% could own two-thirds of global wealth by 2030', All-Party Parliamentary Group on Inclusive Growth (17 April 2018): https://www.inclusivegrowth.co.uk/oecd-press-release/.

30 The calculation is this: if aggregate total wealth of the top 1% and bottom 99% grows at the same rates as observed between 2008 and 2017, the wealth of the top 1% increases by around 6% per year, from around $140 trillion in 2017 to $305 trillion in 2030. The wealth of the bottom 99% increases by around 3% per year, from around $140 trillion in 2017 to $195 trillion in 2030.

Chapter 2: The Cost of Affluence

1 Poverty data is published by the UK Department of Work and Pensions. Measuring the data for 2020–21 was complicated by the Coronavirus lockdowns, so this is data for 2019–20, from the Households Below Average Income survey, which collects data at a household level: https://www.gov.uk/government/collections/households-below-average-income-hbai--2.

2 This is the figure for after housing costs.

3 'Access capitalism scandal: A dinner with Prince Charles, then the begging

letter arrived', *The Times* (31 July 2021): https://www.thetimes.co.uk/article/access-capitalism-scandal-a-dinner-with-prince-charles-then-the-begging-letter-arrived-kngkoxqfk.

4   In total, 41% said that what they feared about rising inequality was a rising level of corruption.

5   'The Tax List 2022: the UK's 50 biggest taxpayers revealed', *The Times* (28 January 2022): https://www.thetimes.co.uk/article/the-tax-list-2022-the-uks-50-biggest-taxpayers-revealed-2vohg8fmf.

6   Oliver Bullough, personal interview.

7   Benjamin I. Page, Larry M. Bartels and Jason Seawright, 'Democracy and the Policy Preferences of Wealthy Americans', *Perspectives on Politics*, 11/1 (March 2013): https://doi.org/10.1017/S153759271200360X.

8   'The poor give more', *Greater Good Magazine* (11 August 2010): https://greatergood.berkeley.edu/article/item/the_poor_give_more.

9   'Does wealth reduce compassion?', *Greater Good Magazine* (17 December 2015): https://greatergood.berkeley.edu/article/item/does_wealth_reduce_compassion.

10 Ibid.

11 Ibid.

12 'Affluent people more likely to be scofflaws', *Greater Good Magazine* (28 February 2012): https://greatergood.berkeley.edu/article/item/affluent_people_more_likely_to_be_scofflaws. The research paper in question was Paul K. Piff *et al.*, 'Higher Social Class Predicts Increased Unethical Behavior' *Proceedings of the National Association of Science* (27 February 2012): https://www.pnas.org/doi/full/10.1073/pnas.1118373109.

13 Piff *et al*, ibid.

14 *See* Michael Mechanic, 'Research Proves It: There's No Such Thing as Noblesse Oblige', *Atlantic* (4 April 2021): https://www.theatlantic.com/ideas/archive/2021/04/does-wealth-rob-brain-compassion/618496/. *See also* https://www.ted.com/talks/paul_piff_does_money_make_you_mean.

15 See John Heathershaw *et al.*, 'The UK's kleptocracy problem: how servicing post-Soviet elites weakens the rule of law', Chatham House research paper (8 December 2021): https://www.chathamhouse.org/2021/12/uks-kleptocracy-problem.

16 Dame Margaret Hodge, 'Losing Our Moral Compass: Corrupt Money and Corrupt Politics' (unpublished report), KCL Policy Institute (March 2022).

17 Vaclav Smil, *Growth: From Microorganisms to Megacities* (2019).

18 Quoted in Hodge, op. cit.

19 Chief Secretary to the Treasury, quoted in House of Commons Foreign Affairs Committee, 'The cost of complacency: illicit finance and the war in Ukraine', second report of session 2022–23 (30 June 2022): https://publications.parliament.uk/pa/cm5803/cmselect/cmfaff/168/report.html.

20 Quoted in Daniel Beasley and Susan Hawley, 'Closing the UK's economic crime enforcement gap: Proposals for boosting resources for UK law enforcement to fight economic crime', Spotlight on Corruption (24 January 2022): https://www.spotlightcorruption.org/report/closing-the-

uks-economic-crime-enforcement-gap-proposals-for-boosting-resources-for-uk-law-enforcement-to-fight-economic-crime/.

21   'Risky Business: Kazakhstan, Kazakhmys plc and the London Stock Exchange', Global Witness report (13 July 2020): https://www.globalwitness.org/en/archive/risky-business-kazakhstan-kazakhmys-plc-and-london-stock-exchange/.

22   'Sani Abacha – the hunt for the billions stolen by Nigeria's ex-leader', BBC News (28 January 2021): https://www.bbc.co.uk/news/world-africa-54929254.

23   'Wolf of Wall Street producers to pay $60m to US government', *Guardian* (7 March 2018): https://www.theguardian.com/business/2018/mar/07/wolf-of-wall-street-producers-to-pay-60m-to-us-government.

24   Susan Hawley, George Havenhand and Tom Robinson, 'Red carpet for dirty money', Spotlight on Corruption report (July 2021): https://www.spotlightcorruption.org/wp-content/uploads/2023/01/Golden-Visa-Briefing.-Final1.pdf.

25   'Woman in £16m Harrods spend loses wealth seizure challenge', BBC News (5 February 2020): https://www.bbc.co.uk/news/uk-51387364.

26   '£100bn of property in England and Wales is secretly owned, estimates show', Global Witness (17 March 2019) https://www.globalwitness.org/en/press-releases/100bn-of-property-in-england-and-wales-is-secretly-owned-estimates-show/.

27   'Unexplained Wealth Orders: How to catch the corrupt and corrupt money in the UK', Transparency International (28 April 2017): https://www.transparency.org/en/news/unexplained-wealth-orders-how-to-catch-the-corrupt-and-corrupt-money-in-the.

28   John Heathershaw *et al.*, op. cit.

29   Anthony Sampson, *Anatomy of Britain* (1962).

30   House of Commons Foreign Affairs Committee, 'The cost of complacency', op. cit.

31   Michael Sandel used the phrase in 'The populist backlash has been a revolt against the tyranny of merit' (interview), *Guardian* (6 September 2020): https://www.theguardian.com/books/2020/sep/06/michael-sandel-the-populist-backlash-has-been-a-revolt-against-the-tyranny-of-merit.

32   James Wood, 'It's still Mrs. Thatcher's Britain', *New Yorker* (25 November 2019): https://www.newyorker.com/magazine/2019/12/02/its-still-mrs-thatchers-britain.

33   In doing so, he earned a rebuke from Michael Young, the author of *The Rise of the Meritocracy*, who pointed out, correctly but ineffectually, that he had coined the term 'meritocracy' as a criticism rather than a celebration.

34   Alan B. Krueger, 'The Rise and Consequences of Inequality in the United States', speech (12 January 2012): https://obamawhitehouse.archives.gov/sites/default/files/krueger_cap_speech_final_remarks.pdf.

35   A phrase I owe to Professor Jane Green at Nuffield College.

Chapter 3: The Lack of Affluence

1   As Mr Micawber reminded young David, 'Annual income 20 pounds, annual expenditure 19 pounds, 19 shillings and six pence, result happiness. Annual income 20 pounds, annual expenditure 20 pounds ought and six, result misery.'

2   'Kirstie Allsopp says young people can buy a house if they just give up gym and Netflix', *Joe* (7 February 2022): https://www.joe.co.uk/news/kirstie-allsopp-says-young-people-can-buy-a-house-if-they-just-give-up-gym-and-netflix-315867.

3   McKinsey Global Institute, 'The world at work: Jobs, pay, and skills for 3.5 billion people' (2012), p. 3: https://www.mckinsey.com/~/media/McKinsey/Featured%20Insights/Employment%20and%20Growth/The%20world%20at%20work/mgi%20Global_labor_Full_Report_June_2012.ashx.

4   Bobby Duffy, *Generations* (2021), p. 25.

5   Ibid., p. 27.

6   Ibid., p. 29.

7   Real hourly pay for 18–29 year olds fell 9.2% between 2009 and 2014. Source: George Bangham *et al.*, 'An Intergenerational Audit for the UK: 2019', Resolution Foundation: https://www.resolutionfoundation.org/app/uploads/2019/06/Intergenerational-audit-for-the-UK.pdf.

8   The real-terms non-housing spending of 18–29 year olds was 7% lower, compared to an increase of 11% for 50–64 year olds and 37% for people aged 65 and over. Source: ibid.

9   Amy Borrett, 'How UK house prices have soared ahead of average wages', *New Statesman* (20 May 2021): https://www.newstatesman.com/politics/2021/05/how-uk-house-prices-have-soared-ahead-average-wages.

10 Darren Baxter *et al.*, 'Making a House a Home: Why Policy Must Focus on the Ownership and Distribution of Housing', report, Joseph Rowntree foundation (July 2022), p. 7: https://www.jrf.org.uk/report/making-house-home-why-policy-must-focus-ownership-and-distribution-housing.

11 Ibid., p. 8.

12 The book is *The Pinch: How the Baby Boomers Took Their Children's Future – And Why They Should Give It Back* (2010).

13 UK government, 'Right to Buy: buying your council home': https://www.gov.uk/right-to-buy-buying-your-council-home/discounts.

14 'Right to Buy homes made £2.8m in profit "in weeks"', BBC News (14 March 2019): https://www.bbc.co.uk/news/uk-47443183.

15 House of Commons Library analysis.

16 That is way ahead of the average rises enjoyed by the under-30s (32%), those aged 30–49 (16%), and those aged 50–64 (28%): my analysis, from House of Commons sources.

17 'Should you cash in your pension to become a buy-to-let landlord or keep your retirement savings invested?', *This is Money* (8 March 2015): https://

www.thisismoney.co.uk/money/pensions/article-2970601/Should-cash-pension-buy-let-landlord.html.

18 Cited in, e.g. George Bangham, 'Game of homes: The rise of multiple property ownership in Great Britain', Resolution Foundation (June 2019): https://www.resolutionfoundation.org/app/uploads/2019/06/Game-of-Homes.pdf.

19 Darren Baxter *et al.*, op. cit., p. 13: https://www.jrf.org.uk/report/making-house-home-why-policy-must-focus-ownership-and-distribution-housing.

20 Molly Broome, Ian Mulheirn & Simon Pittaway, Peaked interest? What higher interest rates mean for the size and distribution of Britain's household wealth, Resolution Foundation (July 2023), https://www.resolutionfoundation.org/app/uploads/2023/07/Peaked-interest.pdf.

21 At a rate 1.6 basis points a year; *see*: https://www.nber.org/digest/202212/real-interest-rate-decline-long-historical-perspective.

22 Only the years immediately surrounding the discovery of America outstrip the current cycle by length; *see*: https://bankunderground.co.uk/2017/11/06/guest-post-global-real-interest-rates-since-1311-renaissance-roots-and-rapid-reversals/.

23 Francis Breedon, Jagjit S. Chadha and Alex Waters, 'The Financial Market Impact of UK Quantitative Easing', *BIS Papers*, 65: https://www.bis.org/publ/bppdf/bispap65p_rh.pdf.

24 *See*, for instance, Ian Mulheirn, *Tackling the UK Housing Crisis* (2019); John Lewis and Fergus Cumming, 'Houses are assets not goods: taking the theory to the UK data', Bank Underground (online; 6 September 2019); David Miles and Victoria Munro, 'Home UK house prices and three decades of decline in the risk-free real interest rate', Bank of England Staff Working Paper, 837 (20 December 2019).

25 George Bangham *et al.*, 'Intergenerational Audit…', op. cit.

26 'Household total wealth in Great Britain: April 2018 to March 2020', ONS (2021): https://www.ons.gov.uk/peoplepopulationandcommunity/personalandhouseholdfinances/incomeandwealth/bulletins/totalwealthingreatbritain/latest. As the Resolution Foundation explains, 'To measure them in a consistent way to defined contribution pension pots, the *Wealth and Assets Survey* values defined benefit and annuitized pension rights at the level of the pension pot that would be required to purchase them in the annuities market at that point in time. Rising life expectancies (which have been the main driver of changes in annuity factors and discount rates) and low interest rates have served to continually inflate the value of defined benefit pensions and pensions in payment in each wave of the survey… in the six years to 2012–14, three-quarters of the growth in pension wealth was down to these "valuation" effects rather than active changes in pension saving.'

27 'Over-65s rely heavily on state pension', *FT Advisor* (17 December 2018): https://www.ftadviser.com/pensions/2018/12/17/over-65s-rely-heavily-on-state-pension/.

28 Lucio Baccaro and Jonas Pontusson, 'Rethinking Comparative Political

Economy', *Politics & Society*, 44/2 (2016): https://www.researchgate.net/publication/301303323_Rethinking_Comparative_Political_Economy.

29   'Theresa May and the varieties of capitalism', University of Bath *IPR Blog* (20 July 2016): https://blogs.bath.ac.uk/iprblog/2016/07/20/theresa-may-and-the-varieties-of-capitalism/.

30   *See* Liam Byrne, 'The "grey wall" is still the biggest barrier to a Labour government' (25 January 2022): https://liambyrnemp.wordpress.com/2022/01/25/the-grey-wall-is-still-the-biggest-barrier-to-a-labour-government/.

31   Molly Broome *et al.*, 'An Intergenerational Audit for the UK: 2022', Resolution Foundation: https://www.resolutionfoundation.org/publications/an-intergenerational-audit-for-the-uk-2022/.

32   Laura Gardiner, 'The million dollar be-question: Inheritances, gifts, and their implications for generational living standards, Resolution Foundation' (December 2017): https://www.resolutionfoundation.org/publications/the-million-dollar-be-question-inheritances-gifts-and-their-implications-for-generational-living-standards/.

33   Ibid.

34   According to 'Bringing retirement into focus: 2021', Standard Life (2021): https://lib.standardlife.com/library/uk/retirement-study.pdf.

35   Brian Nolan *et al.*, 'The wealth of families: The intergenerational transmission of wealth in Britain in comparative perspective', Oxford University New Institute for Economic Thinking ((August 2020): https://www.nuffieldfoundation.org/wp-content/uploads/2019/11/Intergenerational-Wealth-Transfers-Report-Aug-2020.pdf.

36   Brooke Harrington, *Capital Without Borders: Wealth Managers and the One Percent* (2016).

37   STEP website: https://www.step.org/about-step.

38   Harrington, ibid., p. 133.

39   Alec Ross, 'The Future of Work and Inequality' (transcript): https://www.inclusivegrowth.co.uk/understand-industries-future/.

40   Dr Carl Frey, 'Automation and the Future of Work: Understanding the Numbers, in Liam Byrne (ed.), 'The Future of Work for the People We Serve: Ten Lessons for the Revolution to Come', (Parliamentary Network on the World Bank and IMF, 2019).

41   Daily Mail, How many jobs will YOUR area lose to robots? Interactive map lays bare how AI could put up to 2.9m people out of work by 2030 – with retail and transport the worst hit, research finds: https://www.dailymail.co.uk/news/article-5820227/Rise-robots-cost-jobs-coal-closures.html.

42   'AI could replace equivalent of 300 million jobs – report', BBC News (28 March 2023): https://www.bbc.co.uk/news/technology-65102150.

43   'Wealth gaps between different ethnic groups in Britain are large and likely to persist', Resolution Foundation (22 December 2020): https://www.resolutionfoundation.org/press-releases/wealth-gaps-between-different-ethnic-groups-in-britain-are-large-and-likely-to-persist/. Figures estimate

'family wealth per adult'.

44 Phoebe Arslanagic-Wakefield, 'Everything you need to know about the "gender wealth gap"', *Prospect* (14 January 2020): https://www.prospectmagazine.co.uk/other/gender-wealth-gap-women-investing.

45 'America is moving toward a caste society', Macleans (8 April 2014): https://www.macleans.ca/society/america-is-moving-toward-a-caste-society/.

46 Robert D. Putnam, *Our Kids: The American Dream in Crisis* (2015), p. 36.

47 Ibid.

48 Ibid, p. 320.

49 See David Adler & Ben Ansell (2020) Housing and populism, West European Politics, 43:2, 344–365.

50 'Amygdala hijack' – a term first developed by psychologist Daniel Goleman in his book *Emotional Intelligence: Why It Can Matter More Than IQ* (1995).

51 Liam Byrne, 'Our laws are completely inadequate for dealing with interference in our democracy', The House (4 January 2018): https://www.politicshome.com/thehouse/article/our-laws-are-completely-inadequate-for-dealing-with-interference-in-our-democracy.

52 A phrase I owe to Peter Mair.

53 *See*, for example, Liam Byrne, 'Our laws...', op. cit.

54 Steve Pincus, *1688: The First Modern Revolution* (2011).

55 As happened, for example, in late eighteenth-century France or late seventeenth-century England, or the fledgling opposition movements that survived repression, as in Cuba and China.

56 Secessionist political parties are seeking at least a vote on independence in Belgium (Flanders), Canada (Quebec), Denmark (Faroe Islands and Greenland), Finland (Åland), France (Brittany and Corsica), Germany (Bavaria), Italy (Veneto and Sardinia), Spain (Catalonia, the Balearics, the Basque Country, Navarre, Canary Islands and Galicia), the UK (Scotland and Wales) and the United States (Alaska and Puerto Rico).

Chapter 4: All Hail the Market!

1 Henry Kissinger, *Diplomacy* (1994; 2012 edition), p. 765.

2 Key legislation and agencies of the time included the Wagner Act, the Fair Labour Standards Act, the Social Security Act, the Works Progress Administration, the US Housing Authority and the Farm Security Administration.

3 'Walter Lippmann, political analyst, dead at 85', *New York Times* (15 December 1974): https://www.nytimes.com/1974/12/15/archives/walter-lippmann-political-analyst-dead-at-85-walter-lippmann.html.

4 Walter Lippmann, *The Good Society* (1937), p. 31.

5 Karl Popper, *The Poverty of Historicism* (revised edition, 1957; reprinted 2002), pp. 89–90.

6 Quoted in Daniel Stedman Jones, *Masters of the Universe: Hayek, Friedman, and the Birth of Neoliberal Politics* (2014), p. 48.

7 Friedrich Hayek, *The Road to Serfdom* (1944; 2001 edition), p. 44.

8 'Business People: Neglected economist honored by president', *New York Times* (19 November 1991): https://www.nytimes.com/1991/11/19/business/business-people-neglected-economist-honored-by-president.html.

9 Hayek, ibid., p. 36.

10 'Ludwig von Mises, economist, author, and teacher, dies at 92', *New York Times* (11 October 1973): https://www.nytimes.com/1973/10/11/archives/ludwig-von-mises-economist-author-and-teacher-champion-of-the.html.

11 Quoted in Daniel Stedman Jones, op. cit., p. 56.

12 Friedman noted Dicey's argument: 'Legislation, he argued, is dominated by the underlying current of opinion, but only after a considerable lag. Men legislate on the basis of the philosophy they imbibed in their youth, so some twenty years or more may elapse between a change in the underlying current of opinion and the resultant alteration in public policy. Dicey sets 1870 to 1890 as the period in which public opinion in England turned away from individualism (Manchester liberalism) and toward collectivism; yet he points out that economic legislation was not strongly affected by the new trend of opinion until after the turn of the century.' *See* Milton Friedman, 'Neo-Liberalism and Its Prospects' (1951). Lippmann, by contrast, asserted: 'It may be said, I believe, that between, say, 1848 and 1870 the intellectual climate of western society began to change. At some time in that period the intellectual ascendancy of the collectivist movement began.'

13 Ludwig von Mises, *Bureaucracy* (1944; 2007 edition), Chapter 6.

14 Hayek, op. cit., p. 6.

15 Eric Beinhocker, *The Origin of Wealth: Evolution, Complexity, and the Radical Remaking of Economics* (2007), p. 36.

16 'Paul A. Samuelson: Biographical', Nobel Prize website: https://www.nobelprize.org/prizes/economic-sciences/1970/samuelson/biographical/.

17 Paul Samuelson, *Economics* (3rd edition, 1955), p. 212.

18 Richard H. Thaler, 'The Evolution of Economics and *Homo Economicus*', *Chicago Booth Review* (17 June 2015): https://www.chicagobooth.edu/review/the-evolution-of-economics-and-homo-economicus.

19 Michael C. Jensen, 'Some Anomalous Evidence Regarding Market Efficiency, *Journal of Financial Economics*, 6/2–3 (1978), pp. 95–101: https://papers.ssrn.com/sol3/papers.cfm?abstract_id=244159.

20 'Greenspan - I was wrong about the economy. Sort of', *Guardian* (24 October 2008): https://www.theguardian.com/business/2008/oct/24/economics-creditcrunch-federal-reserve-greenspan.

21 Michael Foucault, comments in '14 February 1979: The Modernity of Neoliberalism', see: https://digressionsnimpressions.typepad.com/digressionsnimpressions/2020/08/14-february-1979-foucault-on-neoliberalism-xviii.html.

22 'Milton Friedman, free markets theorist, dies at 94', *New York*

Times (16 November 2006): https://www.nytimes.com/2006/11/16/business/17friedmancnd.html.

23 Milton Friedman, *Capitalism and Freedom* (1962; 2002 edition), p. 8.

24 Though he added the rider, 'Provided the transaction is bilaterally voluntary and informed.'

25 Steven F. Hayward, 'Opinion: Why Ronald Reagan's "A Time for Choosing" endures after all this time', *Washington Post* (23 October 2014): https://www.washingtonpost.com/opinions/why-ronald-reagans-a-time-for-choosing-endures-after-all-this-time/2014/10/23/d833c49e-587a-11e4-bd61-346aee66ba29_story.html.

26 Joseph did not argue that full employment *per se* created inflation, but rather that 'It is the means adopted by successive governments to achieve a high level of employment which are the cause of inflation. Instead of dealing with the real obstacles to fuller employment which are often very specific, governments try the panacea, the universal healer, excess demand.' Now, Joseph freely admitted that his prescription would create unemployment – but he at least acknowledged that 'there is no magic cure for these problems' and, further, that 'In economics there is not and cannot be one cure. Economics is a matter of balance.' He argued, too, for 'reform of employment services, re-training, mobility of labour, reform of housing policy'.

27 Ian Gilmour, *Dancing With Dogma: Britain Under Thatcherism* (1992), p. 2.

28 Robert Atkinson, *Supply Side Follies: Why Conservative Economics Fails, Liberal Economics Falters, and Innovation Economics is the Answer* (2007), p. 55.

29 Quoted, ibid., p. 32.

30 Milton Friedman, 'The social responsibility of business is to increase its profits', *New York Times Magazine* (13 September 1970).

31 Tom Copeland, Tim Koller and Jack Murrin, *Valuation* (3rd edition, 2000), p. 4.

32 Ibid.

33 It fell as low as 55% in 1995.

34 From House of Commons Library analysis.

Chapter 5: A Licence to Profit

1 Estimated via The National Archives' Currency Convertor: https://www.nationalarchives.gov.uk/currency-converter/#currency-result.

2 This was the conclusion of a House of Commons committee (1604) considering a bill for free trade.

3 *See* Liam Byrne, *Dragons: How Ten Entrepreneurs Built Britain* (2016).

4 At an event I organized for Parliamentarians in Church House.

5 Philippe Aghion, Céline Antonin and Simon Bunel, *The Power of Creative Destruction: Economic Upheaval and the Wealth of Nations* (2021).

6 *See* Jared Diamond, *Guns, Germs and Steel* (1997), for a classic illustration.

7   A reference I owe to Barry Weingast. *See* Adam Smith, *The Wealth of Nations*, Book III, Chapter I ('Of the Natural Progress of Opulence in Different Nations') and Chapter III ('On the Rise and Progress of Cities and Towns'.

8   Gordon Tullock, 'The Welfare Costs of Tariffs, Monopolies, and Theft', *Economic Enquiry*, 5/3 (1967): https://onlinelibrary.wiley.com/doi/pdf/10.1111/j.1465-7295.1967.tb01923.x.

9   Robert J. Shiller, 'The best, brightest, and least productive?', Project Syndicate (20 September 2013): https://www.project-syndicate.org/commentary/the-rent-seeking-problem-in-contemporary-finance-by-robert-j--shiller-2013-09.

10 L.J. Alston, 'New institutional economics', in *The New Palgrave Dictionary of Economics* (2nd Edition, 2008).

11 Douglass C. North, John Joseph Wallis and Barry R. Weingast, *Violence and Social Orders: A Conceptual Framework for Interpreting Recorded Human History* (2009; 2013 edition), p. 252.

12 ibid, p. 258.

13 Walter Scheidel, *The Great Leveller: Violence and the History of Inequality, from the Stone Age to the Twenty-First Century* (2017), pp. 52–3.

14 Michael Hudson, 'The toll booth economy', Counterpunch (20 May 2009): https://www.counterpunch.org/2009/05/20/the-toll-booth-economy/.

15 Philippe Aghion *et al.*, op. cit.

16 Daron Acemoglu and James Robinson, '10 reasons countries fall apart', *News Ghana* (26 June 2012).

17 Philippe Aghion *et al.*, op. cit.

18 UK Government, Wealthy External Forum: https://www.gov.uk/government/groups/high-net-worth-unit-external-stakeholder-forum#membership.

19 'Lobbying fears as MPs' interest groups receive £13m from private firms', *Guardian* (17 February 2022): https://amp.theguardian.com/politics/2022/feb/17/lobbying-fears-as-mps-interest-groups-receive-13m-from-private-firms.

20 '55 Tufton Street: The other black door shaping British politics', BBC News (26 September 2022): https://www.bbc.co.uk/news/uk-politics-63039558.

21 My own analysis, aggregated from line items.

22 '20% of UK political donations come from just ten men', openDemocracy (21 July 2021): https://www.opendemocracy.net/en/dark-money-investigations/20-political-donations-come-just-ten-men/.

23 'One in 10 Tory peers have given more than £100,000 to party', *Guardian* (29 December 2022). https://www.theguardian.com/politics/2022/dec/29/one-in-10-tory-peers-have-given-more-than-100000-to-party.

Chapter 6: The Feathering of Fortune

1 Pope Benedict XVI, encyclical letter *Caritas in veritate* (29 June 2020): https://www.vatican.va/content/benedict-xvi/en/encyclicals/documents/hf_ben-xvi_enc_20090629_caritas-in-veritate.html.

2 Marc Orlitzky, 'free market', in *Encyclopedia Britannica*: https://www.britannica.com/topic/free-market. (Accessed 26 June 2023.)

3 Samuel Bowles, 'Marx and modern microeconomics', CEPR (21 April 2018): https://voxeu.org/article/marx-and-modern-microeconomics.

4 Brooke Harrington, 'The Populism of Transnational Plutocrats', Chapter 16 in Magnus Feldmann and Glenn Morgan (eds), *Business and Populism: The Odd Couple?* (2023).

5 Joseph E. Stiglitz, 'Rewriting the rules of the American economy', report (2015): https://rooseveltinstitute.org/wp-content/uploads/2015/05/RI-Rewriting-the-Rules-201505.pdf.

6 Joseph E. Stiglitz, *The Price of Inequality* (2012).

7 Ibid., 'Rewriting...', op. cit.

8 David Ricardo, *On the Principles of Political Economy and Taxation* (1817)

9 *See* J. M. Neeson, *Commoners: Common Right, Enclosure and Social Change in England, 1700–1820* (1994). Over 4,000 enclosure bills were passed between 1730 and 1839, but the process was far simpler after the General Enclosure Act of 1801.

10 Erskine May defines these as 'legislation of a special kind for conferring particular powers or benefits on any person or body of person – Including individuals, local authorities, companies, or corporations – in addition to or in conflict with the general law'. Quoted in Julian Hoppit, 'Patterns of Parliamentary Legislation, 1660–1800', *Historical Journal*, 39/1 (1996), p. 131.

11 Sir Edward Coke, *The Institutes of the Laws of England* (1628).

12 B.B. Schofield, 'The Promotion of the Cromford Canal act of 1789: A Study in Canal Engineering', *Bulletin of the John Rylands Library*, 64/1 (1981), pp. 246–78.

13 *Hansard*, Liverpool and Manchester Railway bill, standing orders (2 March 1825). The railway would not prove of benefit to Huskisson himself, who, famously, was fatally struck by Stephenson's engine *Rocket* at the opening ceremonies.

14 *See* 'Open Access 2.0: Bringing lobbying out of the shadows', Transparency International UK news (27 August 2020): https://www.transparency.org.uk/lobbying-uk-search-meetings-Robert-Jenrick-Richard-Desmond-Westferry.

15 'Half of England is owned by less than 1% of the population', *Guardian* (17 April 2019): https://www.theguardian.com/money/2019/apr/17/who-owns-england-thousand-secret-landowners-author.

16 HMRC, 'Property rental income statistics: 2022': https://www.gov.uk/government/statistics/property-rental-income-statistics-2022/property-rental-income-statistics-2022.

17 UK Parliament, 'Tax reliefs: Twentieth report of session 2022–23': https://publications.parliament.uk/pa/cm5803/cmselect/cmtreasy/723/report.html#heading.1.

18 *See* Mariana Mazzucato, Josh Ryan-Collins and Giorgos Gouzoulis, 'Theorising and mapping modern economic rents', a UCL IIPP working paper (2020), for a longer discussion: https://www.ucl.ac.uk/bartlett/public-purpose/wp2020-13.

19 In 1795, a challenge to Boulton and Watt's patent went all the way to the High Court. In January 1799, the Court of the King's Bench unanimously decided for Boulton and Watt, unlocking an enormous £9 million in royalties. *See* Jenny Uglow, *The Lunar Men: Five Friends Whose Curiosity Changed the World*, pp. 468–9.

20 IPR, 'Fast Facts 2017': https://assets.publishing.service.gov.uk/government/uploads/system/uploads/attachment_data/file/581279/Fast-Facts-2017.pdf.

21 'Charges for the use of intellectual property, receipts (BoP, current US$) – United Kingdom', World Bank: https://data.worldbank.org/indicator/BX.GSR.ROYL.CD?locations=GB.

22 UK Government, 'Patent Box relief statistics: September 2022': https://www.gov.uk/government/statistics/patent-box-reliefs-statistics/patent-box-relief-statistics-september-2022.

23 Marianna Mazzucato, 'State of innovation: Busting the private-sector myth', *New Scientist* online (21 August 2013): https://www.newscientist.com/article/mg21929310-200-state-of-innovation-busting-the-private-sector-myth/.

24 *See* Soshana Zuboff, *The Age of Surveillance Capitalism: The Fight for a Human Future at the New Frontier of Power* (2019), p. 93.

25 UK Government, Defamation Act 2013: https://www.legislation.gov.uk/ukpga/2013/26/section/5.

26 'Net digital advertising revenue share of major ad-selling online companies worldwide from 2016 to 2023', Statista: https://www.statista.com/statistics/290629/digital-ad-revenue-share-of-major-ad-selling-companies-worldwide/.

27 This, argued Gresham, led to foreign merchants demanding payment in 'good' coins rather than bad, and so good coins were exported while bad coins stayed in England, a phenomenon immortalized as 'Gresham's law' whereby 'bad money drives out good'. By November 1559, the queen was convinced, and the following September 1560, the proclamation was issued effectively recalling all the kingdom's currency and reissuing it with a higher and more consistent gold and silver content.

28 Sir Robert Southwell to Samuel Pepys, quoted in Sir John Clapham, *The Bank of England: A History* (1944), p. 14.

29 Ibid., p.16.

30 Andrew G. Haldane, 'Who owns a company?', speech to University of Edinburgh Corporate Finance Conference (22 May 2015).

31 Deborah Hardoon and Kaori Shigiya, 'Financing inequality', paper

for FCA (7 April 2017): https://www.fca.org.uk/publication/research/financing-inequality.pdf

32 House of Commons Library, 'Bank rescues of 2007–09: outcomes and cost': https://commonslibrary.parliament.uk/research-briefings/sn05748/.

33 Marilyne Tolle, 'Inequality: reframing the debate, reforming institutions and rooting out rent-seeking', Bank Underground (2015): https://bankunderground.co.uk/2015/08/07/inequality-reframing-the-debate-reforming-institutions-and-rooting-out-rent-seeking/amp/.

34 Bank of England, 'Quantitative easing': https://www.bankofengland.co.uk/monetary-policy/quantitative-easing.

35 Philip Bunn, Alice Pugh and Chris Yeates, 'The distributional impact of monetary policy easing in the UK between 2008 and 2014', Bank of England Staff Working Paper 720 (March 2018): https://www.bankofengland.co.uk/-/media/boe/files/working-paper/2018/the-distributional-impact-of-monetary-policy-easing-in-the-uk-between-2008-and-2014.pdf.

36 Economic Affairs Committee, 'Quantitative easing: A dangerous addiction?', 1st Report of Session 2019–21 (16 July 2021): https://publications.parliament.uk/pa/ld5802/ldselect/ldeconaf/42/4202.htm

37 'In associations based on mutual exchange,' wrote Aristotle, 'the bond of union is this sort of justice, namely reciprocity in accordance with a proportion rather than with arithmetic equality. In fact, it is by proportional requital that the city holds together.'

38 Quoted in Lionel Robbins, *A History of Economic Thought: The LSE Lectures* (2000), Chapter 1.

39 *See* John W. Baldwin, 'The Medieval Theories of the Just Price: Romanists, Canonists, and Theologians in the Twelfth and Thirteenth Centuries', *Transactions of the American Philosophical Society*, new series, 49/4 (1959), p. 63.

40 Ibid., p. 21.

41 Ibid., p. 59.

42 Steven Epstein, 'The Theory and Practice of the Just Wage', *Journal of Mediaeval History*, 17/1 (1991), p. 58.

43 Ibid., p. 58.

44 Matthew 10:10; Luke 10:7.

45 Quoted in John W. Baldwin, op. cit., pp. 60 and 66.

46 He famously noted that 'it is not from the benevolence of the butcher, the brewer or the baker that we expect our dinner but from their regard to their own interest'.

47 McKinsey Global Institute, 'The world at work: Jobs, pay, and skills for 3.5 billion people', report (1 June 2012): https://www.mckinsey.com/featured-insights/employment-and-growth/the-world-at-work.

48 In his *American Capitalism* (1952).

49 Lorna Booth, 'Procurement statistics: a short guide', House of Commons briefing (26 July 2022): https://researchbriefings.files.parliament.uk/documents/CBP-9317/CBP-9317.pdf.

50   ONS, 'Pandemic-related loan guarantee schemes': https://obr.uk/forecasts-in-depth/tax-by-tax-spend-by-spend/pandemic-related-loan-guarantee-schemes/.

Chapter 7: Malfunctioning Markets

1   Michael E. Porter, *On Competition* (1998), p. 21.
2   OECD, 'Oligopoly markets': https://www.oecd.org/daf/competition/oligopoly-markets.htm.
3   In *The Wealth of Nations*, Book I, Chapter X.
4   Herb Simon, quoted in Brian Loasby, *Knowledge, Institutions and Evolution in Economics* (1999; 2002 edition), p. 7.
5   *See*, for example, Horst Hanusch and Andreas Pyka, 'Principles of Neo-Schumpeterian Economics', *Cambridge Journal of Economics*, 31/2 (2007), pp. 275–89; and more recently, Philippe Aghion, Céline Antonin and Simon Bunel, *The Power of Creative Destruction: Economic Upheaval and the Wealth of Nations* (2021).
6   Joseph A. Schumpeter, *Capitalism, Socialism and Democracy* (1942), p. 83.
7   Ibid., pp. 89–90.
8   Philippe Aghion *et al.*, op. cit.
9   Joseph A. Schumpeter, op. cit., p. 99.
10   Philippe Aghion *et al.*, op. cit.
11   'Too much of a good thing' *Economist* (26 March 2016): https://www.economist.com/news/briefing/21695385-profits-are-too-high-america-needs-giant-dose-competition-too-much-good-thing.
12   The revenue share of the top four firms in each industry has risen from 26% to 32%.
13   From census data: https://obamawhitehouse.archives.gov/sites/default/files/page/files/20151016_firm_level_perspective_on_role_of_rents_in_inequality.pdf.
14   'Dynamism has declined across Western economies', *Economist* (15 November 2018): https://www.economist.com/special-report/2018/11/15/dynamism-has-declined-across-western-economies
15   Torsten Bell and Dan Tomlinson, 'Is everybody concentrating? Recent trends in product and labour market concentration in the UK', Resolution Foundation briefing (July 2018): https://www.resolutionfoundation.org/app/uploads/2018/07/Is-everybody-concentrating_Recent-trends-in-product-and-labour-market-concentration-in-the-UK-1-1.pdf.
16   Scott Corfe, 'Competition, Not Concentration', Social Market Foundation report (31 July 2018), p. 9: https://www.smf.co.uk/publications/competition-not-concentration/.
17   *See* for instance how the game plan for conquering competition in the tech industry was set out in a seminal article of the early 1990s: Charles R. Morris and Charles H. Ferguson, 'How Architecture Wins Technology Wars', *Harvard Business Review* (March–April 1993): https://hbr.

org/1993/03/how-architecture-wins-technology-wars.

18 Congressional Research Service, 'Global Research and Development Expenditures: Fact Sheet' (updated 14 September 2022): https://sgp.fas. org/crs/misc/R44283.pdf

19 European Union, '2022 EU Industrial R&D Investment Scoreboard': https://iri.jrc.ec.europa.eu/sites/default/files/contenttype/ scoreboard/2022-12/EU%20RD%20Scoreboard%202022%20 FINAL%20online_0.pdf.

20 'Global ad spend has slowed but 2020 looks set to be a bumper year', CNBC (24 October 2019): https://www.cnbc.com/2019/10/24/global-ad-spend-has-slowed-but-2020-looks-set-to-be-a-bumper-year.html.

21 Advertising spend data from 'World's largest advertisers in 2021', Marketing Mind: https://adage.com/article/datacenter/25-top-advertisers-including-amazon-alibaba-loreal-and-pg-worlds-largest-advertisers-2022/2433306

22 'Facebook Acquisitions: The Complete List' (2022), Techwyse: https:// www.techwyse.com/blog/general-category/facebook-acquisitions-infographic/.

23 *See* 'Global value chains shed new light on trade', Brookings (10 July 2017): https://www.brookings.edu/blog/order-from-chaos/2017/07/10/ global-value-chains-shed-new-light-on-trade/.

24 *See* 'Labour Market Monopsony: Trends, Consequences, and Policy Responses', White House Council of Economic Advisors Issue Brief (October 2016): https://obamawhitehouse.archives.gov/sites/default/files/ page/files/20161025_monopsony_labor_mrkt_cea.pdf.

25 Ibid.

26 *Wealth of Nations*, Book 1, Chapter 8.

27 This was Engels' comment, approving the theory of 'Lexis' in the preface to the third volume of Marx's *Capital*.

28 Some 30 million American workers are covered by non-compete agreements. *See* 'Labour Market Monopsony…', op. cit.

29 Ibid.

30 David Autor *et al.*, 'The Fall of the Labor Share and the Rise of Superstar Firms', *Quarterly Journal of Economics*, 135/2 (May 2020), pp. 645–709: https://academic.oup.com/qje/article/135/2/645/5721266.

31 Federico J. Diez *et al.*, 'Global market power and its macroeconomic implications', IMF working paper (15 June 2018): https://www.imf.org/ en/Publications/WP/Issues/2018/06/15/Global-Market-Power-and-its-Macroeconomic-Implications-45975.

32 IMF, private correspondence.

33 Vernon L. Smith and Bart J. Wilson, *Humanomics: Moral Sentiments and the Wealth of Nations For the 21st Century* (2019), p. xiii.

34 Richard H. Thaler, *Misbehaving: The Making of Behavioural Economics* (2015). These scholars include Herb Simon, Brian Loasby, Gerd Gigerenzer, Daniel Kahneman and, of course, Richard Thaler.

35 Quoted in Daniel Kahneman, *Thinking, Fast and Slow* (2012).

36 Gerd Gigerenzer, *Rationality For Mortals: How People Cope With Uncertainty* (2008).

37 Ibid., p. 20.

38 The well-known Prisoner's Dilemma is the classic example of not exerting rational self-interest. *See*, for example: https://www.investopedia.com/terms/p/prisoners-dilemma.asp.

39 Vernon L. Smith and Bart J. Wilson, op. cit., p 128.

40 Ibid., p. xiv.

41 See Edmund T. Rolls, *Emotion Explained* (2007) p. 426.

42 Ibid., p. 446.

43 Quoted in Gerd Gigerenzer, op. cit., p. 14.

44 Carmen M. Reinhart and Kenneth S. Rogoff, *This Time is Different: Eight Centuries of Financial Folly* (2011), p. 141.

45 In the big five crashes in advanced economies since the late 1970s (Spain in 1977, Norway in 1987, Finland and Sweden in 1991, and Japan in 1992), house prices boomed for between four and six years before the crisis. This time was no different, except that the asset bubble was a *global* phenomenon.

46 Mervyn King, though he later pointed out that this overstates the size of the banking sector.

47 Some $13.4 trillion in mortgage-backed securities were issued between 2001 and 2006. By 2005, home equity withdrawals in the United States peaked at an annualized rate of $1 trillion dollars.

48 US Financial Crisis Inquiry Commission, 'Final report on the causes of the financial and economic crisis in the United States' (2011), p. xvii: https://www.govinfo.gov/app/details/GPO-FCIC.

49 Adam Blundell Wignall and Paul Atkinson, 'The sub-prime crisis: Causal distortions and regulatory reform', Reserve Bank of Australia Annual Conference (2008): https://www.rba.gov.au/publications/confs/2008/blundell-wignall-atkinson.html.

50 US Financial Crisis Inquiry Commission, op. cit., p. 1.

51 'Greenspan - I was wrong about the economy. Sort of', *Guardian* (24 October 2008): https://www.theguardian.com/business/2008/oct/24/economics-creditcrunch-federal-reserve-greenspan.

52 ONS, 'Economic Review' (August 2010), p. 12.

53 'Super rich have already recovered from pandemic losses – but it could take the poor a decade, Oxfam warns', CNBC (25 January 2021): https://www.cnbc.com/2021/01/25/oxfam-mega-rich-have-already-recovered-losses-from-covid-pandemic.html.

54 James Meade, op. cit., p. 43.

Chapter 8: Empowering the People

1 John F. Kennedy, 'Historic Speeches', Kennedy Presidential Library and Museum: https://www.jfklibrary.org/learn/about-jfk/historic-speeches/

acceptance-of-democratic-nomination-for-president.

2   'Fifty years ago we landed on the moon. Why should we care now?', *New York Times* (14 June 2019): https://www.nytimes.com/2019/06/14/books/review/moon-landing-anniversary.html.

3   'Presidential historian Douglas Brinkley talks JFK, moonshots and Apollo 11', Space.com (20 June 2019): https://www.space.com/douglas-brinkley-jfk-moonshot-book-apollo-program.html.

4   Douglas Brinkley, *American Moonshot: John F. Kennedy and the Great Space Race* (2019).

5   Ben Pimlott, *Harold Wilson* (1992), p. 302.

6   Richard Crossman, *The Backbench Diaries* (1981), p. 1026.

7   Tony Benn, *Out of the Wilderness: Diaries 1963–67* (1987), p. 66.

8   Speech opening the Science Debate at the Labour Party's Annual Conference, Scarborough, 1963, in Harold Wilson, *Purpose in Politics: Selected Speeches* (1964).

9   Cabinet Office, 'Getting on, getting ahead: A discussion paper: analysing the trends and drivers of social mobility' (2008): https://dera.ioe.ac.uk/id/eprint/8835/.

10 Adam Corlett, 'Charting the UK's lost decade of income growth', Resolution Foundation (5 March 2020): https://www.resolutionfoundation.org/comment/charting-the-uks-lost-decade-of-income-growth/.

11 'Secretary Janet Yellen on modern supply side economics and the Tobin Center', Yale University Office of the President (4 April 2023): https://president.yale.edu/president/yale-talk/secretary-janet-yellen-modern-supply-side-economics-and-tobin-center.

12 'At Yale, Treasury Secretary Yellen emphasizes nexus of research and policy', *Yale News* (4 April 2023): https://news.yale.edu/2023/04/04/yale-treasury-secretary-yellen-emphasizes-nexus-research-and-policy

13 Or, as former Google CEO and chairman, Eric Schmidt, recently put it; 'Technology is the engine that powers superpowers'. *See* https://carnegieendowment.org/files/Bateman_US-China_Decoupling_final.pdf.

14 National Academies of Sciences, Engineering, and Medicine, *Rising Above the Gathering Storm: Energizing and Employing America for a Brighter Economic Future*, executive summary (2007): http://www.nap.edu/openbook.php?record_id=11463&page=1. The 85% refers to the work of Robert Solow and Moses Abramovitz published in the middle 1950s, which demonstrated that as much as 85% of measured growth in US income per capita during the 1890–1950 period could not be explained by increases in the capital stock or other measurable inputs. The unexplained portion, referred to alternatively as the 'residual' or 'the measure of ignorance,' has been widely attributed to the effects of technological change.

15 Martin Rees, 'Unless we get smarter, we'll get poorer', *Daily Telegraph* (22 October 2008): http://www.telegraph.co.uk/comment/personal-view/3562991/Unless-we-get-smarter-well-get-poorer.html.

16   Congressional Research Service, 'Global Research and Development Expenditures', op. cit.

17   Richard Jones, 'The UK's innovation deficit & how to repair it', SPERI Paper No.6 (2013): http://speri.dept.shef.ac.uk/wp-content/uploads/2013/10/SPERI-Paper-No.6-The-UKs-Innovation-Deficit-and-How-to-Repair-it-PDF-1131KB.pdf.

18   Anne Green, 'Skills for competitiveness: Country report for United Kingdom', OECD Local Economic and Employment Development (LEED) working paper (2012): http://dx.doi.org/10.1787/5k9bb1vc6skf-en.

19   ONS, 'International comparisons of UK productivity (ICP), final estimates: 2020': https://www.ons.gov.uk/economy/economicoutputandproductivity/productivitymeasures/bulletins/internationalcomparisonsofproductivityfinalestimates/2020.

20   From House of Commons Library research, based on ONS data.

21   David Landes, *The Wealth and Poverty of Nations* (1999), p. 516.

22   Indeed, war itself was a catalyst. European 'discovery' of America unlocked a tidal wave of silver and gold into the invaders' economies, and the fractious British – who spent more than 125 years between 1688 and 1815 in a state of conflict – mobilized a 'fiscal-military state', which raised taxes to buy weapons on such a scale that it triggered an industrial revolution. Between 1750 and 1850, war costs consumed as much as three-quarters of all government expenditure, and British per-capita spending on its army and navy was roughly ten times the scale of China's. *See* Peer Vries, 'Public finance in China and Britain in the long 18th century', LSE Working Papers 167/12 (August 2012), but also John Brewer, *The Sinews of War* (1989) and the 'new China school' of economic history: Richard von Glahn, *The Economic History of China* (2017); R. Bin Wong, *China Transformed* (2000); John King Fairbank, *China: A New History* (1999; 2nd edition, 2006); Leonid Grinin and Andrey Korotayev, *Great Divergence and Great Convergence* (2015); Andre Frank, *ReOrient: Global Economy in the Asian Age* (1988); and Ken Pomeranz, *The Great Divergence* (2000).

23   Robert D. Atkinson and Stephen J. Ezell, *Innovation Economics: The Race for Global Advantage* (2012), pp. 143–52.

24   Rudolf Diesel, quoted in Joel Mokyr, *The Lever of Riches: Technological Creativity and Economic Progress* (1992), p. 155.

25   Philippe Aghion *et al.*, op. cit.

26   Gene M. Grossman and Elhanan Helpman, *Innovation and Growth in the Global Economy* (1991).

27   Philippe Aghion *et al.*, op. cit., p. 70.

28   Most of the early cross-country studies found a negative link between government size (measured as the ratio of public expenditure or tax revenues to GDP) and economic growth. However, most of these studies lacked sufficient controls for other factors affecting growth besides the size of the government.

29   G. Myles (2009), 'Economic Growth and the Role of Taxation - Aggregate Data', OECD Economics Department Working Papers, 714 (2009), Section

1: Introduction: https://www.oecd-ilibrary.org/economics/economic-growth-and-the-role-of-taxation-aggregate-data_222781828316.

30 Ibid. Myles concluded: 'The level of government consumption expenditure was a significant variable in some growth
regressions but this correlation was not robust. Many specifications of tax rate variables have been employed in tax regressions but none has provided a convincing result when other covariates have been included. It is important to note that this is not making the claim that the structure of taxation does not affect the rate of growth.'

31 Åsa Johansson, 'Public finance, economic growth and inequality: A survey of the evidence', OECD Economics Department Working Papers, 1346 (2016): https://doi.org/10.1787/18151973.

32 J. Fournier and Å. Johansson (2016), 'The effect of the size and the mix of public spending on growth and inequality', OECD Economics Department Working Papers, 1344: https://doi.org/10.1787/18151973.

33 Ibid.

34 Åsa Johansson, 'Public Finance…', op. cit.

35 Kyle McNabb, 'Tax Structures and Economic Growth: New Evidence from the Government Revenue Dataset', *Journal of International Development*, 30/2 (13 March 2018), pp. 173–205: https://doi.org/10.1002/jid.3345.

36 'Fiscal policy and long-term growth', IMF policy paper (April 2015): https://www.imf.org/en/Publications/Policy-Papers/Issues/2016/12/31/Fiscal-Policy-and-Long-Term-Growth-PP4964.

37 Kyle McNabb, op. cit.

38 Jens Matthias Arnold *et al.*, 'Tax Policy for Economic Recovery and Growth', *Economic Journal*, 121/550 (February 2011), pp. 59–80; for a summary, *see*: https://cepr.org/voxeu/columns/tax-policy-aid-recovery-and-growth.

39 'UK's regional inequality one of worst in developed world', *Financial Times* (26 November 2019): https://www.ft.com/content/7204c062-1047-11ea-a225-db2f231cfeae.

40 Figures set out in the ONS *Wealth and Assets Survey* for years 2006/08 to 2018/20.

41 *See*, for instance, Paul L. Joskow, 'Introduction to New Institutional Economics: A Report Card' (2004): https://www.researchgate.net/publication/242445070_NEW_INSTITUTIONAL_ECONOMICS_A_REPORT_CARD.

42 Paul M. Romer, 'Beyond classical and Keynesian macroeconomic policy', Policy Options (July–August 1994): https://www.scribd.com/doc/257356022/Beyond-Classical-and-Keynesian-Macroeconomic-Policy.

43 *See* Daron Acemoglu and James Robinson, op. cit. The definition of key institutions is very wide and includes constitutions, political systems, human rights, property rights, laws and courts, money, basic financial institutions, the government's power to tax, along with laws governing migration, trade and foreign investment, plus the institutions of governance – what you might call the 'play of the game' that influences

short-term resource allocation and the day-to-day operation of the economy.

44 Ibid, p. 43.

45 Peter Hall and David Soskice, *An Introduction to Varieties of Capitalism* (2001)

46 Ibid., p. 11.

47 Dan Senor and Paul Singer, *Start-up Nation: The Story of Israel's Economic Miracle* (2011).

48 This would involve expanding earn-while-you-learn routes to Level 5 professional and technical degree programmes, and sort out credit transfer and quality assurance that allows students to seamlessly transfer credits earned from FE to an HE setting. The proposal drew on models like the Warwick Manufacturing Centre and the Sheffield University Advanced Research Centre, and the great work of the UK's Further education colleges, many of which have degree-awarding power.

49 Richard Jones, 'The UK's Innovation Deficit...', op. cit.

50 Around 80% of this is accounted for by the Dedicated Schools Grant, but the rest of the money is split between an extraordinary 148 different programmes distributed by Whitehall diktat.

51 Iain McLean, 'Reconciling public expenditure control with subnational government autonomy', Nuffield College, Gwilym Gibbon Centre for Public Policy Working Paper (2019): https://www.nuffield.ox.ac.uk/media/3240/2019-01-reconciling-public-expenditure-control.pdf.

52 The current system has some advantages because it underpins very significant fiscal redistribution, as Jim Gallagher has discussed; *see*: https://www.nuffield.ox.ac.uk/media/3702/2019-04-pooling-and-sharing-uk-as-fiscal-union.pdf. It means that the richest regions of Britain pool and share up to 10% of their GDP with the rest of the country. This redistribution reflects the differences between the tax revenue and spending levels in different parts of the country, and they are very large. London, the South-East, and the East of England, which together comprise 47% of the UK's economic activity, contribute in absolute terms £16 billion to the North-West; £12 billion to Wales; £10 billion each to Scotland and the East Midlands; and £8 billion to Northern Ireland.

Chapter 9: Paying the People

1 Quoted in Cass Sunstein, *The Second Bill of Rights: FDR's Unfinished Revolution – And Why We Need It More Than Ever* (2006). Kindle edition.

2 Pope Benedict XVI, *Caritas in Veritate*, op. cit.

3 'Law of Partnership', House of Commons *Hansard* (27 June 1854): https://api.parliament.uk/historic-hansard/commons/1854/jun/27/law-of-partnership.

4 'Limited Liability Bill', ibid. (26 July 1855): https://hansard.parliament.uk/

Commons/1855-07-26/debates/032d737a-e4ef-4cde-91f6-a4a46f8327da/
LimitedLiabilityBill.

5   For a longer discussion on this, *see* ONS, 'Estimating the impact of the
self-employed in the labour share' (14 September 2018): https://www.ons.
gov.uk/economy/economicoutputandproductivity/productivitymeasures/
methodologies/estimatingtheimpactoftheselfemployedinthelabourshare.
See also 'Guidance' tab in ONS dataset, 'Labour costs and labour
income, UK' (updated periodically): https://www.ons.gov.uk/economy/
economicoutputandproductivity/productivitymeasures/datasets/
labourcostsandlabourshare.

6   ONS, 'Labour costs…', ibid.

7   'Bet365 gambling boss earns £213m in one year', BBC News (6 January
2023): https://www.bbc.co.uk/news/business-64188805.

8   'Pay for FTSE 100 chiefs rises by 12% despite cost of living crisis',
Financial Times (9 April 2023): https://www.ft.com/content/454a5645-
ccc8-4b20-a5b4-7de65effefef.

9   'Dividends from UK-listed firms up 16.5% in 2022, far outstripping
pay rises', *Guardian* (30 January 2023): https://www.theguardian.com/
money/2023/jan/30/dividends-from-uk-listed-firms-up-165-in-2022-far-
outstripping-pay-rises.

10   'Share buybacks: "the good, the bad and the ugly"', Edentree (28 June
2023): https://www.edentreeim.com/insights/share-buybacks-the-good-the-
bad-and-the-ugly.

11   'High pay hour 2023', High Pay Centre (5 January 2023): https://
highpaycentre.org/high-pay-hour-how-quickly-ceos-earn-the-uk-median-
wage/.

12   'Pension charges and fees explained', *Daily Telegraph* (12 July 2022):
https://www.telegraph.co.uk/financial-services/pensions-advice-service/
pension-charges/.

13   Take for example, a 25-year-old worker saving £3,000 a year. With a 5%
annual return she should enjoy a pot of £362,500 by the age of sixty-five.
Fees of 1.5% per year will knock this down to £253,500. But a fee of 3%
per year would mean costs that eat up two-thirds of best-case aggregate
returns over a lifetime of investing. These fees tend to be well-disguised.
The UK's Transparency Taskforce, for instance, documented well over 100
different fees UK residents pay on their investments. As a result, income in
retirement is set to be lower than it should be.

14   Seven in ten (71%) see raising the minimum wage as a credible policy,
while half (49%) thought it credible to fix the top rate of pay for chief
executives: https://www.kcl.ac.uk/policy-institute/assets/towards-the-
manifestos-solutions-for-tackling-poverty-and-inequality-latest-polling.pdf,
p. 33.

15   I owe the phrase 'civic capitalism' to Professor Colin Hay; *see* 'What
is civic capitalism? An interview with Colin Hay', *Prospect* (6 March
2015): https://www.prospectmagazine.co.uk/politics/47336/what-is-civic-
capitalism-an-interview-with-colin-hay.

16 ONS, *Wealth and Assets Survey*, op. cit.

17 Ben Franklin and Norma Cohen, 'A big bang in pensions?', Centre for Progressive Policy (25 July 2022): https://www.progressive-policy.net/publications/a-big-bang-in-pensions.

18 See Zoë Billingham *et al.*, 'The good life: the role of employers', Centre for Progressive Policy (21 November 2019): https://www.progressive-policy.net/publications/the-good-life-the-role-of-employers.

19 Matthew Taylor's 'Good work: The Taylor Review of modern working practices' (2017) looked at six areas (adapted from the European 'QuInnE' project: Quality of Jobs and Innovation Generated Employment Outcomes). They were: employment quality; wages; education and training; working conditions; work–life balance; and consultative participation and collective representation. The UK government's response followed similar notions: job satisfaction; fair pay; participation and progression; wellbeing, safety and security; and voice and autonomy. The Carnegie Trust/RSA's 'Measuring good work' report (2018) recommended seven slightly different measures, mostly covering the same areas but placing increased focus on the nature of work and on in-work social support. And the Institute for the Future of Work has advanced one of the most comprehensive new proposals for a 'Good Work Charter': https://www.ifow.org/publications/the-ifow-good-work-charter.

20 'Online tool: The CPP Good Employer Index', Centre for Progressive Policy (21 November 2019): https://www.progressive-policy.net/publications/online-tool-the-cpp-good-employer-index.

21 'From tailwinds to turbulence', Boston Consulting Group (BCG) (25 May 2022): https://www.bcg.com/publications/2022/tailwinds-to-turbulence-for-global-assets-under-management.

22 Quoted in James Hawley and Jon Lukomnik, 'The purpose of asset management', Pension Insurance Corporation Working Document (December 2017), p. 6.

23 Sid Azad *et al.*, 'State of the European asset management industry: Adapting to a new normal', McKinsey & Co. (26 November 2019), p. 2: https://www.mckinsey.com/industries/financial-services/our-insights/adapting-to-a-new-normal-in-european-asset-management.

24 'Phil Fisher on diversification', *Value Investing World Newsletter* (28 January 2016), p. 17: https://www.valueinvestingworld.com/2016/01/phil-fisher-on-diversification.html.

25 Mayer, C. (2022), 'Inequality, firms, ownership and governance', IFS Deaton Review of Inequalities.

26 'It's tough at the top as a slew of FTSE chiefs say they've had enough', *The Times* (20 December 2022): https://www.thetimes.co.uk/article/tough-at-the-top-the-busy-exit-door-suggests-a-few-years-is-enough-sfsl3gwv2.

27 'BlackRock CEO Larry Fink tells the world's biggest business leaders to stop worrying about short-term results', *Business Insider* (14 April 2015): https://www.businessinsider.com/larry-fink-letter-to-ceos-2015-4.

28 Made up of annual bonuses (32%) or LTIPs (41%). *See* 'Executive pay

and investment in the UK', BEIS research paper 2021/007, p. 37: https://assets.publishing.service.gov.uk/government/uploads/system/uploads/attachment_data/file/991207/exec-pay-investment-research-report.pdf. Evidence from the USA is much stronger. Between 1980 and 1994, the average value of stock options granted to CEOs of large US companies rose by almost 700%, while salaries and bonuses rose by less than 100%. Since 1994, the trend has only accelerated. In 1994, US CEO compensation was split into roughly one-third salary, one-third bonus and one-third stock and stock options. By 2006, the split was less than half for salary *and* bonus, with more than half paid in stock and stock options. It was a golden dawn for company chiefs. The American Economic Policy Institute found that from '1978 to 2018, CEO compensation grew by 1,007.5%, far outstripping S&P stock market growth (706.7%) and the wage growth of very high earners (339.2%). In contrast, wages for the typical worker grew by just 11.9%.'

29 Andrew G. Haldane, 'Who owns a company?', speech (22 May 2015): https://www.bankofengland.co.uk/-/media/boe/files/speech/2015/who-owns-a-company.pdf.

30 Lynn A. Stout, 'The shareholder value myth', Harvard Law School Forum on Corporate Governance (26 June 2012): https://corpgov.law.harvard.edu/2012/06/26/the-shareholder-value-myth/.

31 Dominic Barton and Marc Wiseman, 'Where boards fall short', Harvard Business Review (January–February 2015): https://hbr.org/2015/01/where-boards-fall-short.

32 In a press release (19 August 2019), the Roundtable announced the adoption of a new Statement on the Purpose of a Corporation, signed by 181 well-known, high-powered CEOs. It explicitly moved 'away from shareholder primacy' as the lodestar for market behaviour and argued instead for a 'modern standard for corporate responsibility' that made a commitment to all stakeholders.

33 'Will Hutton: If we want growth, let's launch an ownership revolution', Labour Tribune MPS (11 October 2022): https://tribunemps.org/will-hutton-if-we-want-growth-lets-launch-an-ownership-revolution.

34 ShareAction's study of the world's seventy-five largest asset managers revealed that one in six did not use their voting rights in more than 10% of the resolutions they could have voted on. https://shareaction.org/wp-content/uploads/2020/11/Voting-Matters-2020.pdf.

35 The Task Force on Climate-related Financial Disclosures (TCFD) establishes a set of eleven clear, comparable and consistent recommended disclosures about the risks and opportunities presented by climate change. The increased transparency encouraged through the TCFD recommendations is intended to lead to decision-useful information and therefore better informed decision-making on climate-related financial risks. *See* https://www.tcfdhub.org/faq/.

36 Ben Franklin and Norma Cohen, op. cit.

37 ONS, 'Annual Survey of Hours and Earning Pension Tables'.

38   The statutory minimum paid in each year is 8% of salary, co-financed by workers, employers and the state. NEST is the default fund into which employers may pay unless they have a scheme of their own.

39   House of Commons Library modelling. *See also* Investment Association, Annual Report (2019), p. 94.

40   James Hawley and Jon Lukomnik, op. cit.

41   The IMF has said that a 3-per-cent decrease in the Gini coefficient, the standard measure of inequality, boosts economic growth by 0.5% a year. *See* 'Redistribution, Inequality, and Growth' (February 2014): https://www.imf.org/external/pubs/ft/sdn/2014/sdn1402.pdf. The OECD, on the other hand, says that if you increase inequality by 3%, then growth slows by 0.35% a year for 25 years: *see* 'Inequality hurts economic growth, finds OECD research' (9 December 2014): https://web-archive.oecd.org/2014-12-09/331636-inequality-hurts-economic-growth.htm.

42   This has been set out with admirable clarity in Jeegar Kakkad, Martin Madsen and Michael Tory, 'Investing in the future: Boosting savings and prosperity for the UK', Tony Blair Institute for Global Change (29 May 2023): https://www.institute.global/insights/economic-prosperity/investing-in-the-future-boosting-savings-and-prosperity-for-the-uk.

43   A line of argument I owe to Professor David Pitt-Watson.

44   Thomas Philippon, 'Has the US Finance Industry Become Less Efficient? On the Theory and Measurement of Financial Intermediation', *American Economic Review*, 105/4 (April 2015), pp. 1408–38: https://www.aeaweb.org/articles?id=10.1257/aer.20120578.

Chapter 10: Supporting the People

1   *See* Paul Addison, *The Road to 1945: British Politics and the Second World War* (1994), pp. 117–18.

2   Frans de Waal, *Mama's Last Hug: Animal Emotions and What They Teach Us About Ourselves* (2019). Kindle edition.

3   Ibid., *The Age of Empathy: Nature's Lessons for a Kinder Society* (2010). Kindle edition.

4   Donald W. Pfaff, with Sandra Sherman, *The Altruistic Brain: How We Are Naturally Good* (2015). Pfaff argues that when we sense the alarm, within mere hundredths of a second we almost instantly visualise a person in distress, blur the ideas with one's own self-image in the cerebral cortex, process the idea in the mind's 'ethical switch' in the prefrontal cortex for a pro-social decision, before instructing the body to act. There is no calculation of a 'bargain' or quid pro quo; 'rather they are precipitated because humans are wired to be altruistic'. p. 62.

5   Ian Morris, *Foragers, Farmers and Fossil Fuels: How Human Values Evolve* (2015), p. 38. Kindle edition.

6   Denis Alexander, 'Cooperation, altruism and naturalism: two lectures on evolutionary themes', Cambridge Research (24 May

2012): https://www.cam.ac.uk/research/discussion/cooperation-altruism-and-naturalism-two-lectures-on-evolutionary-themes.

7   Martin A. Nowak, Corina E. Tarnita and Edward O. Wilson, 'The Evolution of Eusociality', *Nature*, 466 (2010), pp. 1057–1062: https://www.ncbi.nlm.nih.gov/pmc/articles/PMC3279739/.

8   David Sloan Wilson, *This View of Life: Completing the Darwinian Revolution* (2019). Kindle edition, p. 166. Wilson explains that 'Darwin's theory, properly understood is centered on cooperation, and Darwin and others were clear about this from the beginning.'

9   UK Government, White Paper on Social Insurance (1944), paragraph 6.

10 'Making a Contribution: Social Security for the Future', TUC Touchstone Pamphlet 12: https://www.tuc.org.uk/sites/default/files/contributory_benefits.pdf.

11 Guy Standing, 'Basic income as common dividends: Piloting a transformative policy: A report for the Shadow Chancellor of the Exchequer', Progressive Economy Forum (2019).

12 Royal Society of Arts, 'Universal Basic Income' project: https://www.thersa.org/projects/basic-income.

13 'Report on Key Findings from Opinium polling 2023': https://www.inclusivegrowth.co.uk/key-findings-polling-23/.

14 ONS, 'The cost of living, current and upcoming work: February 2023': https://www.ons.gov.uk/economy/inflationandpriceindices/articles/thecostoflivingcurrentandupcomingwork/latest.

15 Like the army veteran forced to bed down at 6:30 p.m. every night in his old army sleeping bag, because he cannot afford the heating; or the grandmother who worked all her life, but now cannot even afford a joint of meat for a Sunday roast.

16 A higher percentage than those who found it credible (40%).

17 Howard Reed and Stewart Lansley, 'Universal Basic Income: An idea whose time has come?', Compass report (2016): https://www.compassonline.org.uk/wp-content/uploads/2016/05/UniversalBasicIncomeByCompass-Spreads.pdf.

18 'Guarantee our essentials: reforming Universal Credit to ensure we can all afford the essentials in hard times', Joseph Rowntree Foundation / Trussell Trust (27 February 2023): https://www.jrf.org.uk/report/guarantee-our-essentials.

19 Meade, op. cit., p. 48, p. 59.

20 Michael Sherraden, *Assets and the Poor: A New American Welfare Policy* (1991; 2015 edition), p. 6.

21 Abigail McKnight, 'Estimates of the asset-effect: The search for a causal effect of assets on adult health and employment outcomes', LSE CASEpapers 149 (2011): https://sticerd.lse.ac.uk/dps/case/cp/CASEpaper149.pdf.

22 C. Gibson-Davis, L.A. Keister and W. Lowell, 'Net Worth Poverty and Child Development', *Socius*, 8 (2022): https://doi.org/10.1177/23780231221111672.

23 'Anxiety nation? Economic insecurity and mental distress in 2020s Britain', Joseph Rowntree Foundation (10 November 2022): https://www.jrf.org.uk/report/anxiety-nation-economic-insecurity-and-mental-distress-2020s-britain.

24 HMRC statistics show that in 2020–21, 52% of up-front tax relief was given to higher-rate taxpayers. *See* 'A blueprint for a better tax treatment of pensions', IFS Report R240 (February 2023), p. 32: https://ifs.org.uk/sites/default/files/2023-02/A-blueprint-for-a-better-tax-treatment-of-pensions.pdf.

25 'Saving savings? Assessing government incentives to put money aside', Resolution Foundation (16 January 2023): https://www.resolutionfoundation.org/events/saving-savings/.

26 Tom Clark, 'Depleted assets?', Joseph Roundtree Foundation blog (11 May 2023): https://www.jrf.org.uk/blog/depleted-assets.

27 UK Government, 'Review of post-18 education and funding' (2022): https://commonslibrary.parliament.uk/research-briefings/sn01079/.

28 Office for Budget Responsibility, 'Welfare spending: universal credit': https://obr.uk/forecasts-in-depth/tax-by-tax-spend-by-spend/welfare-spending-universal-credit/.

29 'Low income' was here defined as those families with a household income of between £11,000 and £15,000.

30 Tom Clark, 'Wealth of evidence? What we know about "asset effects"', Joseph Rowntree Foundation blog (24 April 2023): https://www.jrf.org.uk/blog/wealth-evidence-what-we-know-about-asset-effects.

31 House of Commons Library, 'Student loan statistics: Research briefing' (4 July 2023): https://commonslibrary.parliament.uk/research-briefings/sn01079/.

32 Ian Mulheirn, James Browne, Christos Tsoukalis, 'Housing affordability since 1979: Determinants and solutions', Joseph Rowntree Foundation (18 January 2023): https://www.jrf.org.uk/report/housing-affordability-1979-determinants-and-solutions. According to the report, 'Less generous sub-market rents for social housing contributed five percentage points to the reduction in housing subsidies as a share of aggregate UK housing costs seen between 1979 and 2009–10. The social rented sector shrank from 31% to 17% of the English housing stock and social rents moved from around half to two-thirds of market levels. The abolition of private sector rent controls in the 1980s cut the subsidy to renters by a further five percentage points of total housing costs.'

33 Paul Gregg and Ricky Kanabar, 'Parental homeownership and education: the implications for offspring wealth inequality in GB', UCL Working Paper, 22-01 (June 2023): https://repec-cepeo.ucl.ac.uk/cepeow/cepeowp22-01r2.pdf.

34 'First-time buyer statistics and facts: 2023', (6 March 2023): https://www.money.co.uk/mortgages/first-time-buyer-mortgages/statistics.

35 'Home ownership in Britain has become a hereditary privilege', *Financial Times* (13 July 2023): https://www.ft.com/content/985a608e-17a3-42ff-

abb1-d78a10627a12.

36 Resolution Foundation, Inter-generational Audit, 2022, op. cit., p. 68.

37 Ibid., p. 74.

38 G. Tetlow, 'Pensions tax relief – time for a TEE-brake', Chartered Insurance Industry Thinkpiece, 120 (October 2015): https://www.cii.co.uk/research/2015/october/pensions-tax-relief-time-for-a-tee-brake/.

39 See 'ISA ISA Baby: Assessing the government's policies to encourage household saving', Resolution Foundation briefing (16 January 2023): https://www.resolutionfoundation.org/publications/isa-isa-baby/.

40 Sherraden, op. cit., p. 189.

41 At today's projections (2023), an average earner might look forward to a pension pot of around £182,000, to which the employee has paid £66,000, and the employer £39,000, with the government's role (and compound gains) making up the balance.

42 From 2.1 million in 2011 to 21 million in 2019, and actively contributing members have risen from a low of 0.9 million active members in 2011 to 10.6 million members in 2019. https://commonslibrary.parliament.uk/research-briefings/sn06417/.

43 'Check who to enrol in a workplace pension', Pensions Regulator: https://www.thepensionsregulator.gov.uk/en/business-advisers/automatic-enrolment-guide-for-business-advisers/check-who-to-enrol-in-a-workplace-pension.

44 '6.3 million employees are still without a workplace pension', TUC (4 March 2020): https://www.tuc.org.uk/news/63-million-employees-are-still-without-workplace-pension.

45 Stuart Adam et al., 'A blueprint for a better tax treatment of pensions' IFS report, p. 91 (6 February 2023): https://ifs.org.uk/publications/blueprint-better-tax-treatment-pensions.

46 'Report on Key Findings', op. cit.

47 Stuart Adam et al., op. cit.

48 Ibid., p. 71.

49 UK Government, 'Graduates enjoy £100k earnings bonus over lifetime' (29 February 2020): https://www.gov.uk/government/news/graduates-enjoy-100k-earnings-bonus-over-lifetime.

50 House of Commons Library modelling.

51 The Austrialian loans offer a lifetime maximum loan allocation towards fees for every student, allowing them to retrain throughout their career – regardless of qualification level or previous qualifications – up to a lifetime maximum of £56,000. This is slightly higher (£70,000) for students in medicine, dentistry or veterinary science programmes.

52 Joe Lewis and Paul Bolton, 'The Lifelong Loan Entitlement', House of Commons Library briefing (27 April 2023): https://researchbriefings.files.parliament.uk/documents/CBP-9756/CBP-9756.pdf.

53 Specifically, anyone in receipt of Universal Credit (UC), Working Tax Credit, or eligible for Working Tax Credit and receiving Child Tax Credit.

54 'ISAs Explained', Legal & General: https://www.legalandgeneral.com/
    investments/stocks-and-shares-isa/isas-explained/.
55 That is around 350,000 people since 2016.
56 By the end of 2023–24.
57 'Sidecar savings tools could address two of the biggest financial challenges
    facing UK households, says Nest Insight', press release (26 April 2023):
    https://www.nestinsight.org.uk/sidecar-savings-tools-could-address-two-of-
    the-biggest-financial-challenges-facing-uk-households-says-nest-insight/.
58 Youth home ownership rates rose rapidly from the 1960s: indeed, by 1989
    the majority (51%) of young 'family units' (a single person or couple living
    together) owned their own home (with or without a mortgage). But this
    upward trend then reversed.
59 Resolution Foundation figures. See Home Improvements, Resolution
    Foundation (2010). https://www.resolutionfoundation.org/press-releases/
    up-to-a-third-of-millennials-face-renting-from-cradle-to-grave/.
60 In 2018, for example, the *British Social Attitudes Survey* suggested that
    almost three-quarters (73%) of renters would prefer to own their home if
    they had a free choice. Cited in 'Hope to buy: The decline of youth home
    ownership', Resolution Foundation briefing note (2 December 2021):
    https://www.resolutionfoundation.org/publications/hope-to-buy/.
61 Resolution Foundation, Intergenerational Audit 2022, op. cit., p.85.
62 Building *social* homes would make a difference; indeed experts believe
    that an additional 700,000 social properties would improve levels of
    social renting among lower-income families with children back to the rates
    enjoyed in 1979. See Ian Mulheirn *et al.*, op. cit.
63 Indeed, the Tony Blair Institute noted that if borrowers could access loans
    worth seven times their income, around 40% of young non-homeowners
    would be able to borrow enough to purchase the average first-time-buyer
    property in the region (compared with 20% today). See Ian Mulheirn
    et al., op. cit., p. 17. In Canada and the Netherlands, mortgage lenders
    are required to use state-backed permanent and compulsory mortgage
    insurance when loan-to-value ratios are high. And long-term fixed-
    rate mortgages could be made available by encouraging life insurance
    and pension funds – which invest for the long term – to buy long-term
    mortgages that were both securitized and insured.
64 Such as, perhaps, increasing tax on *second-home* buyers, or increasing the
    stamp duty wedge between new buyers and existing owners.
65 'Report on Key Findings', op. cit.
66 Ian Mulheirn *et al.*, op. cit.
67 'Report on Key Findings', op. cit.
68 'A new generational contract: The final report of the Intergenerational
    Commission', Resolution Foundation (8 May 2018): https://www.
    resolutionfoundation.org/advanced/a-new-generational-contract/.
69 Unsurprisingly, the proposal was much more popular with young people,
    including two thirds (64%) of Gen Z adults, compared to a fifth (21%) of
    baby boomers.

70 The proposal also had less of a generational divide, with approximately two-fifths of Gen Z (40%) and baby boomers (38%) supporting the idea. *See* 'Report on Findings', op. cit.

71 'Mirrlees Review', p. 318. *See* https://ifs.org.uk/mirrlees-review.

Chapter 11: Investing for the People

1 UK Government, 'Government Hospitality wine cellar bi-annual report, 2018 to 2020': https://www.gov.uk/government/publications/government-hospitality-wine-cellar-bi-annual-statement-2018-to-2020/government-hospitality-wine-cellar-bi-annual-report-2018-to-2020.

2 'Government wine committee raises a glass in spirit of defiance', *The Times* (12 March 2010): https://www.thetimes.co.uk/article/government-wine-committee-raises-a-glass-in-spirit-of-defiance-wnrxxdtvrb7.

3 'The sovereign's wealth: UK royal family's finances – explained', *Guardian* (14 September 2022): https://www.theguardian.com/uk-news/2022/sep/14/the-sovereigns-wealth-uk-royal-familys-finances-explained.

4 In 1836, an honest sewer worker followed an old drain into the Bank's basement. He wrote anonymous alerts to the governors, who of course ignored them. Such was the self-confidence of the Bank's high command that they had to be persuaded to meet the worker alone one night in the strongrooms, so that he could prove, by force of his very presence, that new security was needed. The worker's reward was a princely £800 – less than 10% of the value of one of the 13kg bars that sit in the safes today.

5 *See* 'UK taxpayer faces losses after companies backed by Future Fund fail', *Financial Times* (26 January 2023): https://www.ft.com/content/c2158644-fc7a-4864-a68e-097433fc3e20; and "Rishi Sunak can come to our sex parties': behind the mask of Killing Kittens", *The Times* (1 July 2022): https://www.thetimes.co.uk/article/rishi-sunak-can-come-to-our-sex-parties-behind-the-mask-of-killing-kittens-bt8xfhx5v.

6 Credit Suisse, Global Wealth Databook 2022: https://www.credit-suisse.com/media/assets/corporate/docs/about-us/research/publications/global-wealth-databook-2022.pdf.

7 'Richest 1% grab nearly twice as much new wealth as rest of the world put together', Oxfam (16 January 2023): https://www.oxfam.org.uk/media/press-releases/richest-1-grab-nearly-twice-as-much-new-wealth-as-rest-of-the-world-put-together/.

8 Professor Brooke Harrington, private correspondence.

9 Wealth X / Altrata, *World Ultra Wealth Report, 2022*, p. 23: https://altrata.com/reports/world-ultra-wealth-report-2022.

10 Ibid., p. 24.

11 'The Wealth Report', Frank Knight, 16th edition (2022), p. 37: https://www.knightfrank.com/siteassets/subscribe/the-wealth-report-2022.pdf.

12 Ibid.

13 The world's top 1% of most expensive homes can be found in locations

such as Beijing, Singapore, Sydney, Los Angeles, Hong Kong, Vancouver, Paris, New York, London, Berlin, Miami, Cape Town, Sao Paulo and Mumbai. Ibid., p. 57.

14 Ibid.

15 Ibid.

16 Ibid.

17 Andreas Fagereng *et al.* 'Heterogeneity and Persistence in Returns to Wealth', *Econometrica*, 88/1, pp. 115–70: https://onlinelibrary.wiley.com/doi/abs/10.3982/ECTA14835.

18 This data is drawn from analysis of 60% of taxpayers, based on comparing numbers of taxpayers with ONS population estimates for people aged 18 or over for 2018, from NOMIS: https://www.nomisweb.co.uk/.

19 The survey is known to under-report the number of individuals with very high incomes and understate the level of their incomes. An adjustment to correct for this is made to 'very rich' households in FRS-based results using HMRC data.

20 Matt Bruenig, 'Social Wealth Fund For America', People's Policy Project: https://www.peoplespolicyproject.org/projects/social-wealth-fund/.

21 'Rocky ride ahead for Norway's $1.2 trillion wealth fund', *Reuters* (3 May 2022): https://www.reuters.com/world/europe/norway-sovereign-wealth-fund-ceo-warns-rocky-ride-ahead-2022-05-03/.

22 Carys Roberts and Mathew Lawrence, 'Our Common Wealth: A Citizens' Wealth Fund For the UK', IPPR policy paper (April 2018): https://www.ippr.org/files/2018-04/cej-our-common-wealth-march-2018.pdf.

23 'What is a Sovereign Wealth Fund?', SWFI: https://www.swfinstitute.org/research/sovereign-wealth-fund.

24 Elliot Hentov and Jennifer Ale, 'How Do Sovereign Wealth Funds Invest? With Strategic Diversification', State Street Global Investors White Paper (April 2022): https://www.ssga.com/library-content/pdfs/official-institutions-/how-do-sovereign-wealth-funds-invest.pdf.

25 In my polling with the KCL Policy Institute, we asked whether the UK government should create a 'sovereign (or social) wealth fund; it is fair to say that uncertainty was high, with 43% saying they did not know. But among those expressing an opinion, 44% said it was something that government should do – with just 13% saying they should not.

26 Angus J. L. Winchester, *Common Land in Britain: A History from the Middle Ages to the Present Day* (2022).

27 *See* 'Commons Act 2006 Explanatory Notes': https://www.legislation.gov.uk/ukpga/2006/26/notes/division/2?view=plain; *see also* Guy Standing, 'Basic Income as Common Dividends: Piloting a Transformative Policy', report for the Shadow Chancellor of the Exchequer, Progressive Economy Forum (2019): https://www.progressiveeconomyforum.com/wp-content/uploads/2019/05/PEF_Piloting_Basic_Income_Guy_Standing.pdf.

28 Eileen Power, *The Wool Trade in English Medieval History, Being the Ford Lectures* (Oxford University Press, 1941), p. 13.

29 See the work by John Penrose MP: 'The Great Rebalancing: A sovereign wealth fund to make the UK's economy the strongest in the G20', Social Market Foundation (7 November 2016): https://www.smf.co.uk/publications/the-great-rebalancing-a-sovereign-wealth-fund-to-make-the-uks-economy-the-strongest-in-the-g20/; 'Time to think big: A UK Sovereign Wealth Fund', Reform (20 February 2020): https://reform.uk/publications/time-think-big-uk-sovereign-wealth-fund/. John also sponsored a Westminster Hall debate on a 'UK Sovereign Wealth Fund' (14 December 2016): https://hansard.parliament.uk/commons/2016-12-14/debates/D212716E-CFE5-4EDA-9B5E-F52A106E6642/UKSovereignWealthFund.

30 Ibid., 'The Great Rebalancing...'.

31 'First-time buyer average deposit in the United Kingdom (UK) from 2021 to 2022, by region', Statista: https://www.statista.com/statistics/557891/first-time-buyer-average-deposit-by-region-uk/.

32 SWF, 'faqs': https://globalswf.com/faqs.

33 HM Treasury, 'Whole of Government Accounts, 2019–20' (31 March 2020): https://www.gov.uk/government/publications/whole-of-government-accounts-2019-20.

34 In 2011 prices.

35 The IPPR's calculation. See IPPR, Our Common Wealth A Citizens' Wealth Fund for the UK (2018).

36 Bruenig, op. cit., p. 36.

37 Dag Detter, Stefan Fölster and Josh Ryan-Collins, 'Public wealth funds: Supporting economic recovery and sustainable Growth', UCL Institute for Innovation and Public Purpose policy report (2020): https://www.ucl.ac.uk/bartlett/public-purpose/sites/public-purpose/files/final_pwf_report_detter_folster_ryan-collins_16_nov.pdf.

38 HM Treasury, 'Exchange Equalisation Account: Report and Accounts 2021–22': https://assets.publishing.service.gov.uk/government/uploads/system/uploads/attachment_data/file/1092747/E02772868_HC_602_EEA_Report_and_accounts_2021-22_Accessible.pdf.

Chapter 12: Sharing Among the People

1 Quoted in William Edward Hartpole Lecky, *Democracy and Liberty* (1896), Introduction, Vol. I. p. xxxi.

2 Among the non-primates, only lionesses, wolves and African wild dogs hunt together. Among the primates, the tactic is confined to humans, the capuchin monkeys of Central and South America and chimpanzees.

3 The naturalist Edward O. Wilson wrote that 'the condition of multiple generations, organized into groups by means of an altruistic division of labor, was one of the major innovations in the history of life'. He called it 'eusociality'. It is also highly unusual. There are around 2,600 taxonomic families of insects and arthropods. Only fifteen contain eusocial species. Among vertebrates, it is rarer still. It has occurred twice, says Dr Wilson,

in subterranean naked mole rats, and once in the line that led to modern humans: 'Every one [species], without exception, from the two dozen or so insect and crustacean lines to the naked mole rats, defended a nest from which members could forage for enough food to sustain the colony.' See E. O. Wilson, The Social Conquest of Earth (2013).

4   Yuval Noah Harari, *Sapiens: A Brief History of Humankind* (2015), p. 352.

5   Christopher Booker, *The Seven Basic Plots: Why We Tell Stories* (2004).

6   In the words of the nineteenth-century US Supreme Court Justice, Samuel Freeman Miller, regarding the case of *Loan Association v. Topeka* (1874).

7   Carbon taxes are inevitably going to become a big issue. They are beyond the scope of this book, though I suspect they will, in due course, simply punish emitters of carbon to raise money for those who face higher carbon costs without the means to pay.

8   'CASH BACK Ex Chancellor Nadhim Zahawi agrees to pay several million in tax after scrutiny of his family's financial affairs', *Sun* (14 January 2023): https://www.thesun.co.uk/news/21046397/chancellor-nadhim-zahawi-tax/.

9   Abhijit V. Bannerjee and Esther Duflo, *Good Economics For Hard Times: Better Answers to Our Biggest Problems* (2019).

10   Ibid.

11   HMRC, 'Official Statistics: 1. Tax Gaps: Summary' (updated 22 June 2023): https://www.gov.uk/government/statistics/measuring-tax-gaps/1-tax-gaps-summary.

12   *See* Gabriel Zucman, *The Hidden Wealth of Nations: The Scourge of Tax Havens* (English edition, 2015).

13   'How much money is in tax havens?', Tax Justice Network faqs: https://taxjustice.net/faq/how-much-money-is-in-tax-havens/.

14   These figures from 'Equality before the law? HMRC's use of criminal prosecutions for tax fraud and other revenue crimes. A comparison with benefits fraud', TaxWatch (2021): https://www.taxwatchuk.org/wp-content/uploads/2021/02/Equality_Before_The_Law_FINAL.pdf.

15   Judith Freeman, 'The UK General Anti-Avoidance Rule: Transplants and Lessons', *Bulletin for International Taxation* 73/6–7 (June/July 2019), pp. 332–38.

16   The Big Four are Deloitte (formerly Deloitte & Touche); Ernst & Young (EY); KPMG; and Price Waterhouse Cooper (PWC).

17   Including all their lands, buildings, sheep, wethers, swine, goats, cows, calves, oxen, bulls, horses, rounceys, mares, foals, mules and donkeys.

18   'UK household wealth tripled in 20 years: where did it all come from?', Economics Observatory (16 December 2020): https://www.economicsobservatory.com/uk-household-wealth-tripled-20-years-where-did-it-all-come.

19   For tax receipts, see Matthew Keep, 'Tax statistics: An overview', House of Commons Library briefing (5 June 2023): https://researchbriefings.files.parliament.uk/documents/CBP-8513/CBP-8513.pdf.

20 Adam Corlett, 'The shifting shape of UK Tax', Resolution Foundation (November 2019): https://www.resolutionfoundation.org/app/ uploads/2019/11/The-shifting-shape-of-UK-tax.pdf. *See also* Corlett, 'No, the poorest don't pay higher taxes than the richest' (20 June 2018): https:// www.resolutionfoundation.org/comment/no-the-poorest-dont-pay-higher-taxes-than-the-richest/. The Resolution Foundation's analysis is based on the ONS's 'Effects of taxes and benefits on UK household income' (at time of writing, updated to 2020 figures); the taxes covered are shown in Table 2 of the ONS dataset 'Effects of taxes and benefits on household income': https://www.ons.gov.uk/peoplepopulationand community/personalandhouseholdfinances/incomeandwealth/ datasets/theeffectsoftaxesandbenefitsonhouseholdincome financialyearending2014.

21 That comprises 45% income tax plus 2% employee National Insurance contributions. *See* Arun Advani and Andy Summers, 'How much tax do the rich really pay? New evidence from tax microdata in the UK', CAGE Policy Briefing 27 (June 2020): https://warwick.ac.uk/fac/soc/economics/ research/centres/cage/manage/publications/bn27.2020.pdf.

22 The £1 million earnings figure only covers the 60% of adults who are taxpayers. Figures only cover income subject to income tax: although this covers most income, it misses out on income subject to capital gains tax, some social security benefits and income from some tax-efficient savings vehicles, such as ISAs. Tax planning, avoidance and evasion may also affect the figures. Source: House of Commons data.

23 Using anonymized data collected from the personal tax returns. *See* Arun Advani and Andy Summers, op. cit.

24 'Rishi Sunak releases tax return details showing income while chancellor and prime minister', *Sky News* (23 March 2023): https://news.sky.com/ story/rishi-sunak-releases-tax-return-details-showing-income-while-chancellor-and-prime-minister-12840264.

25 James Meade, op. cit., p. 53.

26 Linus Mattauch, 'Reducing wealth inequality through wealth taxes without compromising economic growth', University of Oxford Martin School (31 January 2019): https://www.oxfordmartin.ox.ac.uk/blog/ reducing-wealth-inequality-through-wealth-taxes-without-compromising-economic-growth/.

27 'Solidarity and wealth tax', Policy Department for Budgetary Affairs briefing for European Parliament briefing (April 2022): https://www. europarl.europa.eu/RegData/etudes/BRIE/2022/732005/IPOL_ BRI(2022)732005_EN.pdf.

28 IGM Forum (2019): https://www.kentclarkcenter.org/polls/by-date/ page/4/?y=2019.

29 Arun Advani, David Burgherr and Andy Summers, 'Non-doms: basics and case for reform', briefing note (2022): https://arunadvani.com/papers/AdvaniBurgherrSummers_NondomBasics. pdf.

30 'Abolishing the non-dom regime would raise more than £3.2 billion each year, finds new report', LSE (26 September 2022): https://www.lse.ac.uk/News/Latest-news-from-LSE/2022/i-September-22/Abolishing-the-non-dom-regime-would-raise-more-than-3.2-billion-each-year-finds-new-report.

31 'Exclusive: Majority of UK backs scrapping non-domicile tax status, poll shows', Labour List (14 April 2022): https://labourlist.org/2022/04/exclusive-majority-of-uk-backs-scrapping-non-domicile-tax-status-poll-shows/.

32 Arun Advani et al., 'Fixing National Insurance: A better way to fund social care', CAGE Policy Briefing 33 (September 2021): https://warwick.ac.uk/fac/soc/economics/research/centres/cage/manage/publications/bn33.2021.pdf.

33 In a huge recent poll, the Nuffield College politics professor, Ben Ansell, asked: 'To what extent do you agree or disagree with the following statement: "Realized capital gains should be taxed at the same rate as income in the UK." (By realized capital gains, we mean profits from selling stocks and other assets, and other wealth.)' Over 62% said that they supported the idea, including 50% of Conservatives.

34 'Inheritance Taxation in OECD Countries', OECD report (11 May 2021): https://www.oecd.org/tax/tax-policy/inheritance-taxation-in-oecd-countries-e2879a7d-en.htm.

35 Matthew Keep, 'Tax statistics', op. cit., p. 12.

36 Andrew Dixon et al., 'The Proportional Property Tax Manifesto', Fairer Share (nd), p. 6: https://fairershare.org.uk/wp-content/uploads/2021/10/Fairer-Share_Manifesto.pdf.

37 Ibid.

38 Arun Advani, Emma Chamberlain and Andy Summers, 'A wealth tax for the UK: Executive Summary', Wealth Tax Commission final report (9 December 2020): https://www.wealthandpolicy.com/wp/WealthTaxFinalReport_ExecSummary.pdf.

39 A Green Paper in 1974 proposed a regular wealth tax 'to promote greater social and economic equality', with suggested rates on net wealth ranging from 1% (on £100,000–£300,000) to 5% (on more than £5 million). France, Spain, Norway and Switzerland all have wealth taxes. Most other European countries have repealed their wealth taxes.

40 'Reforms to the taxation of wealth calculator', on Arun Advani's website: https://arunadvani.com/taxreform.html.

Conclusion

1   William Clarke, 'The Basis of Socialism – Industrial', in George Bernard Shaw (ed.), Fabian Essays in Socialism (1889).

2   Sidney Webb, 'The Basis of Socialism – Historic', in ibid.

3   Karl Polanyi, The Great Transformation: The Political and Economic Origins of Our Time (1944; 2002 edition), p. 86.

4 John Ruskin, *'Unto This Last' and Other Essays*, edited by Clive Wilmer (1985), p. 163.

5 Ibid., editorial commentary, p. 158.

6 *See* 'Compare your country: Long-term economic scenarios', drawn from OECD Economic Outlook 109 (October 2021): https://www1. compareyourcountry.org/long-term-economic-scenarios/en/0/c15282 83767118+c1530864012204+c1530864028300+c1530944845410 +c15309448844415/default/all/WLD. Global GDP is forecast to rise from £93.5 trillion in 2023 to £191 trillion by 2060.

7 Martin Wolf's felicitous phrase; *see* his *The Crisis of Democratic Capitalism* (2023). Kindle edition.

8 I am drawing on James Meade's phrasing, op. cit.

9 For the 'oligarchy' quotation, *see* Thomas Piketty, op. cit. For the other quotations, *see* Martin Wolf, op. cit., p. 28.

10 *See* Francis Fukuyama, *Trust: The Social Virtues and the Creation of Prosperity* (1996).

11 In other words, an optimal combination of 'negative liberty', 'positive liberty' and 'republican freedom'. *See* Elizabeth Anderson, *Private Government: How Employers Rule Our Lives (and Why We Don't Talk About It)* (2017) for an excellent summary.

12 Franklin D. Roosevelt, 'State of the Union Message to Congress' (11 January 1944), op. cit.

13 As Alan Thomas put it in his *Republic of Equals: Predistribution and the Property Owning Democracy* (2016), 'The citizen is motivated to take an interest in politics because if she does not she will be at the mercy of other people's interests – and their stance towards her own interests may not be a benevolent one.'

Index